Datsun 1200 Owners Workshop Manual

by J H HAYNES

Associate Member of the Guild of Motoring Writers

and P G STRASMAN, MISTC

Models covered

1171 cc Datsun 1200 Saloon De Luxe, Coupe and **Estate**
First introduced into United Kingdom May **1970**

SBN 0 85696 124 8

© Haynes Publishing Group 1977

ABCDE
FGHIJ
KLMNO
PQR

HAYNES PUBLISHING GROUP
SPARKFORD YEOVIL SOMERSET ENGLAND
distributed in the USA by
HAYNES PUBLICATIONS INC
861 LAWRENCE DRIVE
NEWBURY PARK
CALIFORNIA 91320
USA

Acknowledgements

Our thanks must go to the Nissan Motor Company Limited of Japan for the use of some of their technical illustrations.

Castrol Limited gave their usual help with lubrication and Champion Sparking Plug Company Limited for the provision of spark plug photographs.

Castrol Limited provided lubrication data, and the Champion Sparking Plug Company supplied the illustrations showing the various spark plug conditions.

The bodywork repair photographs used in this manual were provided by Lloyds Industries Limited who supply Turtle Wax, Holts Dupli-Color and a range of other Holts products.

Stanley Randolph page edited the text.

About this manual

The aim of this book is to help you get the best value from your car. It can do so in two ways. First it can help you decide what work must be done, even should you choose to get it done by a garage, the routine maintenance and the diagnosis and course of action when random faults occur. But it is hoped that you will also use the second and fuller purpose by tackling the work yourself. On the simpler jobs it may even be quicker than booking the car into a garage and going there twice, to leave and collect it. Perhaps most important, much money can be saved by avoiding the costs a garage must charge to cover their labour and overheads.

The book has drawings and descriptions to show the function of the various components so that their layout can be understood. Then the tasks are described and photographed in a step by step sequence so that even a novice can cope with complicated work. Such a person is the very one to buy a car needing repair yet be unable to afford garage costs.

The jobs are described assuming only normal spanners are available, and not special tools. But a reasonable outfit of tools will be a worthwhile investment. Many special workshop tools produced by the makers merely speed the work, and in these cases guidance is given as to how to do the job without them, the oft quoted example being the use of a large hose clip to compress the piston rings for insertion in the cylinder. But on a very few occasions the special tool is essential to prevent damage to components, then their use is described. Though it might be possible to borrow the tool, such work may have to be entrusted to the official agent.

To avoid labour costs a garage will often give a cheaper repair by fitting a reconditioned assembly. The home mechanic can be helped by this book to diagnose the fault and make a repair using only a minor spare part. The classic case is repairing a non-charging dynamo by fitting new brushes.

The manufacturer's official workshop manuals are written for their trained staff, and so assume special knowledge; detail is left out. This book is written for the owner, and so goes into detail.

The book is divided into twelve chapters. Each chapter is divided into numbered sections which are headed in bold type between horizontal lines. Each section consists of serially numbered paragraphs.

There are two types of illustration: (1) Figures which are numbered according to Chapter and sequence of occurrence in that Chapter. (2) Photographs which have a reference number on their caption. All photographs apply to the Chapter in which they occur so that the reference figure pinpoints the pertinent section and paragraph number.

Procedures, once described in the text, are not normally repeated. If it is necessary to refer to another Chapter the reference will be given in Chapter number and section number thus: Chapter 1/16.

If it is considered necessary to refer to a particular paragraph in another Chapter the reference is eg, 'Chapter 1/6:5'. Cross references given without use of the word 'Chapter' apply to sections and/or paragraphs in the same Chapter, eg, 'see Section 8' means also 'in this Chapter'.

When the left or right side of the car is mentioned it is as if looking forward.

Great effort has been made to ensure that this book is complete and up to date. The manufacturers continually modify their cars, even in retrospect.

Whilst every care is taken to ensure that the information in this manual is correct no liability can be accepted by the authors or publishers for loss, damage or injury caused by any errors in or omissions from the information given.

Datsun 1200 — 2 door saloon

Datsun 1200 — coupe

As this book has been written in the United Kingdom it uses the appropriate English component names. Some of these differ from those used in America. Normally this causes no difficulty. But to make sure, a glossary is printed below.

Glossary

English	American
Anti-roll bar	Stabiliser or sway bar
Bonnet (engine cover)	Hood
Boot (luggage compartment)	Trunk
Bottom gear	1st gear
Bulkhead	Firewall
Clearance	Lash
Crownwheel	Ring gear (of differential)
Catch	Latch
Camfollower or tappet	Valve lifter or tappet
Cat's eye	Road reflecting lane marker
Circlip	Snap ring
Drop arm	Pitman arm
Drop head coupe	Convertible
Dynamo	Generator (DC)
Earth (electrical)	Ground
Estate car	Station wagon
Exhaust manifold	Header
Fault finding	Trouble shooting
Free play	Lash
Free wheel	Coast
Gudgeon pin	Piston pin or wrist pin
Gearchange	Shift
Gearbox	Transmission
Hood	Soft top
Hard top	Hard top
Half shaft	Axle shaft
Hot spot	Heat riser
Leading shoe (of brake)	Primary shoe
Layshaft (of gearbox)	Counter shaft
Mudguard or wing	Fender
Motorway	Freeway, turnpike etc
Paraffin	Kerosene
Petrol	Gas
Reverse	Back-up
Saloon	Sedan
Split cotter (for valve spring cap)	Lock (for valve spring retainer)
Split pin	Cotter pin
Sump	Oil pan
Silencer	Muffler
Steering arm	Spindle arm
Side light	Parking light
Side marker light	Cat's eye
Spanner	Wrench
Tappet	Valve lifter
Tab washer	Tang: lock
Top gear	High
Transmission	Whole drive line from clutch to axle shaft
Trailing shoe (of brake)	Secondary shoe
Track rod (of steering)	Tie rod (or connecting rod)
Windscreen	Windshield

Miscellaneous points

An 'Oil seal' is fitted to components lubricated by grease!

A 'Damper' is a 'Shock absorber': it damps out bouncing, and absorbs shocks of bump impact. Both names are correct, and both are used haphazardly.

Note that British drum brakes are different from the Bendix type that is common in America, so different descriptive names result. The shoe end furthest from the hydraulic wheel cylinder is on a pivot; interconnection between the shoes as on Bendix brakes is most uncommon. Therefore the phrase 'Primary' or 'Secondary' shoe does not apply. A shoe is said to be Leading or Trailing. A 'Leading' shoe is one on which a point on the drum, as it rotates forward, reaches the shoe at the end worked by the hydraulic cylinder before the anchor end. The opposite is a trailing shoe, and this one has no self servo from the wrapping effect of the rotating drum.

The word 'Tuning' has a narrower meaning than in America, and applies to that engine servicing to ensure full power. The words 'Service' or 'Maintenance' are used where an American would say 'Tune-up'

Contents

Chapter	Section	Page	Section	Page
	Uses of English	4	Routine maintenance	10
	Metric conversion tables	6	Lubrication chart	13
	Dimensions and capacities	9	Ordering spare parts	14
1 Engine	Engine removal	18	Reassembly	28
	Engine dismantling	20	Valve adjustment	31
	Examination and renovation	25	Replacement	33
	Decarbonising	28	Fault finding	34
2 Cooling system	Draining and flushing	35	Thermostat	37
	Filling	36	Water pump	37
	Anti-freeze mixture	36	Fan belt adjustment	37
	Radiator	36	Fault finding	38
3 Fuel system	Air cleaner	40	Carburettor	45
	Fuel pump	41	Exhaust system	53
	Evaporative emission control	43	Fault finding	54
4 Ignition system	Contact breaker points	56	Ignition timing	57
	Condenser	56	Spark plugs	58
	Distributor	56	Fault finding	61
5 Clutch	Adjustment	64	Slave cylinder	67
	Bleeding hydraulic system	67	Release bearing	68
	Master cylinder	67	Fault diagnosis	70
6 Gearbox (manual)	Removal and refitting	73	Steering column gearchange	80
	Dismantling	73	Controlled vacuum advance	80
	Reassembly	77	Fault diagnosis	82
(automatic transmission)	Removal and refitting	85	Fault diagnosis	88
7 Propeller shaft	Universal joints	89	Fault diagnosis	90
	Removal and refitting	89		
8 Rear axle	Removal and refitting	91	Pinion oil seal	95
	Half shafts	93	Differential carrier	95
9 Braking system	Bleeding hydraulic system	99	Wheel cylinders	101
	Drum brakes adjustment	99	Caliper unit	103
	Brake shoes	99	Master cylinder	105
	Flexible hoses	101	Fault diagnosis	108
10 Electrical system	Battery	110	Lamps	116
	Alternator	111	Horns	119
	Starter motor	113	Windscreen wiper	120
	Voltage regulator	115	Fault diagnosis	122
	Fuses	116	Wiring diagrams	124
11 Suspension and steering	Maintenance	129	Front wheel bearings	132
	Stabiliser bar	129	Rear road springs	132
	Track control arm	131	Steering gear	135
	Front suspension struts	131	Fault diagnosis	142
12 Bodywork	Maintenance	144	Door locks	147
	Repairs	144	Bonnet and boot lid	148
	Doors	145	Safety belts	148
	Windscreen glass	145	Heater	148
Index				155

Metric conversion tables

Inches	Decimals	Millimetres	mm	Inches	Inches	mm
			Millimetres to Inches		**Inches to Millimetres**	
			mm	Inches	Inches	mm
1/64	0.015625	0.3969	0.01	0.00039	0.001	0.0254
1/32	0.03125	0.7937	0.02	0.00079	0.002	0.0508
3/64	0.046875	1.1906	0.03	0.00118	0.003	0.0762
1/16	0.0625	1.5875	0.04	0.00157	0.004	0.1016
5/64	0.078125	1.9844	0.05	0.00197	0.005	0.1270
3/32	0.09375	2.3812	0.06	0.00236	0.006	0.1524
7/64	0.109375	2.7781	0.07	0.00276	0.007	0.1778
1/8	0.125	3.1750	0.08	0.00315	0.008	0.2032
9/64	0.140625	3.5719	0.09	0.00354	0.009	0.2286
5/32	0.15625	3.9687	0.1	0.00394	0.01	0.254
11/64	0.171875	4.3656	0.2	0.00787	0.02	0.508
3/16	0.1875	4.7625	0.3	0.01181	0.03	0.762
13/64	0.203125	5.1594	0.4	0.01575	0.04	1.016
7/32	0.21875	5.5562	0.5	0.01969	0.05	1.270
15/64	0.234375	5.9531	0.6	0.02362	0.06	1.524
1/4	0.25	6.3500	0.7	0.02756	0.07	1.778
17/64	0.265625	6.7469	0.8	0.03150	0.08	2.032
9/32	0.28125	7.1437	0.9	0.03543	0.09	2.286
19/64	0.296875	7.5406	1	0.03937	0.1	2.54
5/16	0.3125	7.9375	2	0.07874	0.2	5.08
21/64	0.328125	8.3344	3	0.11811	0.3	7.62
11/32	0.34375	8.7312	4	0.15748	0.4	10.16
23/64	0.359375	9.1281	5	0.19685	0.5	12.70
3/8	0.375	9.5250	6	0.23622	0.6	15.24
25/64	0.390625	9.9219	7	0.27559	0.7	17.78
13/32	0.40625	10.3187	8	0.31496	0.8	20.32
27/64	0.421875	10.7156	9	0.35433	0.9	22.86
7/16	0.4375	11.1125	10	0.39370	1	25.4
29/64	0.453125	11.5094	11	0.43307	2	50.8
15/32	0.46875	11.9062	12	0.47244	3	76.2
31/64	0.484375	12.3031	13	0.51181	4	101.6
1/2	0.5	12.7000	14	0.55118	5	127.0
33/64	0.515625	13.0969	15	0.59055	6	152.4
17/32	0.53125	13.4937	16	0.62992	7	177.8
35/64	0.546875	13.8906	17	0.66929	8	203.2
9/16	0.5625	14.2875	18	0.70866	9	228.6
37/64	0.578125	14.6844	19	0.74803	10	254.0
19/32	0.59375	15.0812	20	0.78740	11	279.4
39/64	0.609375	15.4781	21	0.82677	12	304.8
5/8	0.625	15.8750	22	0.86614	13	330.2
41/64	0.640625	16.2719	23	0.90551	14	355.6
21/32	0.65625	16.6687	24	0.94488	15	381.0
43/64	0.671875	17.0656	25	0.98425	16	406.4
11/16	0.6875	17.4625	26	1.02362	17	431.8
45/64	0.703125	17.8594	27	1.06299	18	457.2
23/32	0.71875	18.2562	28	1.10236	19	482.6
47/64	0.734375	18.6531	29	1.14173	20	508.0
3/4	0.75	19.0500	30	1.18110	21	533.4
49/64	0.765625	19.4469	31	1.22047	22	558.8
25/32	0.78125	19.8437	32	1.25984	23	584.2
51/64	0.796875	20.2406	33	1.29921	24	609.6
13/16	0.8125	20.6375	34	1.33858	25	635.0
53/64	0.828125	21.0344	35	1.37795	26	660.4
27/32	0.84375	21.4312	36	1.41732	27	685.8
55/64	0.859375	21.8281	37	1.4567	28	711.2
7/8	0.875	22.2250	38	1.4961	29	736.6
57/64	0.890625	22.6219	39	1.5354	30	762.0
29/32	0.90625	23.0187	40	1.5748	31	787.4
59/64	0.921875	23.4156	41	1.6142	32	812.8
15/16	0.9375	23.8125	42	1.6535	33	838.2
61/64	0.953125	24.2094	43	1.6929	34	863.6
31/32	0.96875	24.6062	44	1.7323	35	889.0
63/64	0.984375	25.0031	45	1.7717	36	914.4

1   Imperial gallon = 8 Imp pints = 1.16 US gallons = 277.42 cu in = 4.5459 litres

1   US gallon = 4 US quarts = 0.862 Imp gallon = 231 cu in = 3.785 litres

1   Litre = 0.2199 Imp gallon = 0.2642 US gallon = 61.0253 cu in = 1000 cc

Miles to Kilometres		Kilometres to Miles	
1	1.61	1	0.62
2	3.22	2	1.24
3	4.83	3	1.86
4	6.44	4	2.49
5	8.05	5	3.11
6	9.66	6	3.73
7	11.27	7	4.35
8	12.88	8	4.97
9	14.48	9	5.59
10	16.09	10	6.21
20	32.19	20	12.43
30	48.28	30	18.64
40	64.37	40	24.85
50	80.47	50	31.07
60	96.56	60	37.28
70	112.65	70	43.50
80	128.75	80	49.71
90	144.84	90	55.92
100	160.93	100	62.14

lb f ft to Kg f m		Kg f m to lb f ft		lb f/in^2 : Kg f/cm^2		Kg f/cm^2 : lb f/in^2	
1	0.138	1	7.233	1	0.07	1	14.22
2	0.276	2	14.466	2	0.14	2	28.50
3	0.414	3	21.699	3	0.21	3	42.67
4	0.553	4	28.932	4	0.28	4	56.89
5	0.691	5	36.165	5	0.35	5	71.12
6	0.829	6	43.398	6	0.42	6	85.34
7	0.967	7	50.631	7	0.49	7	99.56
8	1.106	8	57.864	8	0.56	8	113.79
9	1.244	9	65.097	9	0.63	9	128.00
10	1.382	10	62.330	10	0.70	10	142.23
20	2.765	20	144.660	20	1.41	20	284.47
30	4.147	30	216.990	30	2.11	30	426.70

Castrol GRADES

Castrol Engine Oils

Castrol GTX

An ultra high performance SAE 20W/50 motor oil which exceeds the latest API MS requirements and manufacturers' specifications. Castrol GTX with liquid tungsten† generously protects engines at the extreme limits of performance, and combines both good cold starting with oil consumption control. Approved by leading car makers.

Castrol XL 20/50

Contains liquid tungsten†; well suited to the majority of conditions giving good oil consumption control in both new and old cars.

Castrolite (Multi-grade)

This is the lightest multi-grade oil of the Castrol motor oil family containing liquid tungsten†. It is best suited to ensure easy winter starting and for those car models whose manufacturers specify lighter weight oils.

Castrol Grand Prix

An SAE 50 engine oil for use where a heavy, full-bodied lubricant is required.

Castrol Two-Stroke-Four

A premium SAE 30 motor oil possessing good detergency characteristics and corrosion inhibitors, coupled with low ash forming tendency and excellent anti-scuff properties. It is suitable for all two-stroke motor-cycles, and for two-stroke and small four-stroke horticultural machines.

Castrol CR (Multi-grade)

A high quality engine oil of the SAE-20W/30 multi-grade type, suited to mixed fleet operations.

Castrol CRI 10, 20, 30

Primarily for diesel engines, a range of heavily fortified, fully detergent oils, covering the requirements of DEF 2101-D and Supplement 1 specifications.

Castrol CRB 20, 30

Primarily for diesel engines, heavily fortified, fully detergent oils, covering the requirements of MIL-L-2104B.

Castrol R 40

Primarily designed and developed for highly stressed racing engines. Castrol 'R' should not be mixed with any other oil nor with any grade of Castrol.
†*Liquid Tungsten is an oil soluble long chain tertiary alkyl primary amine tungstate covered by British Patent No. 882,295.*

Castrol Gear Oils

Castrol Hypoy (90 EP)

A light-bodied powerful extreme pressure gear oil for use in hypoid rear axles and in some gearboxes.

Castrol Gear Oils (continued)

Castrol Hypoy Light (80 EP)

A very light-bodied powerful extreme pressure gear oil for use in hypoid rear axles in cold climates and in some gearboxes.

Castrol Hypoy B (90 EP)

A light-bodied powerful extreme pressure gear oil that complies with the requirements of the MIL-L-2105B specification, for use in certain gearboxes and rear axles.

Castrol Hi-Press (140 EP)

A heavy-bodied extreme pressure gear oil for use in spiral bevel rear axles and some gearboxes.

Castrol ST (90)

A light-bodied gear oil with fortifying additives

Castrol D (140)

A heavy full-bodied gear oil with fortifying additives.

Castrol Thio-Hypoy FD (90 EP)

A light-bodied powerful extreme pressure gear oil. This is a special oil for running-in certain hypoid gears.

Automatic Transmission Fluids

Castrol TQF

(Automatic Transmission Fluid)

Approved for use in all Borg-Warner Automatic Transmission Units. Castrol TQF also meets Ford specification M2C 33F.

Castrol TQ Dexron®

(Automatic Transmission Fluid)

Complies with the requirements of Dexron® Automatic Transmission Fluids as laid down by General Motors Corporation.

Castrol Greases

Castrol LM

A multi-purpose high melting point lithium based grease approved for most automotive applications including chassis and wheel bearing lubrication.

Castrol MS3

A high melting point lithium based grease containing molybdenum disulphide.

Castrol BNS

A high melting point grease for use where recommended by certain manufacturers in front wheel bearings when disc brakes are fitted.

Castrol Greases (continued)

Castrol CL

A semi-fluid calcium based grease, which is both waterproof and adhesive, intended for chassis lubrication.

Castrol Medium

A medium consistency calcium based grease.

Castrol Heavy

A heavy consistency calcium based grease.

Castrol PH

A white grease for plunger housings and other moving parts on brake mechanisms. *It must NOT be allowed to come into contact with brake fluid when applied to the moving parts of hydraulic brakes.*

Castrol Graphited Grease

A graphited grease for the lubrication of transmission chains.

Castrol Under-Water Grease

A grease for the under-water gears of outboard motors.

Anti-Freeze

Castrol Anti-Freeze

Contains anti-corrosion additives with ethylene glycol. Recommended for the cooling systems of all petrol and diesel engines.

Speciality Products

Castrol Girling Damper Oil Thin

The oil for Girling piston type hydraulic dampers.

Castrol Shockol

A light viscosity oil for use in some piston type shock absorbers and in some hydraulic systems employing synthetic rubber seals. It must not be used in braking systems.

Castrol Penetrating Oil

A leaf spring lubricant possessing a high degree of penetration and providing protection against rust.

Castrol Solvent Flushing Oil

A light-bodied solvent oil, designed for flushing engines, rear axles, gearboxes and gearcasings.

Castrollo

An upper cylinder lubricant for use in the proportion of 1 fluid ounce to two gallons of fuel.

Everyman Oil

A light-bodied machine oil containing anti-corrosion additives for both general use and cycle lubrication.

Introduction to the Datsun

The Datsun 1200 is an economy/subcompact car. Conventional to the extreme, front engine, leaf spring solid rear axle and pleasing but not striking bodywork. It's a good car - a rather meaningless statement when normally made but it envelopes the Datsun 1200 well. It is known as the 'Sunny' range. A 2 door saloon, a coupe and an estate (wagon) are available. An automatic transmission is an option instead of the normal 'four on the floor'.

Little has been written about the 1200 because it does not lend itself to being picked out from the mass of other small cars, and little need be said here, suffice to say that it occupies a fully justified standing in the market place with its reliability, economy and efficiency.

General dimensions and capacities

Dimensions (overall)

Length (car)	150.8 in.
(van and estate)	152.2 in.
(coupe)	150.4 in.
Width (all except coupe)	58.9 in.
(coupe)	59.6 in.
Height (all except coupe)	54.7 in.
(coupe)	53.1 in.
Ground clearance	6.7 in.
Wheelbase	90.6 in.

Weights

	lbs
Standard four-door saloon	1532
(with automatic transmission)	1609
De-luxe four door saloon	1576
(with auto-transmission)	1653
Standard two-door saloon	1499
De-luxe two-door saloon	1543
(with auto-transmission)	1620
Standard van	1609
Standard estate car	1609
De-luxe van	1653
De-luxe estate car	1653
Coupe	1565
Coupe (North America)	1609
Two-door saloon (North America)	1587

Routine maintenance

Maintenance is essential for ensuring safety and desirable for the purpose of getting the best in terms of performance and economy from the car. Over the years the need for periodic lubrication - oiling, greasing and so on - has been drastically reduced if not totally eliminated. This has unfortunately tended to lead some owners to think that because no such action is required the items either no longer exist or will last for ever. This is a serious delusion. It follows therefore that the largest initial element of maintenance is visual examination. This may lead to repairs or renewals.

In the summary given here the 'essential for safety' items are shown in **bold type**. These **must** be attended to at the regular frequencies shown in order to avoid the possibility of accidents and loss of life, Other neglect results in unreliability, increased running costs, more rapid wear and more rapid depreciation of the vehicle in general.

EVERY 250 miles travelled or weekly - whichever comes first

STEERING
   Check the tyre pressures.
   Examine tyres for wear or damage.
   Is steering smooth and accurate?

BRAKES
   Check reservoir fluid level.
   Is there any fall off in braking efficiency?
   Try an emergency stop. Is adjustment necessary?

LIGHTS, WIPERS & HORNS
   Do all bulbs work at the front and rear?
   Are the headlamp beams aligned properly?
   Do the wipers and horns work?
   Check windscreen washer fluid level.

ENGINE
   Check the sump oil level and top up if required.
   Check the radiator coolant level and top up if required.
   Check the battery electrolyte level and top up to the level of the plates with distilled water as needed.

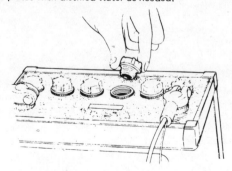

Checking the battery electrolyte level

3,000 miles

EVERY 3,000 miles or 4 monthly, whichever comes first, or earlier if indications suggest that safety items in particular are not performing correctly.

STEERING
Examine all steering linkage rods, joints and bushes for signs of wear or damage.
Check front wheel hub bearings and adjust if necessary.
Check tightness of steering box mounting bolts.
Check the steering box oil level.

BRAKES
Examine disc pads and drum shoes to determine the amount of friction material left. Renew if necessary.
Examine all hydraulic pipes, cylinders and unions for signs of chafing, corrosion, dents or any other form of deterioration or leaks.
Adjust drum type brakes.

SUSPENSION
Examine all nuts, bolts and shackles securing the suspension units, front and rear. Tighten if necessary.
Examine the rubber bushes for signs of wear and play.

ENGINE
Change oil.
Check distributor points gap.
Check and clean spark plugs.

GEARBOX (manual and automatic)
Check oil level and top up if necessary.

CLUTCH
Grease cable lubrication point (mechanical type operation).
Check fluid reservoir level and top up if necessary.

BODY
Lubricate all locks and hinges.
Check that water drain holes at bottom of doors are clear.

6,000 miles

ENGINE
Check fan belt tension and adjust if necessary.
Check cylinder head bolt torque setting.
Check valve clearances and adjust if necessary.
Renew oil filter.
Lubricate distributor.
Clean air cleaner element.
Clean fuel pump.

STEERING
Rotate road wheels and rebalance if necessary.
Dismantle front hubs, clean out old lubricant and repack with fresh grease. Assemble and adjust.

BRAKES
Check pedal free movement and for oil leakage at cylinders.

CLUTCH
Check pedal free movement and for oil leakage at cylinders.

12,000 miles

ENGINE
Check crankcase fume emission valve.
Check fuel storage evaporative emission control system.
Check exhaust emission control system.
Fit new spark plugs.

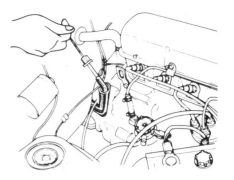

Checking the automatic transmission fluid level

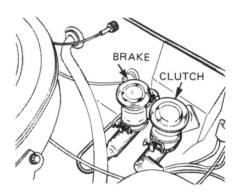

The brake and clutch hydraulic fluid reservoirs

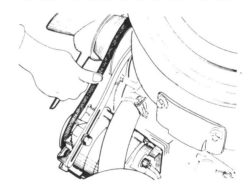

Checking the fan belt tension

Checking the contact breaker points gap

Fit new distributor points.
Clean carburettor float chamber and jets.
Renew fuel line filter unit.
Check HT ignition leads for deterioration.

STEERING
Check wheel alignment.

SUSPENSION
Check shock absorber operation.

TRANSMISSION
Check security of propeller shaft bolts.
Check oil level in rear axle and top up if necessary.

24,000 miles

ENGINE
Flush cooling system and refill with anti-freeze mixture.
Renew air cleaner element.

BRAKES
Lubricate handbrake linkage.

30,000 miles

TRANSMISSION
Drain manual gearbox and refill with fresh oil.
Drain rear axle and refill with fresh oil.
Check propeller shaft universal joints for wear and re-condition if necessary.

STEERING
Grease ball joints.

HEADLIGHTS
Check beams and adjust if required

48,000 miles

BRAKES
Drain hydraulic system, renew all cylinder seals and refill with fresh fluid. Bleed system.

CLUTCH
Drain hydraulic system, renew master and slave cylinder seals, refill with fresh fluid. Bleed system.

Additionally the following items should be attended to as time can be spared:-

CLEANING
Examination of components requires that they be cleaned. The same applies to the body of the car, inside and out, in order that deterioration due to rust or unknown damage may be detected. Certain parts of the body frame, if rusted badly, can result in the vehicle being declared unsafe and it will not pass the annual test for roadworthiness.

EXHAUST SYSTEM
An exhaust system must be leakproof, and the noise level below a certain minimum. Excessive leaks may cause carbon monoxide fumes to enter the passenger compartment. Excessive noise constitutes a public nuisance. Both these faults may cause the vehicle to be kept off the road. Repair or replace defective sections when symptoms are apparent.

Lubricating the clutch operating cable

FUEL STRAINER

Location of the fuel line filter

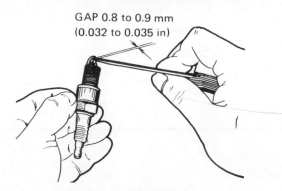

GAP 0.8 to 0.9 mm
(0.032 to 0.035 in)

Checking a spark plug gap

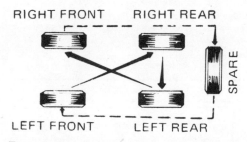

RIGHT FRONT   RIGHT REAR

SPARE

LEFT FRONT   LEFT REAR

Tyre rotation diagram to ensure even wear pattern

Lubrication Chart

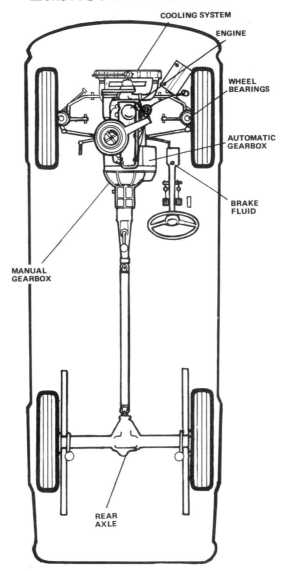

COOLING SYSTEM

ENGINE

WHEEL BEARINGS

AUTOMATIC GEARBOX

BRAKE FLUID

MANUAL GEARBOX

REAR AXLE

Recommended lubricants

Component	Grade	Castrol Grade
Engine	20W/50 Multigrade engine oil	**CASTROL GTX**
Manual Gearbox	Hypoid gear oil 90 EP	**CASTROL HYPOY**
Automatic Transmission		**CASTROL TQF**
Rear Axle/Differential	Hypoid gear oil 90 EP	**CASTROL HYPOY B**
Steering box	Hypoid gear oil 90 EP	**CASTROL HYPOY**
Wheel bearings, suspension joints	High melting point lithium based grease	**CASTROL LM GREASE**
Brake Fluid	Exceeds all required specifications	**CASTROL GIRLING UNIVERSAL BRAKE AND CLUTCH FLUID**
Cooling System	Glycol based anti-freeze mixed with appropriate quantity of water	**CASTROL ANTI-FREEZE**
All body fittings and general oiling	Thin universal oil	**CASTROL EVERYMAN**

Ordering spare parts

Buy genuine Datsun spare parts from a Datsun main dealer. Nothing is to be gained by purchasing spares from other sources. Always give as much information as possible when ordering spare parts. Quote the vehicle model, year of manufacture and body, chassis and engine serial number as appropriate.

Modifications are a continuing and unpublicised process in vehicle manufacture quite apart from major model changes. Spare parts manuals and lists are compiled upon a numerical basis, the individual vehicle numbers being essential to correct identification of the component required.

The vehicle identification number is located on the top surface of the instrument panel cowl and it is visible through the windscreen on vehicles manufactured for and operating in North America.

Vehicles operating in other territories have the identification (chassis) number stamped on the engine compartment rear bulkhead. The key to the vehicle number is as follows.

Prefix	B	R.H. Drive
	L	L.H. Drive
	K	Coupe
	V	Estate car or van
Suffix	U	For North America
	R	Two door model
	T	Manual gearbox
	A	Automatic transmission

The model identification plate is fixed to the engine compartment rear bulkhead. It indicates the type of vehicle, engine capacity, maximum bhp, the wheel base, engine number and vehicle serial number.

The body colour coding is shown on a plate attached to the top surface of the radiator support crossmember. The engine number is duplicated on rear, right hand side of the engine block.

Location of engine serial number

IDENTIFICATION NUMBER

LB10 -XXXXXX

Location of model identification plate

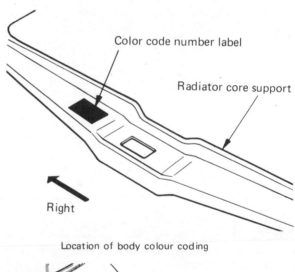

Color code number label

Radiator core support

Right

Location of body colour coding

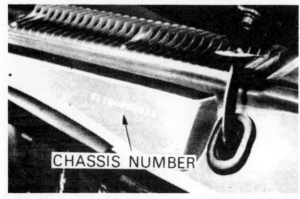

CHASSIS NUMBER

Location of vehicle identification plate (all other territories)

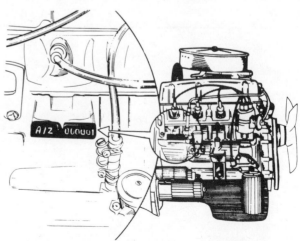

A12 060001

Location of vehicle identification number (North America)

Chapter 1 Engine

Contents

General description	1
Major operations with the engine in position in the vehicle	2
Major operations with the engine removed	3
Method of engine removal	4
Engine removal	5
Engine - separation from manual gearbox	6
Engine - separation from automatic transmission	7
Dismantling the engine - general	8
Removing ancillary engine components	9
Cylinder head - removal	10
Valves - removal	11
Dismantling the rocker assembly	12
Sump - removal	13
Timing cover, gear and chain removal	14
Piston, connecting rod and big-end bearing - removal ...	15
Flywheel - removal	16
Main bearings and crankshaft - removal	17
Piston rings - removal	18
Gudgeon pin - removal	19
Lubrication system - description	20
Oil pump - inspection and servicing	21
Oil pressure relief valve - inspection and servicing	22
Crankcase ventilation control system - description and servicing	23
Engine front mountings - renewal	24
Examination and renovation - general	25
Crankshaft and main bearings - inspection and renovation ...	26
Connecting rods and bearings - examination and renovation	27
Cylinder bores and crankcase - examination and renovation	28
Pistons and piston rings - examination and renovation ...	29
Camshaft and camshaft bearings - examination and renovation	30
Valves and valve seats - examination and renovation ...	31
Valve guides - examination and renovation	32
Timing gears and chain - examination and renovation ...	33
Rockers and rocker shaft - examination and renovation ...	34
Tappets - examination and renovation	35
Flywheel starter ring gear - examination and renovation ...	36
Cylinder head - decarbonising and examination	37
Engine reassembly - general	38
Assembling the engine	39
Engine replacement - general	40
Engine/gearbox - refitting to the vehicle	41
Engine adjustment after major overhaul	42
Fault finding - engine	43

Specifications

(all dimensions in inches unless otherwise stated).

Cylinder block

Material	cast iron
Type	four cylinders, in-line, overhead valve
Capacity	1171 cc
Bore	2.874
Stroke	2.756
Firing order	1 3 4 2
Compression ratio	9 : 1
Oil pressure (hot) at 2000 rev/min.	43 - 50 lb/in^2

Cylinder head

Material	aluminium alloy

Pistons

Type	aluminium, concave head
Bore clearance	0.023 to 0.043
Diameter - standard	2.8727 to 2.8747
- oversize 50	2.8924 to 2.8944
- oversize 100	2.9121 to 2.9140
- oversize 150	2.9318 to 2.9337

Piston rings

Number	two compression (top) one oil control
Ring groove width - compression	0.0787
- oil control	0.1575
Ring side clearance in groove - compression	0.0016 to 0.0027
- oil control	0.0016 to 0.0031
Ring end gap - compression	0.0079 to 0.0138
- oil control	0.0118 to 0.0354

Gudgeon pins

Diameter	0.6869 to 0.6871
Length	2.5681 to 2.5779
Clearance in piston	0.0002 to 0.0003 (at 20ºC ambient)
Interference fit in small end of connecting rod	0.0007 to 0.0013

Crankshaft

Number and type of main bearings	five, shell, detachable
Journal diameter	1.9666 to 1.9671
Maximum journal ovality	less than 0.0012
Crankpin diameter	1.7706 to 1.7701
Maximum crankpin ovality	less than 0.0012
Main bearing thickness	0.0722 to 0.0719
Main bearing clearance	0.0008 to 0.0024
Main bearing clearance (wear limit)	0.0059
End-float	0.0029 to 0.0059 (max. 0.0118)

Connecting rods

Bearing thickness	0.0591 to 0.0594
Big-end end-float	0.0079 to 0.0012
Big-end end-float (wear limit)	less than 0.016
Big-end bearing clearance	0.0008 to 0.0020
Weight difference between rods	not more than 0.18 oz

Camshaft

Number of bearings	five, bored in line
End-float	0.0008 to 0.0031
Lobe lift	0.222
Journal diameter — 1st	1.7237 to 1.7242
2nd	1.7041 to 1.7046
3rd	1.6844 to 1.6849
4th	1.6647 to 1.6652
5th	1.6224 to 1.6229
Bearing inner diameter — 1st	1.7261 to 1.7257
2nd	1.7060 to 1.7050
3rd	1.6868 to 1.6865
4th	1.6667 to 1.6663
5th	1.6247 to 1.6243

Valves

Clearance (hot) inlet and exhaust	0.0138
Clearance (cold) inlet and exhaust	0.0098
Valve head diameter - inlet	1.378
- exhaust	1.142
Valve stem diameter - inlet	0.3138 to 0.3144
- exhaust	0.3128 to 0.3134
Valve length - inlet and exhaust	4.034 to 4.041
Valve lift	0.3346
Valve spring free length	1.831
Valve guide length	2.087
Valve guide height from cylinder head surface	0.709
Valve guide inner diameter - inlet and exhaust	0.3156 to 0.3150
Valve guide outer diameter - inlet and exhaust	0.4737 to 0.4733
Valve stem to guide clearance - inlet	0.0006 to 0.0018
- exhaust	0.0016 to 0.0028
Valve seat width - inlet	0.0512
- exhaust	0.0709
Valve seat angle - inlet and exhaust	45º
Valve seat interference fit - inlet and exhaust	0.0025 to 0.0038
Valve guide interference fit - inlet and exhaust	0.0009 to 0.0017

Timing chain

Type	double roller

Oil pump and lubrication

Type (pump)	rotor, camshaft gear driven
Type (system)	pressure feed
Filter	canister, disposable, full-flow type
Pressure relief valve	ball and spring, non adjustable
Sump and filter capacity	5½ pints

Torque wrench settings

	lb/ft	kg/m
Cylinder head bolts (cold)	40 - 43	5.5 - 6.0
Main bearing cap bolts	36 - 43	5.0 - 6.0
Big-end cap nuts	23 - 28	3.2 - 3.8
Flywheel bolts	47 - 54	6.5 - 7.5
Camshaft gearwheel bolts	29 - 35	4.0 - 4.8
Oil pump body bolts	8 - 12	1.1 - 1.7
Crankshaft pulley bolt	108 - 116	15 - 16
Oil relief valve plug	29 - 36	
Timing cover bolts	5	
Manifold bolts	6.5 - 10	
Clutch bellhousing to engine bolts	12 - 16	
Auto. converter housing to engine	30 - 36	

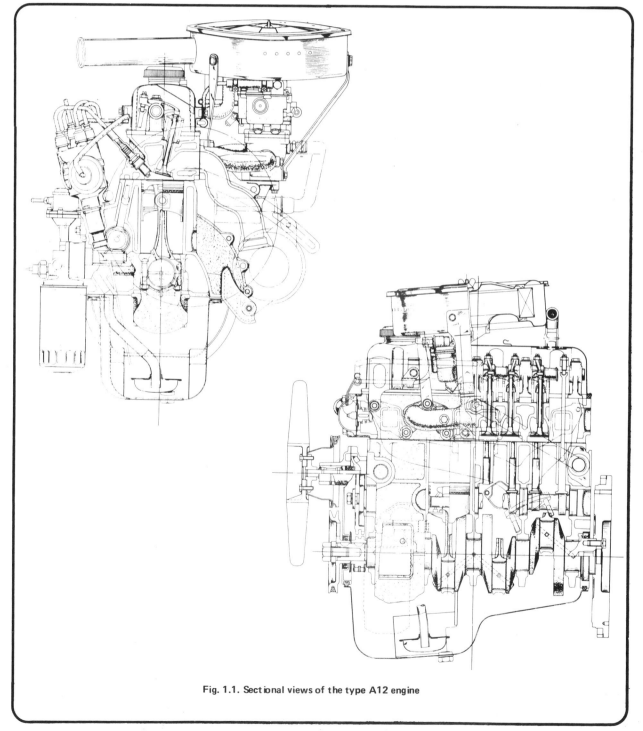

Fig. 1.1. Sectional views of the type A12 engine

1 General description

The engine fitted to all models in the Datsun 1200 range, with the exception of the pick-up, is the type A12. The pick-up available in some markets is fitted with a type A10 engine of 998 cc capacity as are the earlier Datsun 100A models. The A10 engine is similar in general appearance and construction to the larger 1171 cc engine but has only three main crankshaft bearings and embodies a number of light alloy components.

This Chapter describes fully the A12 engine and no further reference to the smaller engine is made.

The A12 engine is front mounted four cylinder, in line, overhead valve, water-cooled design. The cylinder block embodies five main bearings for the crankshaft, the latter being of forged steel construction and incorporates oil drillings for lubrication of the main bearings.

The pistons are made of aluminium with domed crowns, the connecting rods are of forged steel with gudgeon pins which are an interference fit in the connecting rod small ends but fully floating in the pistons.

The cylinder head is of light alloy with pressed in valve seats.

A cast iron crankshaft is fitted, which is supported by five bearings and driven by a double roller chain from the crankshaft. The overhead valve mechanism comprises conventional camshaft operated tappets, push rods and rocker shaft and arms. The valves are fitted with single coil springs and split cotters are employed to retain the valve spring caps.

The inlet manifold is aluminium and the exhaust manifold is cast iron and incorporates a quick warm-up valve.

The power unit is mounted at three points, one each side of the engine crankcase and one below the gearbox housing. The mountings are of the bonded rubber/metal type acting under compression of steel brackets.

2 Major operations with the engine in position in the car

The following major operations can be carried out to the engine with it in place in the body frame:-
1 Removal and replacement of the cylinder head assembly.
2 Removal and replacement of the sump.
3 Removal and replacement of the big end bearings.
4 Removal and replacement of the pistons and connecting rods.
5 Removal and replacement of the timing chain and gears.
6 Removal and replacement of the oil pump.
7 Removal and replacement of the engine front mountings.
8 Removal and replacement of the engine/gearbox rear mounting.

3 Major operations with the engine removed

The following major operations can be carried out with the engine out of the body frame and on the bench or floor:-
1 Removal and replacement of the main bearings.
2 Removal and replacement of the crankshaft.
3 Removal and replacement of the flywheel.
4 Removal and replacement of the crankshaft rear bearing oil seal.
5 Removal and replacement of the camshaft.

4 Method of engine removal

The engine complete with gearbox or automatic transmission unit can be lifted upward and out of the engine compartment. Removal of the engine only is impossible due to the lack of forward clearance required to clear the gearbox primary shaft or drive plate.

5 Engine removal

1 Open the bonnet (hood) unscrew and remove the four hinge securing bolts and lift the lid away.
2 Protect the top surfaces of the front wings with thick covers to prevent scratching during the removal operations.
3 Disconnect the earth lead from the negative terminal of the battery.
4 Drain the cooling system by means of the radiator tap and retain the coolant (if mixed with anti-freeze) in a suitable receptacle for further use unless it is rusty or contaminated.
5 Disconnect the two radiator hoses, remove the four radiator securing bolts and lift the radiator carefully from its location.
6 Disconnect the coil to distributor HT lead.
7 Disconnect the leads to the oil pressure switch and the water temperature transmitter.
8 Disconnect the LT lead from the distributor.
9 Disconnect the cable from the starter motor.
10 Disconnect the fuel supply hose at the fuel pump and plug the hose to prevent loss of fuel.
11 Disconnect the cables from the alternator.
12 Disconnect the heater flow and return water hoses.
13 Remove the air cleaner and then disconnect the accelerator and choke controls from the carburettor.
14 Disconnect the clutch operating cable at its forked clevis (right hand drive vehicles) or an left hand drive vehicles, remove the slave cylinder (one bolt) after disconnecting the operating rod from the clutch release arm. The slave cylinder may then be swung up out of the way without disturbing the hydraulic circuit which would necessitate subsequent bleeding of the system.
15 Disconnect the exhaust pipe down tube from the manifold by unscrewing the two flange securing nuts.
16 Remove the two bolts which secure the starter motor to the clutch bellhousing.
17 Disconnect the reversing lamp switch cables at the gearbox.
18 Disconnect the speedometer drive cable from the gearbox.
19 Mark the edges of the rear axle pinion flange and the propeller shaft mating flange, for exact replacement. Unscrew and remove the four flange securing bolts.
20 Pull the propeller shaft from engagement with the rear of the gearbox.
21 Remove the gearshift lever. With the remote control type lever, disconnect the remote control rod completely from the cross shaft and the actuating lever. With floor mounted gearshift levers, remove the rubber boot, withdraw the lockpin and withdraw the lever, all operations being carried out from within the vehicle interior. On vehicles fitted with automatic transmission, withdraw the securing pins from both ends of the cross shaft and remove the gearshift rod.
22 Fit chains or slings to the engine and using a suitable hoist, lift the engine sufficiently just to take its weight. Unscrew and remove the nuts from the engine rubber insulator mounting blocks, one on each side of the engine.
23 Unscrew and remove the rear mounting bolts and detach the rear mounting. Take care that the rear of the gearbox does not suddenly incline downwards as the mounting is removed and the use of a jack as a support is necessary.
24 Carefully hoist the engine until the front engine mounting brackets clear the mounting pad bolts. Pull the engine/gearbox forwards and hoist it from the engine compartment at a steeply inclined angle.

6 Engine - separation from manual gearbox

1 With the engine and gearbox now removed from the vehicle, unscrew and remove the bolts which connect the clutch bell-housing to the engine block.
2 Pull the gearbox from the engine in a straight line and support the gearbox so that its weight does not hang upon the gearbox primary shaft, even momentarily, whilst it is still engaged with the clutch mechanism.

Fig. 1.2. Removing the radiator (Section 5)

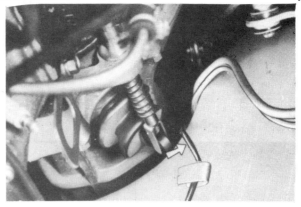

Fig. 1.3. Clutch operating cable connection to rod clevis (right hand drive (Section 5)

Fig. 1.4. Exhaust manifold to downpipe flange nuts (Section 5)

Fig. 1.5. Gearchange selector control rod (Section 5)

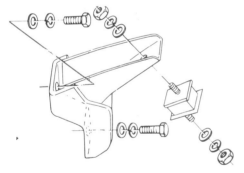

Fig. 1.6. Front engine mounting bracket and insulator (Section 5)

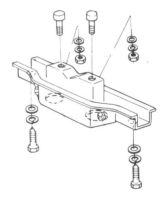

Fig. 1.7. Rear mounting (manual gearbox) (Section 5)

Fig. 1.8. Hoisting the engine/gearbox from the engine compartment (Section 5)

7 Engine - separation from automatic transmission

1 Remove the converter housing dust cover and unscrew and remove the torque converter to drive plate securing bolts. The drive plate will have to be rotated to reach each of the bolts in turn. Mark the relative position of the drive plate to the converter housing using a spirit pen or dab of quick drying paint so that they can be fitted in their original relative positions.
2 Unscrew and remove the bolts which secure the automatic transmission to the engine. Pull the automatic transmission unit from its connection with the engine, keeping it in a straight line and supporting its weight during the operation.

8 Dismantling the engine - general

1 It is best to mount the engine on a dismantling stand but if one is not available, then stand the engine on a strong bench so as to be at a comfortable working height. Failing this, the engine can be stripped down on the floor.
2 During the dismantling process the greatest care should be taken to keep the exposed parts free from dirt. As an aid to achieving this, it is a sound scheme to thoroughly clean down the outside if the engine, removing all traces of oil and congealed dirt.
3 Use paraffin or a good grease solvent such as 'Gunk'. The latter compound will make the job much easier, as, after the solvent has been applied and allowed to stand for a time, a vigorous jet of water will wash off the solvent and all the grease and filth. If the dirt is thick and deeply embedded, work the solvent into it with a wire brush.
4 Finally wipe down the exterior of the engine with a rag and only then, when it is quite clean should the dismantling process begin. As the engine is stripped, clean each part in a bath of paraffin or petrol.
5 Never immerse parts with oilways in paraffin, i.e. the crankshaft, but to clean, wipe down carefully with a petrol dampened rag. Oilways can be cleaned out with wire. If an air line is present all parts can be blown dry and the oilways blown through as an added precaution.
6 Re-use of old engine gaskets is false economy and can give rise to oil and water leaks, if nothing worse. To avoid the possibility or trouble after the engine has been reassembled ALWAYS use new gaskets throughout.
7 Do not throw the old gaskets away as it sometimes happens that an immediate replacement cannot be found and the old gasket is then very useful as a template. Hang up the old gaskets as they are removed on a suitable hook or nail.
8 To strip the engine it is best to work from the top down. The sump provides a firm base on which the engine can be supported in an upright position. When this stage where the sump must be removed is reached, the engine can be turned on its side and all other work carried out with it in this position.
9 Wherever possible, replace nuts, bolts and washers fingertight from wherever they were removed. This helps avoid later loss and muddle. If they cannot be replaced then lay them out in such a fashion that it is clear from where they came.

9 Removing ancillary engine components

1 With the engine removed from the vehicle and separated from the gearbox, the ancillary components should now be removed before dismantling of the engine unit commences.
2 Loosen the alternator mounting bolts and the adjustment strap bolt. Push the alternator in towards the engine and remove the driving belt. Remove the alternator mounting bolts and adjustment strap bolt and lift the unit away.
3 Unscrew the crankshaft pulley securing bolt. This is achieved by using a 'slogger' type ring spanner. One or two hefty clouts with a club hammer on the shaft of the spanner should loosen the nut. It is useless to attempt to unscrew the pulley bolt using

hand pressure as the engine will simply rotate as force is applied.
4 Remove the crankshaft pulley, using two tyre levers if necessary.
5 Unscrew and remove the cartridge type oil filter. It may be necessary to employ a small chain or strap wrench where the filter is stuck tight.
6 Unscrew and remove the bolts which secure the oil pump body to the exterior of the crankcase. Withdraw the oil pump complete with drive gear.
7 Unscrew and remove the spark plugs.
8 Disconnect and remove the vacuum tube which runs between the distributor vacuum capsule and the carburettor.
9 Unscrew and remove the setscrew which retains the distributor plate to the engine crankcase. Withdraw the distributor from its crankcase location.
10 Disconnect the fuel pump to carburettor fuel pipe at the carburettor end. Unscrew and remove the four carburettor to manifold flange nuts and washers. Lift the carburettor away.
11 Unscrew and remove the rocker cover screws and lift off the rocker cover.
12 Unscrew and remove the two thermostat cover retaining bolts and lift the cover away. If it is stuck do not insert a blade and attempt to prise it off as this will damage the mating faces. Tap it sideways with a plastic faced hammer until it is free.
13 Withdraw the thermostat. If it is stuck in its seating, do not try and pull it out with a pair of pliers but cut round its periphery with a sharp pointed knife to free it.
14 Unscrew and remove the manifold securing nuts and withdraw the manifold and gasket.
15 Unscrew and remove the four fan securing bolts and remove the fan and pulley assembly.
16 Unscrew and remove the five nuts which secure the water pump to the upper front face of the timing cover.
17 Unscrew and remove the two securing nuts from the fuel pump and lift it from its crankcase location.

10 Cylinder head - removal

1 Unscrew and remove the five rocker shaft pillar securing bolts. Lift the rocker shaft assembly from the cylinder head.
2 Unscrew each of the cylinder head bolts a turn or two each at a time in the sequence shown in Fig.1.14 finally removing them.
3 Withdraw each of the push rods and keep them in sequence so that they can be returned to their original positions. A piece of wood with two rows of holes drilled in it and numbered will provide a very useful rack for both push rods and valves.
4 Lift off the cylinder head. Should it be stuck, do not attempt to prise it from the engine block but tap it all round using a hardwood block or plastic faced mallet. Remove the cylinder head gasket.

11 Valves - removal

1 The valves can be removed from the cylinder head by the following method. Compress each spring in turn with a valve spring compressor until the two halves of the collets can be removed. Release the compressor and remove the spring and spring retainer.
2 If, when the valve spring compressor is screwed down, the valve spring retaining cap refuses to free to expose the split collet, do not continue to screw down on the compressor as there is a likelihood of damaging it.
3 Gently tap the top of the tool directly over the cap with a light hammer. This will free the cap. To avoid the compressor jumping off the valve spring retaining cap when it is tapped, hold the compressor firmly in position with one hand.
4 Slide the rubber oil control seal off the top of each valve stem and then drop out each valve through the combustion chamber.
5 It is essential that the valves are kept in their correct

21

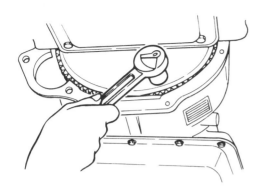

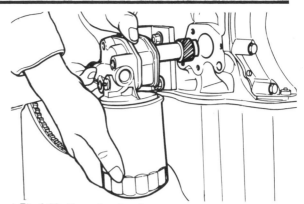

Fig. 1.9. Unscrewing the drive plate to converter bolts (automatic transmission)(Section 7)

Fig. 1.10. Removing the oil pump and filter assembly (Section 9)

Fig. 1.11. Removing the thermostat cover and the thermostat (Section 9)

Fig. 1.12. Removing the manifold and gasket (Section 9)

Fig. 1.13. Removing the water pump (Section 9)

Fig. 1.14. Removal sequence for cylinder head bolts (Section 10)

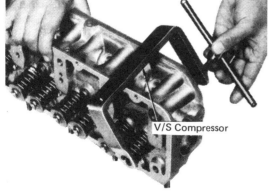

V/S Compressor

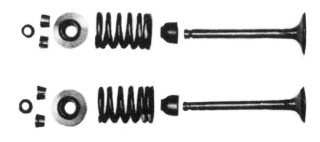

Fig. 1.15. Compressing a valve spring (Section 11)

Fig. 1.16. Components of an inlet and exhaust valve assembly (Section 11)

sequence unless they are so badly worn that they are to be renewed.

12 Dismantling the rocker assembly

1 Components of the rocker assembly are removed simply by sliding the rocker pillars, rocker arms and springs from the shaft, Fig. 1.17.
2 If the original components are to be refitted, identify their fitting sequence with a piece of masking tape.

13 Sump - removal

1 Unscrew and remove the sump drain plug, catching the oil in a container of adequate capacity. Refit the plug.
2 Unscrew and remove the sixteen sump retaining bolts and lift the sump away.
3 The gauze strainer and oil intake pipe will now be exposed and should be detached by removal of the two intake pipe flange securing bolts.

14 Timing cover, gear and chain - removal

1 Unscrew and remove the timing cover securing bolts.
2 Remove the timing cover (the crankshaft pulley already having been removed, Section 9 paragraph 3). The timing cover will incorporate a chain slipper, Fig. 1.18.
3 Withdraw the oil thrower disc from the crankshaft.
4 Unbolt and remove the timing chain tensioner from the front face of the engine block.
5 Unscrew and remove the camshaft gearwheel securing bolt.
6 Remove the camshaft and crankshaft gearwheels simultaneously complete with double roller chain. Use tyre levers behind each gear and lever them equally and a little at a time. If they are stuck on their shafts, the use of a puller may be required.
7 When the gearwheels and chain are removed, extract the Woodruff key from the crankshaft and retain it safely.

15 Piston, connecting rod and big-end bearing - removal

1 With the cylinder head and sump removed undo the big end retaining bolts.
2 The connecting rods and pistons are lifted out from the top of the cylinder block, after the carbon or 'wear' ring at the top of the bore has been scraped away.
3 Remove the big end caps one at a time, taking care to keep them in the right order and the correct way round. Also ensure that the shell bearings are kept with their correct connecting rods and caps unless they are to be renewed. Normally, the numbers 1 to 4 are stamped on adjacent sides of the big end caps and connecting rods, indicating which cap fits on which rod and which way round the cap fits. If no numbers or lines can be found then, with a sharp screwdriver or file, scratch mating marks across the joint from the rod to the cap. One line for connecting rod No.1, two for connecting rod No.2 and so on. This will ensure there is no confusion later as it is most important that the caps go back in the correct position on the connecting rods from which they were removed.
4 If the big end caps are difficult to remove they may be gently tapped with a soft hammer.
5 To remove the shell bearings, press the bearings opposite the groove in both the connecting rod, and the connecting rod caps and the bearings will slide out easily.
6 Withdraw the pistons and connecting rods upwards and ensure they are kept in the correct order for replacement in the same bore. Refit the connecting rod, caps and bearings to the rods if the bearings do not require renewal, to minimise the risk of getting the caps and rods muddled.

16 Flywheel - removal

1 Remove the clutch as described in Chapter 5.
2 Lock tabs are fitted under the six bolts which hold the flywheel to the flywheel flange on the rear of the crankshaft.
3 Unscrew the bolts and remove them.
4 Lift the flywheel away from the crankshaft flange.
NOTE: Some difficulty may be experienced in removing the bolts by the rotation of the crankshaft every time pressure is put on the spanner. To lock the crankshaft in position while the bolts are removed, wedge a block of wood between the crankshaft and the side of the block inside the crankcase.

17 Main bearings and camshaft - removal

1 Unscrew and remove the securing bolts from the main bearing caps. The caps are numbered 1 to 5 starting from the timing cover end of the engine and arrows are marked on the caps and these point towards the timing cover to ensure correct orientation of the caps when refitting.
2 Withdraw the bearing caps complete with the lower halves of the shell bearings.
3 Remove the rear oil seal.
4 Lift the crankshaft from the crankcase and then remove each of the upper halves of the shell bearings.
5 Remove the baffle plate and the mesh screen from the crankcase, Fig. 1.21.
6 With the engine block still inverted, unscrew and remove the two bolts which secure the camshaft end plate. Remove the plate and carefully withdraw the camshaft. Rotate the camshaft during the removal operation and take particular care not to damage the camshaft bearings as the lobes of the cams pass through them.
7 The tappet blocks may now be lifted from their original sequence so that they may be refitted in exactly the same order.
8 The engine is now completely dismantled and the individual components should be examined and serviced as described in later Sections of this Chapter.

18 Piston rings - removal

1 Each ring should be sprung open only just sufficiently to permit it to ride over the lands of the piston body.
2 Once a ring is out of its groove, it is helpful to cut three ¼ in wide strips of tin and slip them under the ring at equidistant points.
3 Using a twisting motion this method of removal will prevent the ring dropping into a empty groove as it is being removed from the piston.

19 Gudgeon pin - removal

1 The gudgeon pins are an interference fit in the connecting rod small ends. It is recommended that removal of the gudgeon pin be left to a service station having a sufficiently powerful press to remove them.
2 Where a press is available to carry out the work yourself, the body of the piston must be supported on a suitably shaped distance piece into which the gudgeon pin may be ejected.

20 Lubrication system - description

The engine lubrication system is of the pressure feed type. An oil pump mounted on the right hand side of the cylinder block is driven by a meshing gear on the camshaft which also drives the distributor drive shaft. Oil is drawn from the sump through a filter screen and tube, pumped by the rotor type pump, through the full flow oil filter to the main crankcase oil

Fig. 1.17. Components of the rocker gear (Section 12)

Fig. 1.18. Removing the timing cover (Section 14)

Fig. 1.19. Removing a piston/connecting rod assembly
(Section 15)

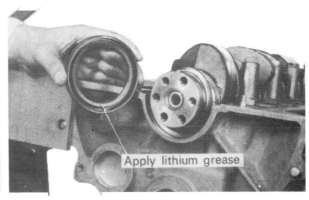

Apply lithium grease

Fig. 1.20. The crankshaft rear oil seal (Section 17)

Fig. 1.21. Removing the baffle plate and gauze screen from the
crankcase (Section 17)

Fig. 1.22. Correct orientation of camshaft thrust plate (Section 17)

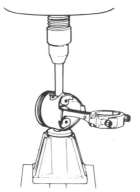

Fig. 1.23. Pressing a gudgeon pin from the connecting rod small
end (Section 19)

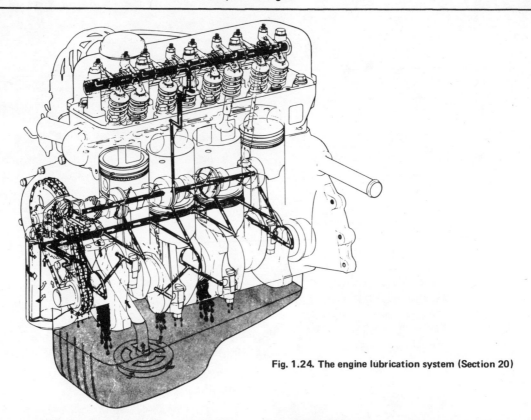

Fig. 1.24. The engine lubrication system (Section 20)

gallery.

The main oil gallery supplies oil to the crankshaft main bearings and big-end bearings through drillings and a regulated quantity of oil ejected from small holes in the connecting rods lubricate the gudgeon pins and cylinder walls.

The timing chain is fed with oil from the main gallery and the chain tensioner is held against the timing chain partly by oil pressure and partly by a coil spring.

The camshaft bearings are lubricated with oil from the main gallery and the rocker shaft and valve gear obtain their lubrication through a drilling from the camshaft centre bearing.

21 Oil pump - inspection and servicing

1 Having removed the oil pump as previously described, unscrew and remove the two cover bolts, extract the inner and outer rotors and drive shaft.

2 Clean all components in paraffin and then check the following clearances using feeler gauges.

Side clearance between inner and outer rotors, not to exceed 0.0047 in.

Clearance between outer rotor and the pump body, between 0.0059 and 0.0083 in.

The end float with the cover fitted should be between 0.0016 and 0.0047 in.

Where measurements are outside the specified tolerances then the oil pump should be renewed as an assembly.

3 Apply a thin coating of gasket cement to the mating surfaces of the body and cover before reassembling and always use a new gasket when refitting the pump to the crankcase.

22 Oil pressure relief valve - inspection and servicing

1 The oil pressure relief valve assembly is screwed into the rear face of the oil pump body. Unscrew the sealing plug and extract the shim, spring and valve.

2 No adjustment of the valve is provided for and the only check that can be carried out is to measure the length of the spring. This should be 1.71 in. The best way to check this is to compare it with a new one.

3 Refit the relief valve components in their correct sequence, check the plug sealing washer and tighten the plug to between 29 and 36 lb/ft torque.

4 In the event of low oil pressure being indicated by the oil warning lamp lighting up, it must not be assumed that the fault lies with the pressure relief valve on the oil pump. Check for (i) blocked filter cartridge (ii) sump oil level correct (iii) oil pressure switch faulty and (iv) general excessive wear in main and big-end bearings. All these factors may be the cause of low oil pressure being indicated.

23 Crankcase ventilator control system - description and servicing

1 The system is designed to extract gas which has passed the pistons and entered the crankcase. These fumes are drawn through a closed circuit with valve to the inlet manifold.

2 During part-throttle openings the vacuum created in the inlet manifold draws fumes through a valve screwed into the side of the inlet manifold and air to replace them is drawn into the clean side of the air cleaner through a hose which connects the air cleaner to the rocker cover and thence to the crankcase.

3 During full thorttle operation, the inlet manifold vacuum is insufficient to draw the crankcase fumes through the valve and the flow is therefore in the reverse direction through the rocker cover to air cleaner hose.

4 The spring loaded valve which is essential to the accurate control of the system should be checked periodically in the following manner. With the engine idling, remove the hose from the valve. If the valve is operating correctly a hissing noise will be evident to prove that air is being admitted by the valve. A high vacuum should also be felt if a finger is placed over the valve inlet. Where these factors are not observed then the valve must be renewed.

5 Occasionally check the hoses for splits and security of connections. Pull a piece of rag through them to clean them.

6 A flame trap is interposed between the air cleaner and the

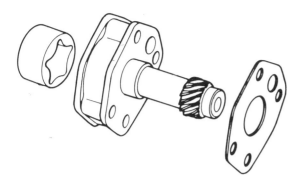

Fig. 1.25. Components of the oil pump (Section 21)

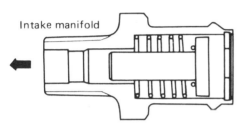

Intake manifold

Fig. 1.26. Sectional view of the crankcase emission control valve
(Section 23)

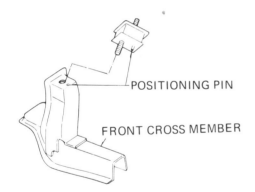

POSITIONING PIN

FRONT CROSS MEMBER

Fig. 1.27. Engine front mounting insulator and support
(Sections 24 and 41)

Clearance limit : 0.30mm (0.0118 in)
Standard : 0.05 to 0.15mm
(0.0020 to 0.0059 in)

Fig. 1.28. Checking the crankshaft end-float (Section 26)

rocker cover to prevent a blow-back from the carburettor reaching the engine interior. Check that this is securely fixed in the hose and regularly wash it free from oil contamination in paraffin, NOT fuel.

24 Engine front mountings - renewal

1   With time the bonded rubber insulators, one on each of the front mountings, will perish causing undue vibration and noise from the engine. Severe juddering when reversing or when moving off from rest is also likely and is a further sign of worn mounting rubbers.
2   The front mounting rubber insulators can be changed with the engine in the car.
3   Apply the handbrake firmly, jack up the front of the car, and place stands under the front of the car.
4   Lower the jack, and place the jack under the sump to take the weight of the engine.
5   Undo the large bolt which holds each of the engine mountings to the body crossmember.
6   Raise the engine sufficiently high to enable the mounting insulator not to be removed from the crankcase bracket and withdraw the insulator.
7   Fitting new flexible insulators is a reversal of removal but note the positioning pin, Fig. 1.27.

26 Examination and renovation - general

With the engine stripped down and all parts thoroughly cleaned, it is now time to examine everything for wear. The following items should be checked and where necessary renewed or renovated as described in the following Sections.

26 Crankshaft and main bearings - inspection and renovation

1   Examine the crankpin and main journal surfaces for signs of scoring or scratches. Check the ovality of the crankpins at different positions with a micrometer. If more than 0.001 in out of round, the crankpin will have to be reground. It will also have to be reground if there are any scores or scratches present. Also check the journals in the same fashion.
2   If it is necessary to regrind the crankshaft and fit new bearings your local Datsun garage or engineering works will be able to decide how much metal to grind off and the size of new bearing shells.
3   Full details of crankshaft regrinding tolerances and bearing undersizes are given in Specifications.
4   The main bearing clearances may be established by using a strip of Plastigage between the crankshaft journals and the main bearing/shell caps. Tighten the bearing cap bolts to a torque of between 36 and 44 lb/ft. Remove the cap and compare the flattened Plastigage strip with the index provided. The clearance should be compared with the tolerances in Specifications.
5   Temporarily refit the crankshaft to the crankcase having refitted the upper halves of the shell main bearings in their locations. Fit the centre main bearing cap only, complete with shell bearing and tighten the securing bolts to between 36 and 44 lb/ft torque. Using a feeler gauge, check the end-float by pushing and pulling the crankshaft, Fig. 1.28. Where the end-float is outside the specified tolerance, the centre bearing cap will have to be renewed.

27 Connecting rods and bearings - examination and renovation

1   Big-end bearing failure is indicated by a knocking from within the crankcase and a slight drop in oil pressure.
2   Examine the big-end bearing surfaces for pitting and scoring. Renew the shells in accordance with the sizes specified in Specifications. Where the crankshaft has been reground, the

correct undersize big-end shell bearings will be supplied by the repairer.

3 Should there be any suspicion that a connecting rod is bent or twisted or the small end bush no longer provides an interference fit for the gudgeon pin then the complete connecting rod assembly should be exchanged for a reconditioned one but ensure that the comparative weight of the two rods is within 0.18 oz.

4 Measurement of the big-end bearing clearances may be carried out in a similar manner to that described for the main bearings in the previous Section but tighten the securing nuts on the cap bolts to between 23 and 28 lb/ft.

28 Cylinder bores and crankcase - examination and renovation

1 The cylinder bores must be examined for taper, ovality, scoring and scratches. Start by carefully examining the top of the cylinder bores. If they are at all worn a very slight ridge will be found on the thrust side. This marks the top of the piston ring travel. The owner will have a good indication of the bore wear prior to dismantling the engine, or removing the cylinder head. Excessive oil consumption accompanied by blue smoke from the exhaust is a sure sign of worn cylinder bores and piston rings.

2 Measure the bore diameter just under the ridge with a micrometer and compare it with the diameter at the bottom of the bore, which is not subject to wear. If the difference between the two measurements is more than 0.008 in then it will be necessary to fit special pistons and rings or to have the cylinders rebored and fit oversize pistons. If no micrometer is available remove the rings from a piston and place the piston in each bore in turn about ¾ in below the top of the bore. If an 0.0012 in feeler gauge slid between the piston and cylinder wall requires more than a pull of between 1.1 and 3.3 lbs to withdraw it, using a spring balance then remedial action must be taken. Oversize pistons are available as listed in Specifications.

3 These are accurately machined to just below the indicated measurements so as to provide correct running clearances in bores bored out to the exact oversize dimensions.

4 If the bores are slightly worn but not so badly worn as to justify reboring them, then special oil control rings and pistons can be fitted which will restore compression and stop the engine burning oil. Several different types are available and the manufacturer's instructions concerning their fitting must be followed closely.

5 If new pistons are being fitted and the bores have not been reground, it is essential to slightly roughen the hard glaze on the sides of the bores with fine glass paper so the new piston rings will have a chance to bed in properly.

29 Pistons and piston rings - examination and renovation

1 If the original pistons are to be refitted, carefully remove the piston rings as described in Section 18.

2 Clean the grooves and rings free from carbon, taking care not to scratch the aluminium surfaces of the pistons.

3 If new rings are to be fitted, then order the top compression ring to be stepped to prevent it impinging on the 'wear ring' which will almost certainly have been formed at the top of the cylinder bore.

4 Before fitting the rings to the pistons, push each ring in turn down to the part of its respective cylinder bore (use an inverted piston to do this and to keep the ring square in the bore) and measure the ring end gap. For compression rings the end gap (measured with a feeler blade) should be between 0.0079 and 0.0138 in and for oil control rings 0.0118 to 0.0354 in.

5 The rings should now be tested in their respective grooves for side clearance. With new rings and pistons the clearance should be between 0.0015 and 0.0027 in for the top two compression

rings and between 0.0015 and 0.0031 in for the bottom oil control ring. Where original rings are being refitted, the maximum side clearance of all rings is 0.0079 in.

6 Where necesary a piston ring which is slightly tight in its groove may be rubbed down holding it perfectly squarely on an oilstone or a sheet of fine emery cloth laid on a piece of plate glass. Excessive tightness can only be rectified by having the grooves machined out.

7 The gudgeon pin should be a push fit into the piston at room temperature. If it appears slack, then both the piston and gudgeon pin should be renewed.

30 Camshaft and crankshaft bearings - examination and renovation

1 Carefully examine the camshaft bearings for wear. If the bearings are obviously worn or pitted then they must be renewed. This is an operation for your local Datsun dealer or local engineering works as it demands the use of specialized equipment. The bearings are removed with a special drift after which new bearings are pressed in, and in-line bored, care being taken to ensure the oil holes in the bearings line up with those in the block.

2 The camshaft itself should show no signs of wear, but, if very slight scoring on the cams is noticed, the score marks can be removed by very gentle rubbing down with a very fine emery cloth. The greatest care should be taken to keep the cam profiles smooth.

3 Examine the skew gear for wear, chipped teeth or other damage.

4 Carefully examine the camshaft thrust plate. Excessive end-float (more than 0.0039 in) will be visually self evident and will require the fitting of a new plate.

31 Valves and valve seats - examination and renovation

1 Examine the heads of the valves for pitting and burning, especially the heads of the exhaust valves. The valve seatings should be examined at the same time. If the pitting on valve and seat is very slight the marks can be removed by grinding the seats and valves together with coarse, and then fine, valve grinding paste.

2 Where bad pitting has occurred to the valve seats it will be necessary to recut them and fit new valves. If the valve seats are so worn that they cannot be recut, then it will be necessary to fit new valve seat inserts. These latter two jobs should be entrusted to the local Datsun agent or engineering works. In practice it is very seldom that the seats are so badly worn that they require renewal. Normally, it is the valve that is too badly worn for replacement, and the owner can easily purchase a new set of valves and match them to the seats by valve grinding.

3 Valve grinding is carried out as follows:-

Smear a trace of coarse carborundum paste on the seat face and apply a suction grinder tool to the valve head. With a semi-rotory motion, grind the valve head to its seat, lifting the valve occasionally to redistribute the grinding paste. When a dull matt even surface finish is produced on both the valve seat and the valve, wipe off the paste and repeat the process with fine carborundum paste, lifting and turning the valve to redistbute the paste as before. A light spring placed under the valve head will greatly ease this operation. When a smooth unbroken ring of light grey matt finish is produced, on both valve and valve seat faces, the grinding operation is completed.

4 Scrape away all carbon from the valve head and the valve stem. Carefully clean away every trace of grinding compound, taking great care to leave none in the ports or in the valve guides. Clean the valves and valve seats with a paraffin soaked rag then with a clean rag, and finally, if an air line is available, blow the valves, valve guides and valve ports clean.

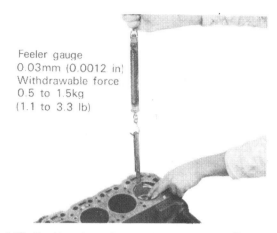

Feeler gauge
0.03mm (0.0012 in)
Withdrawable force
0.5 to 1.5kg
(1.1 to 3.3 lb)

Fig. 1.29. Checking piston clearance in a cylinder bore (Section 29)

Fig. 1.30. Checking piston ring end gap (Section 29)

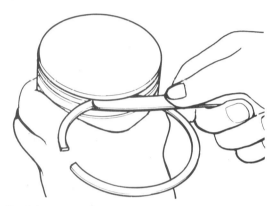

Fig. 1.31. Checking piston ring side clearance (Section 29)

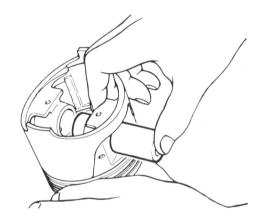

Fig. 1.32. Checking the fit of a gudgeon pin in a piston (Section 29)

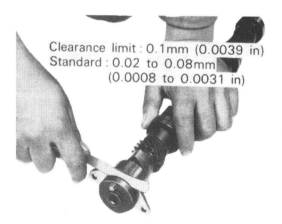

Clearance limit : 0.1mm (0.0039 in)
Standard : 0.02 to 0.08mm
(0.0008 to 0.0031 in)

Fig. 1.33. Checking camshaft end-float (Section 30)

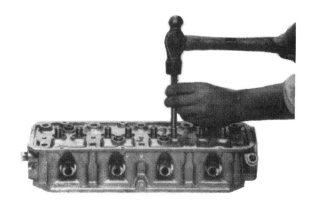

Fig. 1.34. Installing a valve guide (Section 32)

32 Valve guides - examination and renovation

1 Test each valve in its guide for wear. After a considerable mileage, the valve guide bore may wear oval. This can best be tested by inserting a new valve in the guide and moving it from side to side. If the tip of the valve stem deflects by about 0.0080 in. then it must be assumed that the tolerance between **the** stem and guide is greater than the permitted maximum (0.0039 in).

2 New valve guides (oversizes available - see Specifications) may be pressed or drifted into the cylinder head after the worn ones have been removed in a similar manner. The cylinder head must be heated to 200°C before carrying out these operations and although this can be done in a domestic oven, it must be remembered that the new guide will have to be reamed after installation and it may therefore be preferable to leave this work to your Datsun dealer.

33 Timing gears and chain - examination and renovation

1 Examine the teeth on both the crankshaft gear wheel and the camshaft gear wheel for wear. Each tooth forms an inverted 'V' with the gearwheel periphery, and if worn the side of each tooth under tension will be slightly concave in shape when compared with the other side of the tooth, i.e. one side of the inverted 'V' will be concave when compared with the other. If any sign of wear is present the gearwheels must be renewed.

2 Examine the links of the chain for side slackness and renew the chain if any slackness is noticeable when compared with a new chain. It is a sensible precaution to renew the chain at about 30,000 miles (48000 km) and at a lesser mileage if the engine is stripped down for a major overhaul. The actual rollers on a very badly worn chain may be slightly grooved.

34 Rockers and rocker shaft - examination and renovation

1 Thoroughly clean the rocker shaft and then check the shaft for straightness by rolling it on plate glass. It is most unlikely that it will deviate from normal, but if it does, purchase a new shaft. The surface of the shaft should be free from any worn ridges caused by the rocker arms. If any wear is present, renew the shaft,

Check the rocker arms for wear of the rocker bushes, for wear at the rocker arm face which bears on the valve stem, and for wear of the adjusting ball ended screws. Wear in the rocker arm bush can be checked by gripping the rocker arm tip and holding the rocker arm in place on the shaft, noting if there is any lateral rocker arm shake. If shake is present, and the arm is very loose on the shaft, a new bush or rocker arm must be fitted.

Check the tip of the rocker arm where it bears on the valve head for cracking or serious wear on the case hardening. If none is present reuse the rocker arm. Check the lower half of the ball on the end of the rocker arm adjusting screw. Check the pushrods for straightness by rolling them on the bench. Renew any that are bent.

35 Tappets - examination and renovation

Examine the bearing surface of the mushroom tappets which lie on the camshaft. Any indentation in this surface or any cracks indicate serious wear and the tappets should be renewed. Thoroughly clean them out, removing all traces of sludge. It is most unlikely that the sides of the tappets will prove worn, but, if they are a very loose fit in their bores and can readily be rocked, they should be exchanged for new units. It is very unusual to find any wear in the tappets, and any wear is likely to occur only at very high mileages.

36 Flywheel starter ring gear - examination and renovation

1 If the teeth on the flywheel starter ring are badly worn, or if some are missing then it will be necessary to remove the ring and fit a new one, or preferably exchange the flywheel for a reconditioned unit.

2 Either split the ring with a cold chisel after making a cut with a hacksaw blade between two teeth, or use a soft headed hammer (not steel) to knock the ring off, striking it evenly and alternately at equally spaced points. Take great care not to damage the flywheel during this process.

3 Heat the new ring in either an electric oven to about 200°C or immerse in a pan of boiling oil.

4 Hold the ring at this temperature for five minutes and then quickly fit it to the flywheel so the chamfered portion of the teeth faces the gearbox side of the flywheel.

5 The ring should be tapped gently down onto its register and left to cool naturally when the contraction of the metal on cooling will ensure that it is a secure and permanent fit. Great

care must be taken not to overheat the ring, indicated by it turning light metallic blue, as if this happens the temper of the ring will be lost.

37 Cylinder head - decarbonising and examination

1 With the cylinder head removed, use a blunt scraper to remove all trace of carbon and deposits from the combustion spaces and ports. Remember that the cylinder head is aluminium alloy and can be damaged easily during the decarbonising operations. Scrape the cylinder head free from scale or old pieces of gasket or jointing compound. Clean the cylinder head by washing it in paraffin and take particular care to pull a piece of rag through the ports and cylinder head bolt holes. Any grit remaining in these recesses may well drop onto the gasket or cylinder block mating surface as the cylinder head is lowered into position and could lead to a gasket leak after reassembly is complete.

2 With the cylinder head clean test for distortion if a history of coolant leakage has been apparent. Carry out this test using a straight edge and feeler gauges or a piece of plate glass. If the surface shows any warping in excess of 0.0039 in then the cylinder head will have to be resurfaced which is a job for a specialist engineering company.

3 Clean the pistons and top of the cylinder bores. If the pistons are still in the block then it is essential that great care is taken to ensure that no carbon gets into the cylinder bores as this could scratch the cylinder walls or cause damage to the piston and rings. To ensure this does not happen, first turn the crankshaft so that two of the pistons are at the top of their bores. Stuff rag into the other two bores or seal them off with paper and masking tape. The waterways should also be covered with small pieces of masking tape to prevent particles of carbon entering the cooling system and damaging the water pump.

There are two schools of thought as to how much carbon should be removed from the piston crown. One school recommends that a ring of carbon shuold be left round the edge of the piston and on the cylinder bore wall as an aid to low oil consumption. Although this is probably true for early engines with worn bores, on later engines the thought of the second school can be applied: which is that for effective decarbonisation all traces of carbon should be removed.

If all traces of carbon are to be removed, press a little grease into the gap between the cylinder walls and the two pistons which are to be worked on. With a blunt scraper carefully scrape away the carbon from the piston crown, taking great care not to scratch the aluminium. Also scrape away the carbon from the surrounding lip of the cylinder wall. When all carbon has been removed, scrape away the grease which will now be contaminated with carbon particles, taking care not to press any into the bores. To assist prevention of carbon build-up the piston crown can be polished with a metal polish such as Brasso. Remove the rags or masking tape from the other two cylinders and turn the crankshaft so that the two pistons which were at the bottom are now at the top. Place rag or masking tape in the cylinders which have been decarbonised and proceed as just described.

If a ring of carbon is going to be left round the piston then this can be helped by inserting an old piston ring into the top of the bore to rest on the piston and ensure that the carbon is not accidentally removed. Check that there are no particles of carbon in the cylinder bores. Decarbonising is now complete.

38 Engine reassembly - general

1 To ensure maximum life with minimum trouble from a rebuilt engine, not only must everything be correctly assembled, but everything must be spotlessly clean, all the oilways must be clear, locking washers and spring washers must always be fitted where indicated and all bearing and other working surfaces must be thoroughly lubricated during assembly.

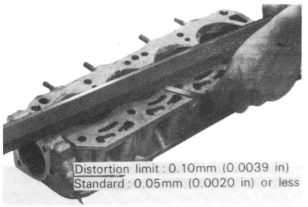

Fig. 1.35. Testing for cylinder head distortion, using a straight edge (Section 37)

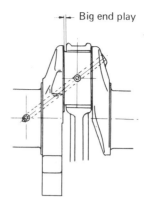

Fig. 1.36. Oil hole positions prior to checking big-end end play (Section 39)

2 Before assembly begins renew any bolts or studs the threads of which are in any way damaged, and whenever possible use new spring washers.

3 Apart from your normal tools, a supply of clean rag; an oil can filled with engine oil (an empty plastic detergent bottle thoroughly cleaned and washed out, will invariably do just as well); a new supply of assorted spring washers; a set of new gaskets; and a torque spanner, should be collected together.

39 Assembling the engine

1 Check the cylinder block for cracks, probe the oil passages and holes with a piece of wire and clean the external surfaces.

2 Renew all gaskets and seals and use plenty of clean engine oil to lubricate the components as they are installed. Observe absolute cleanliness.

3 Lubricate and refit the tappet blocks to their original locations with the engine block in the inverted position.

4 Oil the camshaft bearings and gently slide the camshaft into position taking care not to scratch or damage the bearing surfaces as the cam lobes pass through.

5 Fit the camshaft locking plate so that the word 'lower' is to the bottom when the engine is the right way up. Tighten the securing bolts to 3.6 lb/ft.

6 Install the main bearing shells into their crankcase locations and into the bearing caps. Oil the bearing surfaces and carefully lower the crankshaft into position in the crankcase.

7 Fit the main bearing caps complete with shells. These are numbered 1 to 5 from the timing cover end and the centre cap is flanged to take up the thrust of the crankshaft end-float. Tighten the main bearing cap bolts to a torque of between 36 and 43 lb/ft. The arrow on each cap should point towards the timing cover.

8 Check the crankshaft rotates smoothly and test the end-float (Section 26).

9 Fit a new rear oil seal and the flywheel, using new locking tabs and tightening the bolts to between 47 and 54 lb/ft.

10 The piston rings will have been fitted to the pistons (Section 29) and the connecting rods fitted with new bearings, pistons and gudgeon pins, as required (Sections 27 and 29). Arrange the piston ring gaps, each at an equidistant point of a circle so that they do not line up and cause gas blow-by. Liberally lubricate the rings and piston surfaces and insert the connecting rod into the cylinder bore so that the mark 'F' faces towards the timing cover. Ensure that if the original pistons are being fitted then they are returned to their original cylinders.

11 Using a piston ring compressor, place the shaft of a hammer on the piston crown and strike the hammer head with the hand. This force should be quite sufficient to drive the piston, rod assembly down its bore. Where this action does not have the desired effect then the piston rings have not been sufficiently compressed or the piston ring end gaps are incorrect.

12 Connect each big-end to its appropriate crankshaft journal

and fit the big-end cap complete with shell. The caps and rods are numbered 1 to 4 commencing at the timing gear end of the engine and when correctly fitted will have the cap and rod numbers adjacent. Tighten the big-end bolt nuts to between 23 and 27.5 lb/ft. Use plenty of oil when fitting the connecting rods to the crankshaft and turn the crankshaft so that each big-end bearing is engaged when the respective crankshaft journal is at its lowest point.

13 Check the end-float of each connecting rod big-end after installation. this should be between 0.0079 and 0.0118 in when the crankshaft is aligned as shown in Fig. 1.36.

14 Refit the crankcase baffle and gauze filter screen.

15 Temporarily refit the camshaft and crankshaft sprockets. Test their alignment and adjust if necessary by installing shims which are available for fitting beneath the crankshaft sprocket.

16 Place the crankshaft and camshaft sprockets within the timing chain and fit both sprockets complete with timing chain to the crankshaft and camshaft simultaneously. When correctly installed, a line drawn through the sprocket centres should also pass through the crankshaft dowel hole and the crankshaft sprocket keyway. A double check is the alignment of the sprocket dot punch marks and the matching marks on the chain side plates, Fig. 1.37. Installation of the timing gear will call for rotation of the camshaft and the crankshaft and repositioning of the camshaft sprocket within the loop of the chain on a trial and error basis until the alignment is correct.

17 When the timing is correct, tighten the camshaft sprocket securing bolt to between 29 and 35 lb/ft torque.

18 Fit the timing chain tensioner and tighten the securing bolts.

19 Check that the gap between the body of the tensioner and the rear face of the slipper does not exceed 0.591 in. Fig. 1.38. If the gap is greater than specified, either the chain has stretched badly or the tensioner slipper has worn away and in either event the component must be renewed.

20 Fit the oil thrower disc to the crankshaft ensuring that the projecting rim is towards the timing cover.

21 Drift out the timing cover oil seal using a piece of tubing for this purpose. Fit a new seal, ensuring that the lips face inwards. Renew the chain slipper if it is worn.

22 Apply a thin film of gasket cement to the mating surfaces of the timing cover and the cylinder block. Stick a new gasket in position on the block, checking carefully that the bolt holes are aligned with it. Secure the cover with the retaining bolts and tighten them to a torque of 5 lb/ft.

23 Refit the oil pump intake pipe and gauze filter.

24 Apply a thin film of gasket cement to the lower face of the crankcase and stick a new sump gasket into position so that the holes in the gasket are in alignment with the bolt holes of the crankcase. Apply more gasket cement to the mating surfaces of the sump, being patricularly liberal with it at the front and rear and in the corners adjacent to the main bearing caps and timing cover. Offer up the sump and insert the securing bolts. Tighten them progressively in diametrically opposite sequence.

25 The cylinder head should now be reassembled ready for

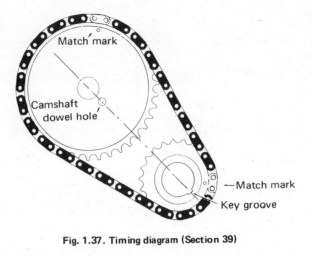

Fig. 1.37. Timing diagram (Section 39)

Fig. 1.38. Correct fitting of the timing chain tensioner (Section 39)

Fig. 1.39. Cylinder head bolt tightening sequence (Sections 39 and 42)

Fig. 1.40. Checking a valve clearance (Section 39)

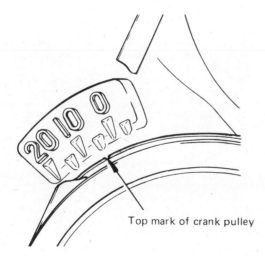

Fig. 1.41. Crankshaft and timing cover timing marks (Section 39)

Fig. 1.42. Correct positioning of distributor rotor after installation (engine at TDC) (Section 39)

bolting to the engine. Place the cylinder head on its side and having oiled the valve guides, insert the valves in their original locations or the seats into which they were previously ground (Section 31).

26 To each valve in turn, fit a new oil seal, a new valve spring (if the engine has covered more than 20,000 miles) the valve spring cup and insert. Compress each spring in turn sufficiently to permit the split cotters to be inserted in the cut-out in the valve stem. Release the compressor gently and check that the cotters have not been displaced.

27 When all valves have been fitted, place the cylinder head face down on the bench and using a hammer and a block of wood strike the end of each valve stem squarely to settle the valve components.

28 Thoroughly clean the faces of the cylinder head and the cylinder block using a non-fluffy rag and fuel.

29 The cylinder head gasket is of laminated type, having a steel sheet surface on one side and this surface should make contact with the face of the cylinder block. Due to the possibility of oil leakage from the cylinder head gasket on the push-rod side, the gasket has been partially treated with sealant in this area only. It is recommended however that both the mating faces of head and block are smeared with a thin coat of non-setting gasket cement as this will help to protect the surface of the alloy head against corrosion as well as providing a reliable seal.

30 Place the gasket in position on the block (steel side down, jointing material visible). Lightly smear the threads of the cylinder head bolts with heavy grade grease and push two of the bolts through the head so that as the head is gently lowered into position they will serve as locating dowels to locate the gasket and head.

31 Note that one bolt head is marked T, this must be screwed into number one position, Fig. 1.39..

32 Fit the remaining bolts and tighten them progressively a turn or two at a time each, in the sequence shown, to a torque of between 40 and 43 lb/ft.

33 Refit the push-rods in their original locations.

34 Refit the rocker shaft assembly tightening the pillar bolts to a torque of between 15 and 18 lb/ft. Tighten the centre bolts first and work outwards.

35 Fit a new exhaust manifold gasket and fit the manifold, securing nuts and washers. Tighten to a torque of between 6.5 and 10 lb/ft.

36 Oil the crankshaft pulley shank and having checked that the Woodruff key is in position, push it carefully into position through the timing cover oil seal. Tighten the pulley securing bolt to between 109 and 116 lb/ft. The teeth of the flywheel ring gear may be jammed with a large screwdriver to prevent the pulley and crankshaft rotating during the tightening operation.

37 The valve clearances should now be adjusted. Rotate the engine during the adjustment procedure by using a spanner or socket on the crankshaft pulley bolt.

38 The valve clearances obviously will have to be set with the engine cold to start with but when the unit is refitted to the vehicle and run up to normal operating temperature then they will have to be checked and readjusted when the engine is hot.

39 The valve adjustments may be made with the engine cold but are more accurate when the engine is hot. The importance of correct rocker arm/valve stem clearances cannot be overstressed as they vitally affect the performance of the engine. If the clearances are set too open, the efficiency of the engine is reduced as the valves open late and close earlier than was intended. If, on the other hand the clearances are set too close there is a danger that the stems will expand upon heating and not allow the valves to close properly which will cause burning of the valve head and seat and possible warping.

40 It is important that the valve clearance is set when the tappet of the valve being adjusted is on the heel of the cam (the lowest point) so that the valve is fully seated. One of two methods may be employed, first place a finger over No 1 spark plug hole, turn the engine and as soon as compression is felt, either observe the piston crown until it reaches its highest point (TDC) and descends about 1/8th inch or using a length of wire as a measure

stop rotating the engine when the wire has passed its highest point and descended about 1/8th inch. Both the valves for No 1 cylinder may be set (inlet and exhaust valve clearance 0.014 in).

41 The firing order is 1-3-4-2 and the alternative method of valve clearance adjustment which avoids the necessity of turning the engine excessively is to apply the adjustment sequence shown in the following table.

Valve fully open	Check & Adjust	Clearance
Valve No. 8	Valve No. 1	0.014 inch
Valve No. 6	Valve No. 3	0.014 inch
Valve No. 4	Valve No. 5	0.014 inch
Valve No. 7	Valve No. 2	0.014 inch
Valve No. 1	Valve No. 8	0.014 inch
Valve No. 3	Valve No. 6	0.014 inch
Valve No. 5	Valve No. 4	0.014 inch
Valve No. 2	Valve No. 7	0.014 inch

Counting from the timing cover end of the engine, inlet valves are nos. 2-3-6-7, exhaust valves are nos. 1-4-5-8.

42 Adjustment of the clearance is made by conventional screw and locknut. Insert the feeler blade between the rocker arm face and the valve stem end face. Loosen the locknut, turn the screw until the blade cannot be withdrawn and then loosen the screw until the blade can be withdrawn just, (stiffly), by a hard pull. Holding the slotted adjustment screw quite still, tighten the locknut with a ring spanner. When all the valve clearances have been adjusted, recheck them again before fitting the rocker box cover complete with a new sealing gasket.

43 Using a new gasket, fit the oil pump to the crankcase, checking that the drive gear meshes correctly.

44 Screw a new oil filter cartridge into position. Lightly grease the rubber sealing ring before fitting it and tighten it by hand pressure only.

45 Using new gaskets, refit the thermostat, thermostat cover, water pump and fan.

46 Fit the alternator to its mountings and reconnect the slotted adjustment strap.

47 Locate the fan belt over the crankshaft, water pump and alternator pulleys and then prise the alternator away from the engine until the belt has a total deflection of ½ in at the centre of its longest run. Tighten the adjustment strap bolt and mounting bolts of the alternator.

48 Fit the carburettor to the manifold and the fuel pump to the crankcase, ensuring that new gaskets similar to those originally fitted are used.

49 Reconnect the fuel pipe between the pump and the carburettor.

50 The distributor should now be refitted. To do this, turn the engine until No 1 cylinder is at TDC. This position can be observed from the alignment of the crankshaft pulley and timing cover marks, Fig. 1.41. A secondary check can be made by seeing that both the inlet and exhaust valves of No 1 cylinder are fully closed.

51 When installed, the distributor rotor should take up the position shown in Fig. 1.42. To achieve this, hold the distributor over the engine and position the rotor as shown. Now turn the rotor approximately 60° in a clockwise direction, this is to compensate for movement of the rotor as the distributor is pushed into mesh with the camshaft gear. The action of meshing will return the rotor to the position illustrated which shows the rotor pointing to No 1 spark plug HT lead segment in the distributor cap. Tighten the distributor clamp plate bolt.

52 Fit the spark plugs, correctly cleaned and gapped (Chapter 4).

53 Connect the plug leads and crankcase ventilation hose.

54 Refit the clutch assembly to the flywheel (Chapter 5), and mate the gearbox to the engine, tightening the bolts which secure the clutch bellhousing to the engine to a torque of 12-16 lb/ft.

55 In the case of vehicles fitted with automatic transmission, ensure that the alignment marks made on the drive plate and converter housing before removal are mated. Tighten the housing

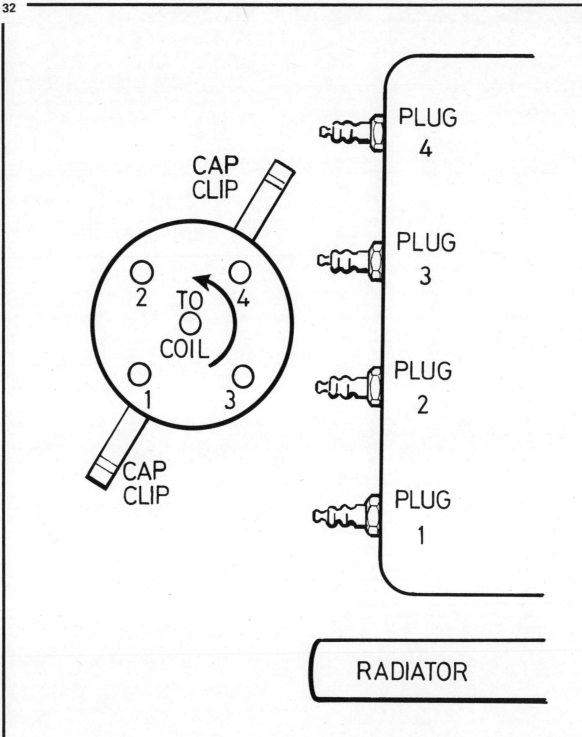

Fig. 1.43. Connecting sequence of HT leads (Section 39)

H 3001

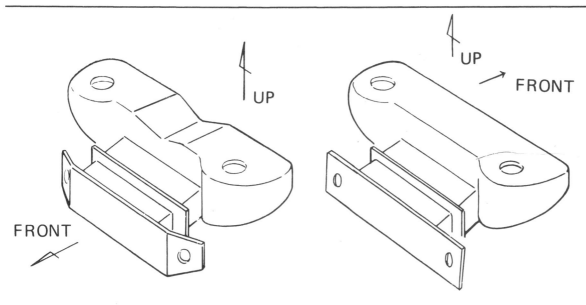

FOR MANUAL TRANSMISSION   FOR AUTOMATIC TRANSMISSION

Fig. 1.44. Gearbox rear mountings (Section 39)

to engine bolts to a torque of 30-36 lb/ft.

56 Once the gearbox or automatic transmission is coupled to the engine block, refit the front engine mounting brackets and the rear mounting assembly. The type of rear mounting differs according to the type of transmission, Fig. 1.44.

57 Fit suitable slings to the engine/gearbox unit and prepare the hoist for lifting the power unit back into the vehicle.

40 Engine replacement - general

1 Although the engine can be replaced with one man and a suitable winch, it is easier if two are present, one to lower the engine into the engine compartment and the other to guide the engine into position and to ensure it does not foul anything.

2 At this stage one or two tips may come in useful. Ensure all the loose leads, cables, etc. are tucked out of the way. If not it is easy to trap one and so cause much additional work after the engine is replaced.

3 Two pair of hands are better than one when refitting the bonnet. Do not tighten the bonnet securing bolts fully until it is ascertained that the bonnet is on straight.

41 Engine/gearbox - refitting to the vehicle

1 Raise the engine/gearbox unit and either roll the vehicle forward under it or if the hoist is mobile roll it forward so that the unit is suspended above the engine compartment.

2 Lower the engine into the engine compartment at a steep angle with the gearbox inclined downwards to the rear. Ensure that nothing is fouled during the operation.

3 Fit the rear mounting bolts while the unit is still suspended employing a jack if necessary to raise the gearbox sufficiently to engage them.

4 Fit the engine front mounting pads, Fig. 1.27, and lower the engine into position. Remove the engine slings and hoist.

5 Refit the starter motor and connect the cable.

6 Refit the propeller shaft, ensuring that the rear flange marks made before removal are aligned.

7 Remove the plug and reconnect the fuel line to the fuel pump.

8 Refit the gearshift lever and the speedometer to drive cable to the gearbox.

9 Reconnect the reversing lamp leads.

10 Connect the exhaust down pipe.

11 Reconnect the clutch cable or hydraulic slave cylinder according to vehicle type.

12 Reconnect the choke and accelerator controls and refit the air cleaner.

13 Reconnect the LT lead to the distributor, the HT lead between the distributor and the coil.

14 Connect the oil pressure and water temperature leads.

15 Refit the radiator and heater hoses.

16 Connect the negative battery lead.

17 Refit the bonnet.

18 Refill the cooling system (Chapter 2).

19 Refill the engine sump with the correct grade and quantity of oil.

20 Check the level of oil in the manual gearbox or automatic transmission.

42 Engine adjustment after major overhaul

1 With the engine refitted to the vehicle, give a final visual check to see that everything has been reconnected and that no loose rags or tools have been left within the engine compartment.

2 Turn the engine slow running screw in about ½ turn, (to increase slow running once the engine is started). (Chapter 3).

3 Pull the choke fully out and start the engine. This may take a little longer than usual as the fuel pump and carburettor bowl will be empty and need initial priming.

4 As soon as the engine starts, push the choke in until the engine runs at a fast tickover and examine the engine for leaks. Check particularly the water hoses and oil filter and fuel hose unions.

5 Run the vehicle on the road until normal operating temperature is reached. Check the valve clearances while the engine is hot as described in Section 39 of this Chapter. Readjust engine tickover.

6 After 500 miles running, the engine oil should be changed particularly where the majority of the internal components have been renewed or reconditioned.

7 After 500 miles, check the torque setting of the cylinder head bolts with the cylinder head COLD. Follow the tightening sequence given in Fig. 1.39.

Fault finding - Engine

Symptom	Reason/s	Remedy
Engine will not turn over when starter switch is operated •	Flat battery Bad battery connections Bad connections at solenoid switch and/or starter motor Starter motor jammed	Check that battery is fully charged and that all connections are clean and tight. Where a pre-engaged starter is fitted rock the car back and forth with a gear engaged. If this does not free pinion remove starter.
	Defective solenoid	Bridge the main terminals of the solenoid switch with a piece of heavy duty cable in order to operate the starter.
	Starter motor defective	Remove and overhaul starter motor.
Engine turns over normally but fails to start	No spark at plugs	Check ignition system according to procedures given in Chapter 4.
	No fuel reaching engine	Check fuel system according to procedures given in Chapter 3.
	Too much fuel reaching the engine (flooding)	Check the fuel system as above.
Engine starts but runs unevenly and misfires	Ignition and/or fuel system faults	Check the ignition and fuel systems as though the engine had failed to start.
	Incorrect valve clearances	Check and reset clearances.
	Burnt out valves	Remove cylinder head and examine and overhaul as necessary.
	Worn out piston rings	Remove cylinder head and examine pistons and cylinder bores. Overhaul as necessary.
Lack of power	Ignition and/or fuel system faults	Check the ignition and fuel systems for correct ignition timing and carburettor settings.
	Incorrect valve clearances	Check and reset the clearances.
	Burnt out valves	Remove cylinder head and examine and overhaul as necessary.
	Worn out piston rings	Remove cylinder head and examine pistons and cylinder bores. Overhaul as necessary.
Excessive oil consumption	Oil leaks from crankshaft rear oil seal, timing cover gasket and oil seal, rocker cover gasket, oil filter gasket, sump gasket, sump plug washer	Identify source of leak and renew seal as appropriate.
	Worn piston rings or cylinder bores resulting in oil being burnt by engine	Fit new rings or rebore cylinders and fit new pistons, depending on degree of wear.
	Worn valve guides and/or defective valve stem seals	Remove cylinder heads and recondition valve stem bores and valves and seals as necessary.
Excessive mechanical noise from engine	Wrong valve to rocker clearances	Adjust valve clearances.
	Worn crankshaft bearings	Inspect and overhaul where necessary.
	Worn cylinders (piston slap)	
	Slack or worn timing chain and sprockets	Adjust chain and/or inspect all timing mechanism.

NOTE: When investigating starting and uneven running faults do not be tempted into snap diagnosis. Start from the beginning of the check procedure and follow it through. It will take less time in the long run. Poor performance from an engine in terms of power and economy is not normally diagnosed quickly. In any event the ignition and fuel systems must be checked first before assuming any further investigation needs to be made.

Chapter 2 Cooling system

Contents

General description 1	Thermostat - removal, testing, refitting 7
Cooling system - draining 2	Water pump - description 8
Cooling system - flushing 3	Water pump - removal and refitting 9
Cooling system - filling 4	Fan belt - adjustment, removal, refitting 10
Anti-freeze mixture 5	Water temperature gauge - fault finding 11
Radiator - removal, inspection, cleaning, refitting 6	Fault finding - cooling system 12

Specifications

System type	thermo syphon with pump assistance
Radiator type	corrugated fin
Filler cap opening pressure	13 lb/in^2
Thermostat type	wax pellet
starts to open	75 to 78°C (USA 80.5 to 83.5°C, Canada 86.5 to 89.5°C)
Coolant capacity	
with heater	5 litres (8.80 pints)
without heater	4.2 litres (7.10 pints)
Torque wrench settings	
Water pump body securing nuts	7 - 10 lb/ft (0.967 - 1.382 kg/m)

1 General description

The cooling system comprises the radiator, top and bottom water hoses, water pump, cylinder head and block water jackets, radiator cap with pressure relief valve and flow and return heater hoses. Some models are fitted with an expansion tank. The thermostat is located in a recess at the front of the cylinder head. The principle of the system is that cold water in the bottom of the radiator circulates upwards through the lower radiator hose to the water pump, where the pump impeller pushes the water round the cylinder block and head through the various cast-in passages to cool the cylinder bores, combustion surfaces and valve seats. When sufficient heat has been absorbed by the cooling water, and the engine has reached an efficient working temperature, the water moves from the cylinder head past the now open thermostat into the top radiator hose and into the radiator header tank.

The water then travels down the radiator tubes when it is rapidly cooled by the in-rush of air. when the vehicle is in forward motion. A four bladed fan, mounted on the water pump pulley, assists this cooling action. The water, now cooled, reaches the bottom of the radiator and the cycle is repeated.

When the engine is cold the thermostat remains closed until the coolant reaches a pre-determined temperature (see Specifications). This assists rapid warming-up.

Water temperature is measured by an electro-sensitive capsule located immediately below the thermostat housing. Connection between the transmitter capsule and the facia gauge is made by a single cable and Lucar type connector. The cooling system also provides the heat for the heater. The heater matrix is fed directly with water from the hottest part of the engine - the cylinder head - returning through a connection on the bottom radiator hose.

2 Cooling system - draining

1 Should the system have to be left empty for any reason both the cylinder block and radiator must be drained, otherwise with a partly drained system corrosion of the water pump impeller seal face may occur with subsequent early failure of the pump seal and bearing.

2 Place the car on a level surface and have ready a container having a capacity of two gallons which will slide beneath the radiator and sump.

3 Move the heater control on the facia to HOT and unscrew and remove the radiator cap. If hot, unscrew the cap very slowly, first covering it with a cloth to remove the danger of scalding when the pressure in the system is released.

4 Unscrew the radiator drain tap at the base of the radiator and then when coolant ceases to flow into the receptacle, repeat the operation by unscrewing the cylinder block plug located on the left hand side of the engine. Retain the coolant for further use, if it contains anti-freeze.

3 Cooling system - flushing

1 The radiator and waterways in the engine after some time may become restricted or even blocked with scale or sediment which reduce the efficiency of the cooling system. When this condition occurs or the coolant appears rusty or dark in colour the system should be flushed. In severe cases reverse flushing may be required as described later.

2 Place the heater controls to the HOT position and unscrew

fully the radiator and cylinder block drain taps.

3   Remove the radiator filler cap and place a hose in the filler neck. Allow water to run through the system until it emerges from both drain taps quite clear in colour. Do not flush a hot engine with cold water.

4   In severe cases of contamination of the coolant or in the system, reverse flush by first removing the radiator cap and disconnecting the lower radiator hose at the radiator outlet pipe.

5   Remove the top hose at the radiator connection end and remove the radiator as described in Section 7.

6   Invert the radiator and place a hose in the bottom outlet pipe. Continue flushing until clear water comes from the radiator top tank.

7   To flush the engine water jackets, remove the thermostat as described later in this Chapter and place a hose in the thermostat location until clear water runs from the water pump inlet. Cleaning by the use of chemical compounds is not recommended.

4   Cooling system - filling

1   Place the heater control to the HOT position.

2   Screw in the radiator drain tap finger tight only and close the cylinder block drain tap.

3   Pour coolant slowly into the radiator so that air can be expelled through the thermostat pin hole without being trapped in a waterway.

4   Fill to the correct level which is 1 inch below the radiator filler neck and replace the filler cap.

5   Run the engine, check for leaks and recheck the coolant level.

6   On vehicles fitted with an expansion tank, check that the radiator overflow tube is correctly connected and that the tank is filled with coolant to the level indicated.

5   Anti-freeze mixture

1   The cooling system should be filled with Castrol Anti-freeze solution in early Autumn. The heater matrix and radiator bottom tank are particularly prone to freeze if anti-freeze is not used in air temperatures below freezing. Modern anti-freeze

solutions of good quality will also prevent corrosion and rusting and they may be left in the system to advantage all year round, draining and refilling with fresh solution each year.

2   Before adding anti-freeze to the system, check all hose connections and check the tightness of the cylinder head bolts as such solutions are searching. The cooling system should be drained and refilled with clean water as previously explained, before adding anti-freeze.

3   The quantity of anti-freeze which should be used for various levels of protection is given in the table below, expressed as a percentage of the system capacity.

Anti-freeze volume	Protection to	Safe pump circulation
25%	$-26^{\circ}C$ ($-15^{\circ}F$)	$-12^{\circ}C$ ($10^{\circ}F$)
30%	$-33^{\circ}C$ ($-28^{\circ}F$)	$-16^{\circ}C$ ($3^{\circ}F$)
35%	$-39^{\circ}C$ ($-38^{\circ}F$)	$-20^{\circ}C$ ($- 4^{\circ}F$)

4   Where the cooling system contains an anti-freeze solution any topping up should be done with a solution made up in similar proportions to the original in order to avoid dilution.

5   On vehicles fitted with an expansion tank, ensure that it is filled to the correct level with the same strength of anti-freeze mixture.

6   Radiator - removal, inspection, cleaning, refitting

1   Drain the cooling system as described in Section 2.

2   Disconnect the top hose from the radiator header tank pipe and the overflow tube from the reservoir (if fitted).

3   Disconnect the bottom hose from the radiator outlet pipe.

4   Unscrew and remove the six retaining bolts which secure the radiator to the front engine compartment mounting panel.

5   Lift out the radiator, taking care not to damage the cooling fins. Do not allow anti-freeze solution to drop onto the bodywork during removal as damage may result.

6   Radiator repair is best left to a specialist but minor leaks may be tackled with Holts Radweld.

7   The radiator matrix may be cleared of flies by brushing with a soft brush or by hosing.

8   Flush the radiator as described in Section 3 according to its degree of contamination. Examine and renew any hoses or clips

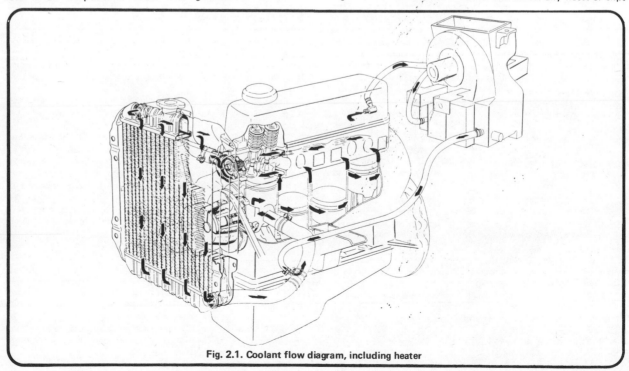

Fig. 2.1. Coolant flow diagram, including heater

which have deteriorated.

9 Examine the plastic drain tap and its rubber washer, renewing if suspect.

10 Replacement of the radiator is a reversal of the removal procedure. Refill and check for leaks as described in Section 4.

7 Thermostat - removal, testing, refitting

1 A faulty thermostat can cause overheating or slow engine warm up. It will also affect the performance of the heater.

2 Drain off enough coolant through the radiator drain tap so that the coolant level is below the thermostat housing joint face. A good indication that the correct level has been reached is when the cooling tubes are exposed when viewed through the radiator filler cap.

3 Unscrew and remove the two retaining bolts and withdraw the thermostat cover sufficiently to permit the thermostat to be removed from its seat in the cylinder head.

4 To test whether the unit is serviceable, suspend the thermostat by a piece of string in a pan of water being heated. Using a thermometer, with reference to the opening and closing temperature in Specifications, its operation may be checked. The thermostat should be renewed if it is stuck open or closed or it fails to operate at the specified temperature. The operation of a thermostat is not instantaneous and sufficient time must be allowed for movement during testing. Never replace a faulty unit - leave it out if no replacement is available immediately.

5 Replacement of the thermostat is a reversal of the removal procedure. Ensure the mating faces of the housing are clean. Use a new gasket with jointing compound. The word TOP which appears on the thermostat face must be visible from above.

8 Water pump - description

The water pump is of conventional impeller type, driven by the fan belt. The impeller chamber is built into, and forms part of, the timing cover. The water pump detachable body is of die-cast aluminium in which runs the shaft. The shaft is fitted with bearings which are a shrink fit in the body and in the event of leakage or failure of the water pump, then it must be renewed as an assembly on an exchange basis.

9 Water pump - removal and refitting

1 Drain the cooling system, retaining tthe coolant if required for further use.

2 Slacken the alternator mountings and adjustment strap bolt, push the alternator in towards the engine and slip the fan belt from the driving pulleys.

3 Unscrew and remove the four bolts which secure the fan and pulley to the water pump flange, remove the fan and pulley.

4 Unscrew and remove the securing nuts and bolts from the water pump housing flange and withdraw the water pump. Should the pump be stuck to the face of the timing cover, do not attempt to prise the mating flange apart as this will damage the soft aluminium and cause leaks after refitting. Grip the shaft extension housing firmly and lever from side to side to break the seal.

5 Refitting is a reversal of removal but ensure that the mating faces are clean and free from old pieces of gasket. Use a new gasket coated both sides with jointing compound and tighten the securing nuts to a torque of between 7 and 10 lb/ft.

6 Adjust the tension of the fan belt as described in Section 10 of this Chapter.

7 Refill the cooling system (Section 4).

10 Fan belt - adjustment, removal, refitting

1 The correct tension of the fan belt must be maintained for it

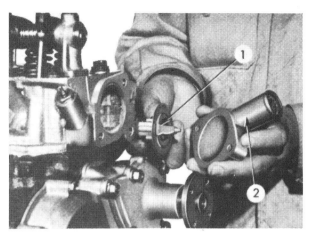

FIG. 2.2. REMOVING THE THERMOSTAT (SECTION 7)

1 thermostat   2 cover

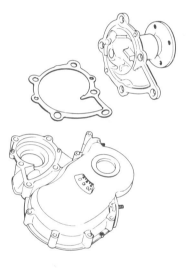

Fig. 2.3. Components of the water pump (Section 8)

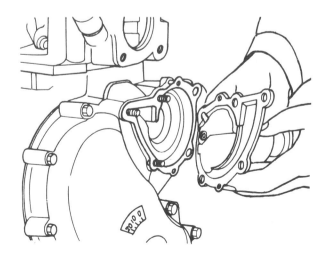

Fig. 2.4. Withdrawing the water pump body (Section 9)

is very important. If it is overtightened then the bearings in the water pump and the alternator may wear prematurely. If it is slack, it will slip and cause overloading and a discharged battery through low alternator output.

2   The fan belt is correctly tensioned when a total movement of ½ in can be obtained at the centre of the longest run of the belt.

3   Always adjust the fan belt with the engine cold. Slacken the alternator mounting bolts and the slotted adjustment strap bolt. Prise the alternator away from the engine until the correct tension is obtained. It will be easier to achieve the correct tension if the alternator bolts are only slackened sufficiently to permit it to move stiffly. Always recheck the fan belt tension after the alternator mounting and adjustment strap bolts have been tightened.

11 Water temperature gauge - fault finding

1   Correct operation of the water temperature gauge is very important as the engine can otherwise overheat without it being observed.

2   The gauge is an electrically operated instrument comprising a transmitter unit screwed into the front of the cylinder head and transmitting through a Lucar type connector and cable to the dial mounted on the facia instrument panel. The instrument only operates when the ignition is switched on.

3   Where the water temperature gauge reads high-low intermittently, or not at all, then first check the security of the connecting cable between the transmitter unit and the gauge.

4   Disconnect the Lucar connector from the transmitter unit, switch on the ignition when the gauge should read COLD. Now earth the cable to the engine block when the gauge needle should indicate HOT. This test proves the gauge to be functional and the fault must therefore lie in the cable or transmitter unit. Renew as appropriate.

5   If the fuel gauge shows signs of malfunction at the same time as the water temperature gauge then a fault in the voltage stabilizer may be the cause.

Fault finding - Cooling system

Symptom	Reason/s	Remedy
Overheating	Low coolant level	Top up.
	Slack fan belt	Adjust tension.
	Thermostat not operating	Renew.
	Radiator pressure cap faulty or of wrong type	Renew.
	Defective water pump	Renew.
	Cylinder head gasket blowing	Fit new gasket.
	Radiator core clogged	Clean.
	Radiator blocked	Reverse flush.
	Binding brakes	Rectify.
	Bottom hose or tank frozen	Drain and refill with anti-freeze.
Engine running too cool	Defective thermostat	Renew.
	Faulty water temperature gauge	Renew.
Loss of coolant	Leaking radiator or hoses	Renew or tighten.
	Cylinder head gasket leaking	Renew gasket.
	Leaking cylinder block core plugs	Renew.
	Faulty radiator filler cap or wrong type fitted	Renew with correct type.

Chapter 3 Fuel system

Contents

General description 1
Air cleaner - servicing 2
Air cleaner - automatic temperature control type 3
Fuel filter - servicing 4
Fuel pump - description 5
Fuel pump - testing 6
Fuel pump - removal and refitting 7
Fuel pump - dismantling, inspection, reassembling 8
Fuel tank and fuel lines - description and servicing 9
Evaporative emission control (fuel storage) - description and checking 10
Fuel tank level transmitter - removal and refitting 11
Accelerator linkage - adjustment 12
Carburettor - general description 13
Slow running - adjustment 14
Float level - adjustment 15

Fast idle adjustment - manually operated choke 16
Fast idle adjustment - automatically operated choke ... 17
Vacuum break - adjustment (automatic choke) 18
Choke valve release - adjustment (automatic choke) ... 19
Dashpot adjustment (automatic transmission) 20
Setting the housing cover (automatic choke) 21
Primary and secondary throttle butterfly valves - adjustment of interlock mechanism 22
Carburettor - removal and refitting 23
Carburettors - dismantling and reassembly general 24
Carburettor (manual choke) - dismantling and reassembly ... 25
Carburettor (automatic choke) - dismantling and reassembly 26
Exhaust emission control - adjustment and maintenance ... 27
Exhaust system - description and servicing 28
Fault finding 29

Specifications

Fuel pump ... ... mechanical, driven by camshaft eccentric
   Output ... ... 450 cc per minute
   Static fuel pressure ... ... 2.6 lb/in^2

Fuel tank
   Location ... ... rear mounted
   Capacity:
      saloon ... ... 8.75 Imp galls/40 litres/10.5 US galls
      estate and coupe ... ... 8.5 Imp galls/38 litres/10 US galls

Air cleaner
   Type (up until 1972) ... ... normal, paper element
      (after 1972) ... ... automatic temperature control

Carburettors
   Type (up to 1972) ... ... Hitachi DCG - 306 manual choke
      (after 1972 (manual gearbox) ... ... Hitachi DCH - 306 - 4 (auto. choke)
      (automatic transmission) ... ... Hitachi DCH - 306 - 5 (auto. choke)

	DCG - 306		DCH - 306	
	PRIMARY	SECONDARY	PRIMARY	SECONDARY
Manifold ports (diameter)	1.024 in.	1.181 in.	1.024 in.	1.181 in.
Choke tube (diameter)	0.787 in.	1.024 in.	0.787 in.	1.024 in.
Main jet	98	135	95	140
Main air bleed	80	80	80	80
Slow jet	43	50	43	50
Slow air bleed	220	100	215	100
Power jet	60		60	
Accelerator pump ejector nozzle	0.0197 in.		0.0197 in.	

1 General description

The fuel system comprises a rear mounted tank from which fuel is drawn through a filter by means of a mechanically operated pump mounted on the right hand side of the crankcase. The fuel pump is operated by an eccentric on the camshaft and delivers fuel, under pressure, to a twin choke carburettor. The carburettor type varies according to the vehicle model and date of manufacture and reference should be made to Specifications for full details. Vehicles built before 1972 are fitted with a manually operated choke. Later vehicles have an electrically-operated automatic choke.

All vehicles are fitted with a crankcase fume emission control system (see Chapter 1) and 1972 onward vehicles operating in North America, are fitted with a full exhaust emission control system and automatic temperature control air cleaner to reduce noxious exhaust gases to the minimum.

A full description of each component of the fuel system is to be found in the following Sections of this Chapter.

2 Air cleaner - servicing

1 The standard air cleaner comprises a body in which is housed a paper element type filter, a lid and the necessary connecting hoses and brackets.

2 Every 24,000 miles the element should be renewed. Other than renewal, no servicing is required.

3 Unscrew and remove the wing nut which secures the air cleaner lid in position, remove the lid and extract the paper element.

4 Wipe the interior of the air cleaner body free from oil and dirt and install the new element.

3 Air cleaner - automatic temperature control type

1 This type of air cleaner is designed to keep air being drawn into the engine for combustion purposes at a consistent temperature of about 43°C. The system is installed to assist in reducing pollution emitted from the exhaust and consists, essentially, of a temperature sensor and air control valves.

2 The temperature sensor will actuate the air control valve so that the correct mixture of hot air from the exhaust manifold and cold air entering the air cleaner inlet tube will be supplied to the carburettor at the specified temperature irrespective of the operating temperature of the engine itself.

3 Regular maintenance of this type of air cleaner is not required beyond renewal of the element as described for standard air cleaner in the preceding Section.

However, in the event of a fault developing and evidence of increased exhaust fumes being emitted, carry out the following operations.

4 Check the security, condition and correct location of all vacuum and air supply hoses, (Fig. 3.3).

5 With the engine at normal operating temperature, switch off the ignition and holding a mirror to reflect the interior of the air cleaner intake pipe, check the position of the valve. The valve should be closed to exhaust manifold heated air. If this is not the case, check the valve linkage.

6 Disconnect the vacuum hose which connects the vacuum capsule (2) to the inlet manifold, (Fig. 3.5.) Suck the tube to actuate the vacuum capsule and check that the valve closes to cold air intake. If this is not the case then the air cleaner must be renewed as an assembly.

7 With the engine cold, check that the ambient temperature of the sensor is below 30°C.

8 Using a mirror as previously described, check that the valve is in the 'open to cold air' position.

9 Start the engine and run it at idling speed, the valve should close immediately to cold air and permit exhaust manifold heated air to be drawn into the cleaner.

10 As the engine warms up observe that the valve gradually opens to permit the entry of cold air into the air cleaner intake tube.

11 If the valve does not operate correctly at within the temperature range 38 to 55°C (checked by using a thermometer adjacent to its location) remove and renew the sensor unit by bending back the tabs of its retaining clips.

4 Fuel filter - servicing

1 The fuel filter is located in the tank to pump hose and is of the sealed paper element type.

2 Every 12,000 miles, renew the filter. It is preferable to carry out this operation when the fuel tank level is low otherwise when the fuel hoses are disconnected from the filter, the tank line will have to be plugged to prevent loss of fuel.

3 Check that the new filter is installed in the correct attitude, (Fig. 3.7.)

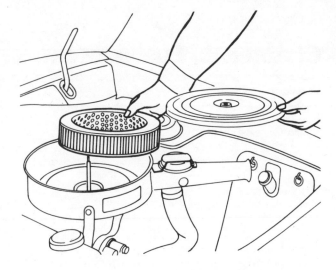

Fig. 3.1. Fitting a new air cleaner element (Section 2)

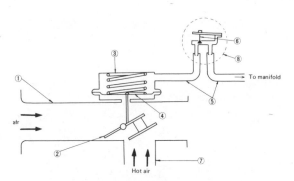

FIG. 3.2. AUTOMATIC TEMPERATURE CONTROL AIR CLEANER - AIR FLOW DIAGRAM (SECTION 3)

1   air intake
2   air control valve
3   diaphragm spring
4   diaphragm
5   vacuum hoses
6   air bleed valve (partially open)
7   hot air intake
8   sensor assembly

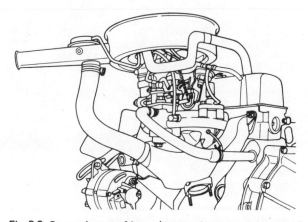

Fig. 3.3. Correct layout of hoses (automatic temperature control type air cleaner) (Section 3)

5 Fuel pump - description

The fuel pump is actuated by the movement of its rocker arm on a camshaft eccentric. This movement is transferred to a flexible diaphragm which draws the fuel from the tank and pumps it under pressure to the carburettor float chamber. Inlet and outlet valves are incorporated to control the flow of fuel irrespective of engine speed.

6 Fuel pump - testing

Presuming that the fuel lines and unions are in good condition and that there are no leaks anywhere, check the performance of the fuel pump in the following manner: Disconnect the fuel pipe at the carburettor inlet union, and the high tension lead to the coil, and with a suitable container or a large rag in position to catch the ejected fuel, turn the engine over on the starter motor solenoid. A good spurt of petrol should emerge from the end of the pipe every second revolution.

7 Fuel pump - removal and refitting

1 Disconnect the fuel pipes by unscrewing their two unions on the fuel pump which is located on the right hand side of the engine. Where the fuel tank contains more than a small amount of fuel it will probably be necessary to plug the inlet fuel line from the tank.
2 Remove the two nuts which secure the fuel pump to the crankcase. Lift away the pump noting carefully the number of gaskets used between the pump and crankcase mating faces.

8 Fuel pump - dismantling, inspection, reassembly

1 Scratch a mark across the edges of the upper and lower body flange to ensure easy refitting.
2 Unscrew and remove the body securing screws (17) and their lock washers (18) (Fig. 3.9.)
3 Remove the cover screw (7) washer (8) cover (5) and the gasket (6).

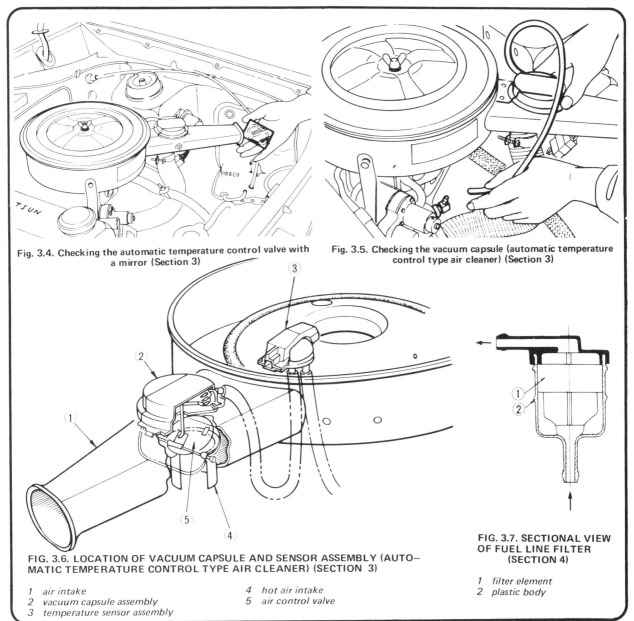

Fig. 3.4. Checking the automatic temperature control valve with a mirror (Section 3)

Fig. 3.5. Checking the vacuum capsule (automatic temperature control type air cleaner) (Section 3)

FIG. 3.6. LOCATION OF VACUUM CAPSULE AND SENSOR ASSEMBLY (AUTO—MATIC TEMPERATURE CONTROL TYPE AIR CLEANER) (SECTION 3)

1 air intake
2 vacuum capsule assembly
3 temperature sensor assembly
4 hot air intake
5 air control valve

FIG. 3.7. SECTIONAL VIEW OF FUEL LINE FILTER (SECTION 4)

1 filter element
2 plastic body

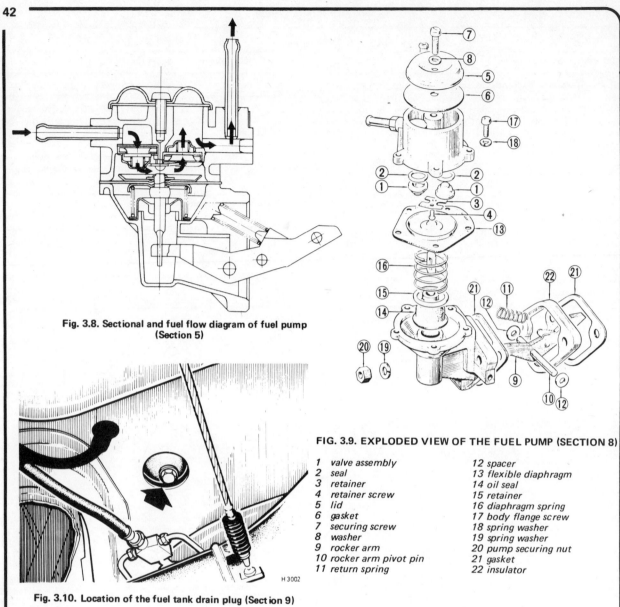

Fig. 3.8. Sectional and fuel flow diagram of fuel pump
(Section 5)

FIG. 3.9. EXPLODED VIEW OF THE FUEL PUMP (SECTION 8)

1 valve assembly
2 seal
3 retainer
4 retainer screw
5 lid
6 gasket
7 securing screw
8 washer
9 rocker arm
10 rocker arm pivot pin
11 return spring

12 spacer
13 flexible diaphragm
14 oil seal
15 retainer
16 diaphragm spring
17 body flange screw
18 spring washer
19 spring washer
20 pump securing nut
21 gasket
22 insulator

Fig. 3.10. Location of the fuel tank drain plug (Section 9)

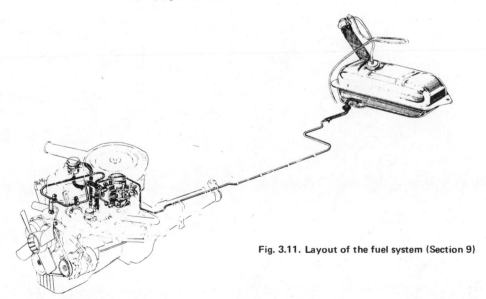

Fig. 3.11. Layout of the fuel system (Section 9)

4 Unscrew and remove the inlet and outlet fuel pipe connecting stubs.

5 Unscrew and remove the two screws from the valve retainer (3). Withdraw the two valves (1) and the valve washers (2).

6 Press the diaphragm (13) downwards and then grip the top of the pull rod and move the bottom end of the rod so that a sideways movement will disengage it from the rocker arm link. The diaphragm, diaphragm spring, lower body and washer may then be withdrawn.

7 The rocker arm pin (10) is an interference fit and if it is essential to remove it, then it should be pressed or drifted out.

8 Check all components for wear and renew as necessary. Hold the diaphragm up to the light and inspect for splits or pin holes. Check the upper and lower body halves for cracks.

9 Reassembly is a reversal of dismantling. Apply grease to the rocker arm mechanism and install a new cover gasket.

10 When the pump has been reassembled, test its efficiency by either placing a finger over the inlet pipe and actuating the rocker arm when a good suction noise should be heard by connecting it to the tank fuel line and after actuating the rocker arm a few times, each successive stroke should be accompanied by a well defined spurt of fuel from the outlet pipe.

11 Refit the pump as described in the preceding Section.

9 Fuel tank and fuel lines - description amd servicing

1 The fuel tank is rear mounted and varies in capacity according to vehicle model. Filler tube, vent pipes and fuel lines are connected to the tank by flexible tubing. The fuel level gauge (next Section) is mounted in the top of the tank and a drain plug is conveniently located.

2 To remove the fuel tank, drain the tank and then disconnect the fuel line connector.

3 Remove the cover and trim from the floor of the luggage boot, disconnect the electrical leads to the fuel level transmitter.

4 Unscrew and remove the securing bolts and anchor plates from the fuel tank flanges, (Fig. 3.12).

5 Loosen the filler hose clip and withdraw the tank from its location.

6 If the tank contains a lot of sediment or sludge, shake it vigorously using two or three changes of paraffin and then allow it to drain thoroughly.

7 Should a leak develop in the fuel tank do not be tempted to solder over the hole. Fuel tank repair is a specialist job and unless lengthy safety precautions are observed can be a very dangerous procedure. It is probably as cheap these days to buy a new tank rather than have the faulty one repaired.

8 Occasionally drain the tank when there is very little fuel left in it so that any accumulated water or sediment will be flushed out and discarded. This action will safeguard the tank against corrosion and help to prevent clogging of the fuel line filter.

9 Refitting the fuel tank is a reversal of removal, check that the vent tubes which are connected to the filler neck are not trapped

and are securely clipped in position.

10 The installation components vary in detail between the different models but the operations described in this Section apply.

10 Evaporative emission control (fuel storage) - description and checking

1 This system is designed to prevent vapour from the tank escaping to atmosphere and is fitted to vehicles operating in areas where stringent anti-pollution regulations are enforced.

2 The system comprises a tight sealing filler cap, a vapour-liquid separator, a vent line and a flow guide valve.

3 The principle of operation is such that with the engine switched off, the vent line, the separator and fuel tank are filled with fuel vapour. When the pressure of this vapour reaches a pre-determined level it actuates a flow guide valve and passes to the crankcase. When the engine is started, the vapour which has accumulated in the crankcase, manifold and air cleaner is drawn into the inlet manifold for combustion within the engine cylinders. When the vapour pressure in the system becomes negative, then the flow guide valve will permit entry of fresh air to the fuel tank from the air cleaner.

4 Periodic preventative maintenance of the system should be carried out. Inspect all hoses and the fuel filler cap for damage or deterioration. Leakage at the fuel cap can only be determined by fitting a three-way connector, cock and manometer (U shaped glass tube will do) into the vent line as shown, (Fig. 3.14).

5 Blow through the cock until the level in the U tube is approximately at the higher level illustrated. Close the cock and after a period of 2½ minutes check that the level in the U tube has not dropped more than indicated in the illustration. If the levels in the U tube quickly become equalised, then the filler cap is not sealing correctly.

6 Assuming the previous test has proved satisfactory, again blow into the U tube and shut the cock. Remove the filler cap quickly when the height of the liquid in the U tube should immediately drop to zero, failure to do this will indicate a clogged or obstructed vent line.

7 The fuel filler cap incorporates a vacuum release valve and this may be checked by gently sucking with the mouth. A slight

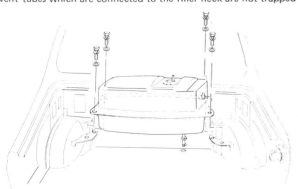

Fig. 3.12. Fuel tank securing bolts and anchor plates (Section 9)

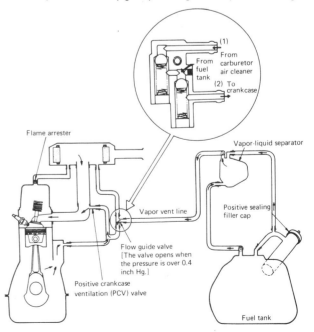

Fig. 3.13. Diagram of the fuel storage system fume emission control system (Section 10)

44

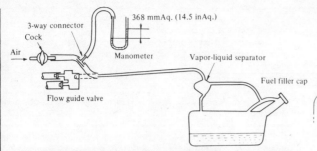

Fig. 3.14. Diagram for checking serviceability of components used in the fuel storage system fume emission control system (Section 10)

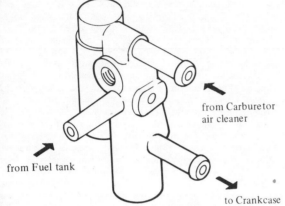

from Carburetor air cleaner

from Fuel tank

to Crankcase

Fig. 3.16. Fuel system flow valve, located in engine compartment (Section 10)

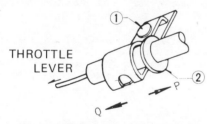

THROTTLE LEVER

FIG. 3.18. ADJUSTMENT DIAGRAM FOR ACCELERATOR CABLE (SECTION 12)

1 clamp bolt
2 outer cable socket

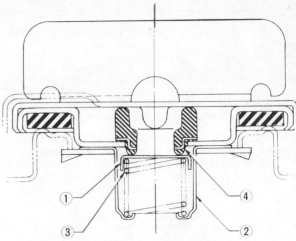

FIG. 3.15. SECTIONAL VIEW OF THE FUEL TANK FILLER CAP VALVE (SECTION 10)

1 valve
2 valve housing
3 spring
4 valve seat

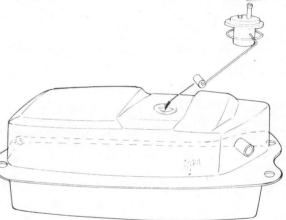

Fig. 3.17. Location of fuel tank transmitter and float assembly (Section 11)

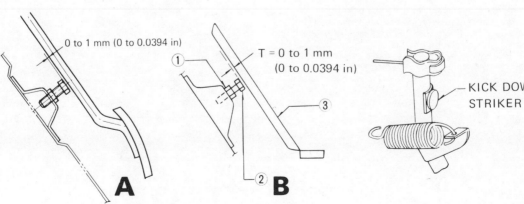

0 to 1 mm (0 to 0.0394 in)

T = 0 to 1 mm (0 to 0.0394 in)

KICK DOWN SWITCH STRIKER

A

B

FIG. 3.19. ACCELERATOR PEDAL STOP CLEARANCE (SECTION 12)

Fig. 3.20. Accelerator pedal kick-down switch contact (automatic transmission) (Section 12)

A left hand drive
B right hand drive
1 locknut
2 stop bolt

resistance accompanied by a click shows the valve is in good condition. Further suction will cause the resistance to cease as soon as the valve clicks.

8 To check the operation of the flow guide valve, apply air pressure from a tyre pump in the following sequence:

a) Air applied to fuel tank nozzle should emerge freely from crankcase nozzle.

b) Air applied to crankcase nozzle should not enter or emerge from any other nozzle.

c) Air applied to air cleaner nozzle should emerge from one or both of the other two nozzles.

Any deviations from the foregoing tests will necessitate renewal of the components as assemblies.

11 Fuel tank level transmitter - removal and refitting

1 Disconnect the battery.

2 Provided the fuel tank is not too full, the transmitter may be removed without draining the tank.

3 Disconnect the trim and floor cover in the luggage boot.

4 Disconnect the electrical lead from the unit.

5 Using a screwdriver, unscrew the locking plate which secures the unit to the tank orifice by a bayonet action.

6 Withdraw the unit and sealing washer taking care not to damage or bend the float mechanism.

7 Refitting is a reversal of removal but always use a new sealing washer.

12 Accelerator linkage - adjustment

1 After a considerable mileage, the accelerator cable may stretch and the following adjustment may be carried out to remove the slack.

2 Check the security of the inner cable to the accelerator pedal and the threaded portion of the outer cable which is held by a nut to the engine bulkhead. Loosen clamp 1 and pull the outer cable in the direction P, (Fig. 3.18) until any further movement would cause the throttle arm on the carburettor to move. Now ease the outer cable in the opposite direction Q no more than 0.050 in. Tighten the clamp.

3 The accelerator pedals on left and right hand drive models are fitted with an adjustable stop and although the pedal pad itself differs in design between the two models, each must have a clearance with the pedal fully depressed and the throttle lever on the carburettor fully open, (Fig. 3.19).

4 Never attempt to bend the accelerator pedal arm to correct the clearance but only adjust the stop bolt by first loosening the locknut. Before carrying out any adjustment to the stop bolt always check the cable setting as described earlier in this Section.

5 With automatic transmission vehicles, the accelerator pedal arm is fitted with a kick down switch striker button.

13 Carburettor - general description

The carburettor fitted to all models is of downdraught twin choke type. Until 1972, a manually operated choke version DCG 306, was fitted and after this date an automatic electrically heated choke is fitted, DCH 306 - 4. Vehicles fitted with automatic transmission have a similar carburettor, modified to suit the slightly different operating requirements, DCH 306 - 5. Full specifications of the carburettors used in all vehicles of the range are given in the Specifications Section of this Chapter.

The carburettor is conventional in operation and incorporates a primary and main jet system and a mechanically operated accelerator pump.

a) Manually operated choke: This comprises a butterfly valve which closes one of the venturi choke tubes and is so synchronized with the throttle valve plate that the latter opens sufficiently to provide a rich mixture and an increased slow running speed for easy starting.

Fig. 3.21. Hitachi model DCG 306 carburettor (Section 13)

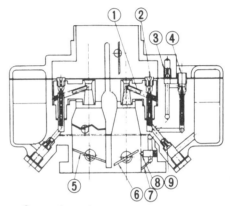

FIG. 3.22. LOCATION OF JETS IN DCG 306 CARBURETTOR (SECTION 13)

1 primary main nozzle
2 primary main air bleed
3 primary slow air bleed
4 primary slow jet
5 secondary throttle valve
6 primary throttle valve
7 idle hole
8 by-pass hole
9 primary main jet

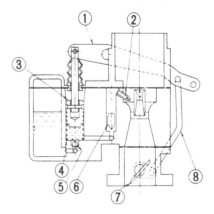

FIG. 3.23. COMPONENTS OF THE ACCELERATOR PUMP (MODEL DCG 306) (SECTION 13)

1 operating lever
2 pump nozzle
3 piston
4 return spring
5 inlet valve
6 outlet valve
7 primary throttle valve
8 operating rod

b) Automatic choke: This is essentially an electrically heated bi-metal strip. When the engine is switched on, the bi-metal strip which is linked to the now fully closed choke valve (cold engine) is heated electrically and over a pre-set period causes the choke valve to open until its fully open position coincides with the engine reaching normal operating temperature.

For idling and slow running, the fuel passes through the slow running jet, the primary slow air bleed and the secondary slow air bleed. The fuel is finally ejected from the by-pass and idle holes, (Fig. 3.22).

The accelerator pump is synchronized with the throttle valve. During periods of heavy acceleration, the pump which is of simple piston and valve construction, provides an additional metered quantity of fuel to enrich the normal mixture. The quantity of fuel metered can be varied according to operating climatic conditions by adjusting the stroke of the pump linkage.

The secondary system provides a mixture for normal motoring conditions by means of a main jet and air bleed. The float chamber is fed with fuel pumped by the mechanically operated pump on the crankcase. The level in the chamber is critical and must at all times be maintained as specified, (Section 15).

14 Slow running - adjustment

1 Run the engine to normal operating temperature and then set the throttle adjusting screw (1) (Fig. 3.25) to provide an engine speed of 800 rpm with the gear selector lever in neutral ('N' automatic transmission). If the vehicle is fitted with a tachometer then the setting of engine speed will be no problem. Where an instrument is not available then a useful guide may be obtained from the state of the ignition warning lamp. This should be just going out at the correct idling speed.
2 Setting of the mixture screw (2) may be carried out using 'Colortune' or a vacuum gauge attached to the inlet manifold. In either case follow the equipment manufacturer's instructions.
3 In certain territories, the use of a CO_1 meter is essential and if this is used then the throttle adjusting screw and the mixture screw must be turned to provide a reading on the meter of 1.5% ± 0.5% at the specified engine idling speed.
4 As a temporary measure, the adjustment screws may be rotated progressively, first one and then the other until the engine idles at the correct speed without any 'hunting' or stalling. Turning the mixture screw clockwise weakens the mixture and anti-clockwise richens it. Never screw the mixture screw in too far so that it is forced into its seat or damage to the needle point of the screw will result. On later type carburettors this cannot happen as a travel stop is fitted. Should this cap be inadvertently removed then it must be reset in accordance with the diagram, (Fig. 3.26).

15 Float level - adjustment

1 Where the appropriate adjustments have been carried out and there is evidence of fuel starvation or conversely, flooding or excessively rich mixture, the float level should be checked.
2 Remove the carburettor as described in Section 23.
3 Disconnect choke connecting rod, accelerator pump lever and return spring.
4 Unscrew and remove the five securing screws which secure the upper choke chamber to the main body.
5 Turn the float chamber upside down and check the dimension H with the float hanging down under its own weight, (Fig. 3.27).
6 Now gently push the float upwards to the full extent of its travel and check the clearance 'h' between the end face of the inlet needle valve and the float tongue. Adjustment to correct either of these dimensions is carried out by bending the float tongue or the stopper tag (3).

16 Fast idle adjustment - manually operated choke

1 Ensure that the choke control is fully out and that the air cleaner having been removed, the choke butterfly valve can be seen to be in the fully closed position.
2 Check the position of the primary throttle valve plate. This should be open sufficiently to give a clearance of 0.0480 in between the edge of the plate and the venturi wall, (Fig. 3.28).
3 Where adjustment is required, bend the choke connecting rod.

17 Fast idle adjustment - automatically operated choke

1 Unscrew and remove the three screws which secure the automatic choke housing. Note the index setting and remove the cover.
2 Within the choke housing, set the fast idle arm on the second step of the fast idle cam.
3 Turn the fast idle adjusting screw so that the clearance between the edge of the primary throttle valve plate and the choke tube wall is 0.033 in (manual gearbox) or 0.044 in (automatic transmission), (Fig. 3.30).
4 When starting the engine from cold after this adjustment, if the engine idles too roughly or too slowly, increase the clearance by 0.004 in. Conversely if the engine idles too fast, reduce the clearance by 0.004 in.
5 When adjustment is complete, refit the cover, aligning the cover and body index marks in their original positions.

18 Vacuum break - adjustment (automatic choke)

1 Close the choke valve and hold it closed by the use of a temporary rubber band, (Fig. 3.31).
2 Grip the vacuum break stem with a pair of pliers and detach it from the capsule diaphragm. Measure the dimension 'B' which should be 0.0450 in (manual) or 0.048 in (automatic). Adjust if necessary by bending the vacuum break rod carefully.
3 Refit the break stem to the diaphragm.

19 Choke valve release - adjustment (automatic choke)

1 Repeat operation 1 of the preceding Section.
2 Actuate the throttle linkage so that the primary and secondary throttle valves are fully closed. This will be easier if the throttle return valve return spring is first removed.
3 Measure clearance C, (Fig. 3.32). The clearance should be 0.079 in. If incorrect, bend the shaft which connects the throttle lever to the choke valve release.

20 Dash pot - adjustment (automatic transmission)

1 This device is only fitted to vehicles having automatic transmission.
2 Run the engine to normal operating temperature.
3 Actuate the throttle linkage by hand until the dashpot just impinges upon the return spring lever. At this position the engine tachometer should register 2000 rpm. If this is not the case, adjust the dashpot stop nut.
4 Finally when the engine is running at 3,000 rpm release the throttle linkage and ensure that the engine speed falls smoothly from this level to 1000 rpm in about five seconds. If the speed does not fall smoothly and progressively then the dashpot is probably worn and must be renewed.

21 Setting the housing cover (automatic choke)

1 If the choke cover and body index marks are observed before

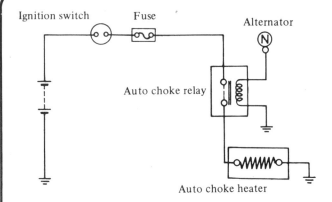

Ignition switch   Fuse   Alternator
Auto choke relay
Auto choke heater

Fig. 3.24. Circuit diagram - automatic choke (Section 13)

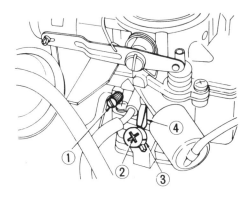

FIG. 3.25. SLOW-RUNNING ADJUSTMENT SCREWS
(SECTION 14)

1 *throttle screw*   3 *mixture screw limiter*
2 *mixture screw*   4 *mixture screw*
                                 limiter travel stop

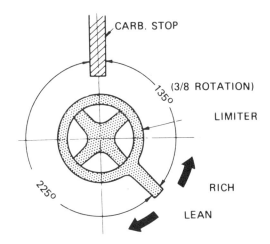

CARB. STOP
(3/8 ROTATION)
135°   LIMITER
225°
RICH
LEAN

Fig. 3.26. Setting diagram for mixture screw travel limiter
(Section 14)

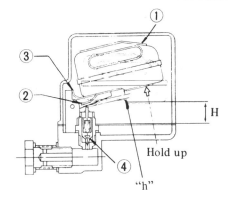

H
Hold up
"h"

FIG. 3.27. FLOAT LEVEL SETTING DIAGRAM (SECTION 15)

1 *float*   3 *float stop*
2 *float tang*   4 *inlet needle valve*

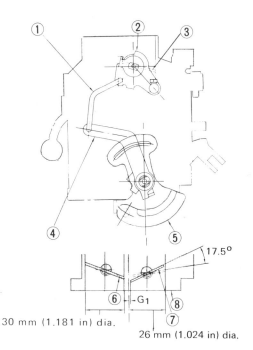

17.5°
30 mm (1.181 in) dia.
26 mm (1.024 in) dia.

FIG. 3.28. FAST IDLE SETTING DIAGRAM - MANUALLY
OPERATED CHOKE (SECTION 16)

1 *connecting rod*   6 *secondary throttle*
2 *choke lever*   *butterfly valve*
3 *choke butterfly valve*   7 *primary throttle*
4 *choke connecting lever*   *butterfly valve*
5 *throttle lever*   8 *carburettor body*

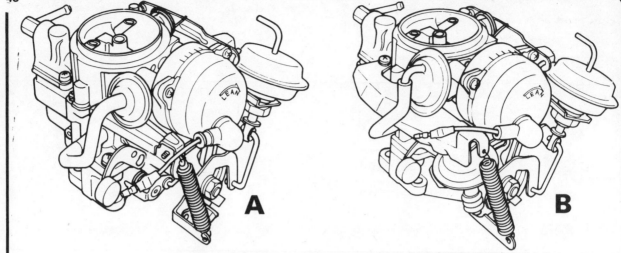

FIG. 3.29. AUTOMATIC CHOKE TYPE CARBURETTOR (SECTION 17)

A   type DCH - 306 - 4 for manually operated gearbox

B   type DCH - 306 - 5 for automatic transmission (note dashpot)

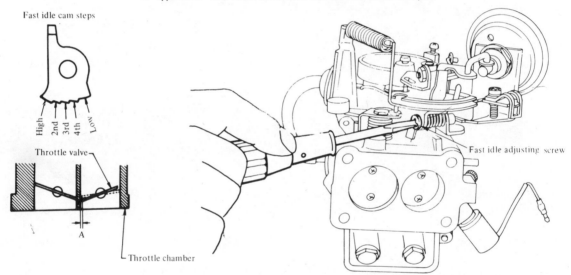

Fig. 3.30. Adjusting the fast idle setting on an automatic choke carburettor (Section 17)

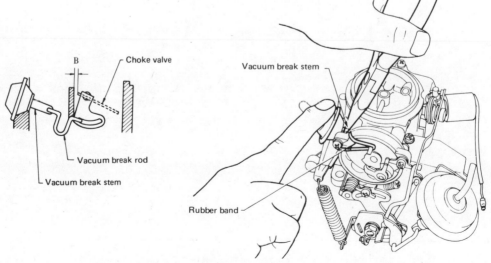

Fig. 3.31. Adjusting the vacuum break (automatic choke carburettor (Section 18)

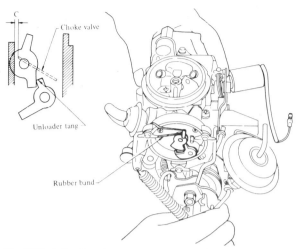

Fig. 3.32. Adjusting the choke valve release (automatic choke carburettor) (Section 19)

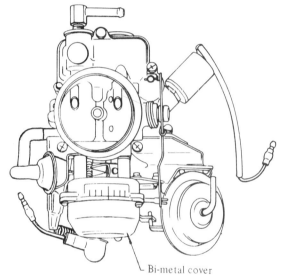

Fig. 3.34. Setting the housing cover - automatic choke carburettor (Section 21)

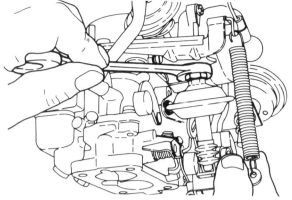

Fig. 3.33. Dashpot adjustment - automatic transmission (Section 20)

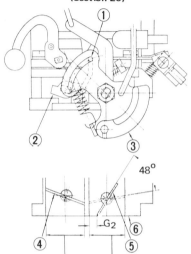

30 mm (1.181 in) dia.   26 mm (1.024 in) dia.

FIG. 3.35. SETTING DIAGRAM - PRIMARY AND SECON-DARY THROTTLE BUTTERFLY VALVES INTERLOCK MECHANISM (SECTION 22)

1 connecting rod
2 lever
3 throttle lever
4 secondary throttle butterfly valve
5 primary throttle butterfly valve
6 carburettor body

removal of the cover and then the cover is refitted in its original position, the setting of the automatic choke will not be disturbed. Where, however, new components have been fitted or due to changing characteristics of the engine because of wear or tuning, adjustment of the automatic choke is required, proceed in the following manner.

2 Release the choke cover screws enough to allow it to rotate. Set the cover so that the **centre** index and scale marks are in alignment. When the engine is started if there is any tendency to over-choke then rotate the cover in a clockwise direction. If there is any tendency to stall or hesitate, turn the cover in an anti-clockwise direction. Do not turn the cover more than half a division of the scale before retesting the starting performance. Re-tighten the cover screws.

3 Where there is evidence that the bi-metal resistance is un-serviceable, this should be tested by connecting a sensitive ohmmeter between the choke heater wire terminal and the carburettor body. With the ignition on, the resistance should range from 9.2 to 9.6 ohms.

22 Primary and secondary throttle butterfly valves - adjustment of interlock mechanism

1 Actuate the primary throttle valve until the secondary

throttle valve is just about to open. Measure the distance (G2) between the edge of the primary valve plate and the wall of the bore, this should be 0.23 in. (Fig. 3.35).

2 If the clearance requires adjustment, bend the rod which connects the two throttle plates.

23 Carburettor - removal and refitting

1 Remove the air cleaner assembly.
2 Disconnect the fuel and vacuum hoses from the carburettor, also the choke and accelerator controls (choke heater cable 1972 model vehicles).
3 Remove the four nuts and washers which secure the carburettor to the inlet manifold.
4 Lift the carburettor from the manifold and discard the flange gasket.
5 Refitting is a reverse of removal, always use a new flange gasket.

24 Carburettors - dismantling and reassembly - general

1 With time the component parts of the Hitachi carburettor will wear and petrol consumption will increase. The diameter of

50

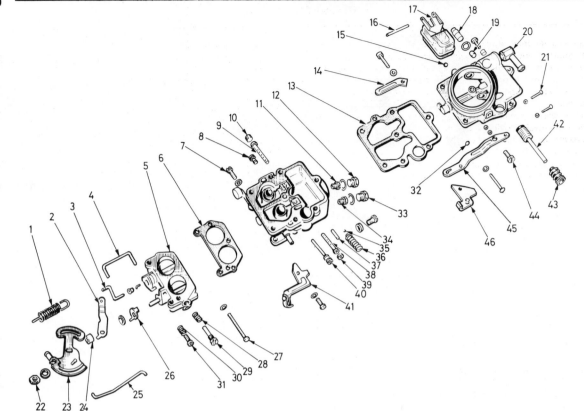

FIG. 3.36. EXPLODED VIEW OF THE TYPE DCG - 306 MANUALLY OPERATED CHOKE CARBURETTOR (SECTION 25)

1 return spring	13 float chamber gasket	25 accelerator pump rod	36 piston return spring
2 choke lever	14 spring support	26 plate	37 weight
3 rod	15 secondary slow air bleed	27 screw	38 primary emulsion tube
4 choke connecting rod	16 float pivot pin	28 mixture screw spring	39 primary main air bleed
5 throttle chamber	17 float	29 mixture screw	40 primary slow jet
6 gasket	18 inlet needle valve	30 throttle screw spring	41 accelerator cable connector
7 screw	19 filter	31 throttle adjusting screw	42 accelerator pump piston
8 secondary slow jet	20 choke chamber assembly	32 primary slow air bleed	43 accelerator pump cover
9 secondary emulsion tube	21 screw	33 power valve	44 accelerator pump lever shaft
10 secondary main air bleed	22 nut	34 primary main jet	45 accelerator pump lever
11 secondary main jet	23 throttle lever	35 ball	46 choke cable connector
12 drain plug	24 sleeve		

Fig. 3.38. Components removed to gain access to accelerator pump, (manual choke carburettor) (Section 25)

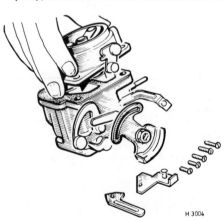

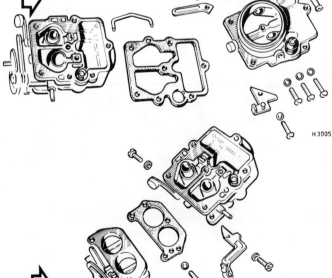

Fig. 3.37. Removing the choke chamber from a manually operated choke carburettor (Section 25)

Fig. 3.39. The throttle chamber removed from a manual choke carburettor (Section 25)

drillings and jet may alter, and air and fuel leaks may develop round spindles and other moving parts. Because of the high degree of precision involved it is recommended that an exchange rebuilt carburettor is purchased. This is one of the few instances where it is better to buy a new component rather than to rebuild the old one.

2 The accelerator pump itself may need attention and gaskets may need renewal. Providing care is taken there is no reason why the carburettor may not be completely reconditioned at home, but ensure a full repair kit can be obtained before you strip the carburettor down. NEVER poke out jets with wire or similar to clean them but blow them out with compressed air or air from a car tyre pump.

25 Carburettor (manual choke) - dismantling and reassembly

1 The main jets and needle valves are accessible from the exterior of the carburettor.

2 These should be unscrewed, removed and cleaned by blowing them through with air from a tyre pump; never probe a jet or needle valve seat with wire.

3 Detach the choke chamber by removing the connecting rod, accelerator pump lever, return spring and the five securing screws.

4 The primary and secondary emulsion tubes are accessible after removing the main air bleeds.

5 Remove the accelerator pump cover, retaining the spring, piston and ball valve carefully.

6 Separate the float chamber from the throttle housing by unscrewing and removing three securing screws. Slide out the float pivot pin and remove the float.

7 Unless imperative, do not dismantle the throttle butterfly valves from their spindles.

8 Take great care when disconnecting the interlock rods that they are not bent or twisted or the settings and adjustments will be upset.

9 With the carburettor dismantled, clean all components in clean fuel and blow through the internal body passages with air from a tyre pump.

10 Inspect all components for wear and the body and chamber castings for cracks.

11 Clean the small gauze filter and if corroded or clogged, renew it.

12 If wear is evident in the throttle spindle, the carburettor should be renewed on an exchange basis.

13 Check all jet and air bleed sizes with those specified in Specifications in case a previous owner has changed them for ones of incorrect size.

14 Check the ejection of fuel when the accelerator pump is actuated.

15 Reassembly is a reversal of dismantling using all the items supplied in the repair kit.

16 When the carburettor is being reassembled, check the float movement (Section 15) and when it is refitted to the engine, carry out all the checks and adjustments described in Sections 14, 16, 20 and 22 of this Chapter.

26 Carburettor (automatic choke) - dismantling and reassembly

1 The main jets and needle valves are accessible from the exterior of the carburettor, note the two located beneath the float chamber drain plugs.

2 Detach the throttle return spring.

3 Remove the pivot screw from the accelerator pump lever and detach the lever from the pump piston and the throttle lever rod.

4 On 1972 models fitted with emission control, remove the vacuum hose.

5 Unscrew and remove the automatic choke housing cover (note index setting).

6 Unscrew the two servo diaphragm securing screws and remove the diaphragm.

7 Unscrew and remove the five securing bolts which hold the choke housing in position and remove the housing.

8 Slide out the float pivot pin and remove the float.

9 Unscrew and remove the fuel inlet needle valve.

10 Turn the carburettor upside down and eject the components of the accelerator pump taking care not to lose the ball.

11 From the top flange of the lower body, unscrew the slow air bleeds and the main air bleeds. After removal of the latter, the emulsion tubes may be extracted by turning the carburettor upside down.

12 Separate the throttle chamber from the main carburettor body by removing the three securing screws.

13 Unscrew the mixture screw and remove it together with its coil spring.

14 Do not dismantle further by removing the servo - diaphragm or the throttle butterfly valves unless absolutely essential.

15 Carry out the operations listed in paragraphs 8 to 14 of the preceding Section.

16 Reassembly is a reversal of dismantling using all the items supplied in the repair kit.

17 When the carburettor is being reassembled, check the float movement (Section 15) and when it is refitted to the engine, carry out all the checks and adjustments described in Sections 14, 17, 18, 19, 20, 21 and 22 of this Chapter.

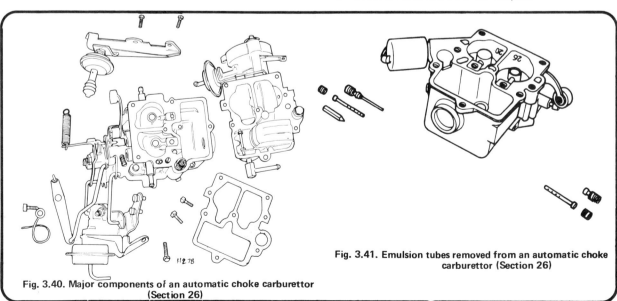

Fig. 3.40. Major components of an automatic choke carburettor (Section 26)

Fig. 3.41. Emulsion tubes removed from an automatic choke carburettor (Section 26)

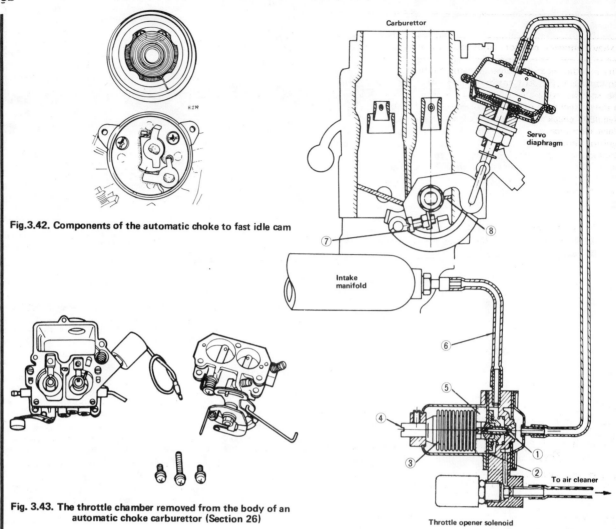

Fig.3.42. Components of the automatic choke to fast idle cam

Fig. 3.43. The throttle chamber removed from the body of an automatic choke carburettor (Section 26)

Fig. 3.45. Diagram of the throttle opener circuit installed to assist in the reduction of exhaust fumes (Section 27)

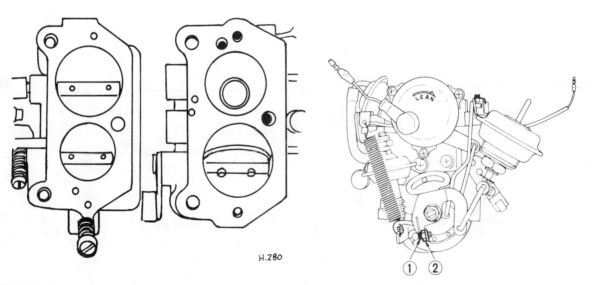

Fig.3.44. The throttle butterfly valves and actuating mechanism (automatic choke carburettor). (Section 26)

Fig. 3.46. Adjusting screw (1) and locknut (2) of servo diaphragm used in fume emission control system (Section 27)

27 Exhaust emission control - adjustment and maintenance

1 The maintenance of a 'clean exhaust' without loss of power or economy is dependent not only upon the correct adjustment of the specific components described in this Section but also upon the correct tune of other components of the engine.

2 Regularly check the adjustment of the following:
a) Valve clearances
b) Ignition timing
c) Contact breaker points
d) Spark plugs
e) Crankcase fume emission control (Chapter 1)
f) All the carburettor adjustments described for automatic choke carburettors in this Chapter.

3 A throttle opening device is fitted which is designed to open the throttle slightly during engine deceleration and to reduce the concentration of unburned hydrocarbons in the exhaust system by admitting a mixture sufficient to maintain complete combustion within the cylinders. The device comprises a servo

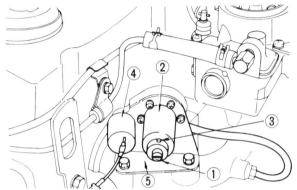

FIG. 3.47. INLET MANIFOLD CONTROL VALVE - OR COMPONENT OF THE FUME EMISSION CONTROL SYSTEM (SECTION 27)

1 adjusting screw
2 control valve body
3 lockscrew

4 throttle opener solenoid
5 control valve assembly
   mounting plate

diaphragm attached to the carburettor and a control valve bolted to the inlet manifold. The system is actuated by vacuum within the inlet manifold.

4 To adjust the system on manual gearbox vehicles, disconnect the electric lead from the air cleaner vacuum valve. On vehicles fitted with automatic transmission, loosen the dashpot until it becomes inoperative.

5 Start the engine and adjust the slow running speed to 700 rpm (manual gearbox) and 750 (automatic transmission) checking with a tachometer.

6 Refer to Fig. 3.45 and detach tube (6) from the inlet manifold. Disconnect the servo to valve tube and fit this directly to the manifold, thus by-passing the valve. The tachometer should now register between 1700 and 1800 rpm. If the reading is outside that specified, loosen the locknut (2) and adjust the screw (1) until the reading is correct, (Fig. 3.46).

7 Reconnect the vacuum tubes in their original positions and then increase the engine speed to 3000 rpm moving the throttle lever by hand. Release the throttle lever abruptly and time the period taken for the engine speed to drop to 1000 rpm this should be between 3.5 and 4.5 seconds (manual gearbox) and 2.5 to 3.5 seconds (automatic transmission). If the time taken for the engine speed to drop is outside the specified limits, loosen the locknut on the valve and adjust the screw, clockwise to increase the period, anti-clockwise to reduce it, (Fig. 3.47).

8 In the event of failure to respond to adjustment with either component, renew as assemblies as they are not capable of repair.

28 Exhaust system - description and servicing

1 All models in the range are fitted with a two section exhaust system. The front downpipe is connected to a socket at the forward end of the silencer and the silencer body and tailpipe are a combined unit.

2 The system is suspended at the silencer by means of rubber rings and at the tailpipe by a flexible strap.

3 Examination of the exhaust pipe and silencers at regular intervals is worthwhile as small defects may be repairable when, if left they will almost certainly require renewal of one of the sections of the system. Also, any leaks, apart from the noise factor, may cause poisonous exhaust gases to get inside the car

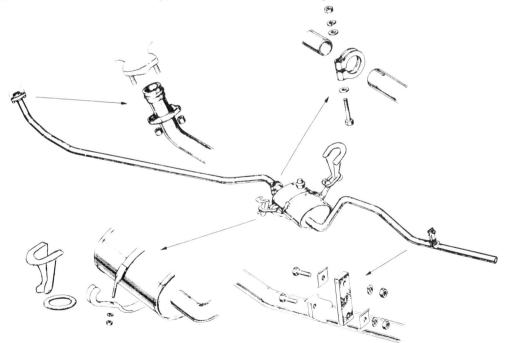

Fig. 3.48. Exploded view of the exhaust system (all models) (Section 28)

which can be unpleasant, to say the least, even in mild concentrations. Prolonged inhalation could cause sickness and giddiness.

4 As the sleeve connections and clamps are usually very difficult to separate it is quicker and easier in the long run to remove the complete system from the car when renewing a section. It can be expensive if another section is damaged when trying to separate a bad section from it.

5 To remove the system first remove the bolts holding the tail pipe bracket to the body. Support the rear silencer on something to prevent cracking or kinking the pipes elsewhere.

6 Unhook the rubber rings supporting the front silencer.

7 Disconnect the manifold to downpipe connecting flange and then withdraw the complete exhaust system from below and out to the rear of the vehicle. If necessary, jack up the rear of the vehicle to provide more clearance.

8 When separating the damaged section to be renewed cut away the damaged part from the adjoining good section rather than risk damaging the latter.

9 If small repairs are being carried out it is best, if possible, not to try and pull the sections apart.

10 Refitting should be carried out after connecting the two sections together. De-burr and grease the connecting socket and make sure that the clamp is in good condition and slipped over the front pipe but do not tighten it at this stage.

11 Connect the system to the manifold and connect the rear support strap. Now adjust the attitude of the silencer so that the tension on the two rubber support rings will be equalized when fitted.

12 Tighten the pipe clamp, the manifold flange nuts and the rear suspension strap bolts. Check that the exhaust system will not knock against any part of the vehicle when deflected slightly in a sideways or upward direction.

Fault finding - Fuel system

Symptom	Reason/s	Remedy
Excessive fuel consumption	Air filter choked	Renew element.
	Leakage from pump, carburettor or fuel lines or fuel tank	Renew or tighten as necessary.
	Float chamber flooding	Check and adjust level.
	Distributor capacitor faulty	Renew.
	Distributor weights or vacuum capsule faulty	Service or renew.
	Mixture too rich	Adjust, see Section 14.
	Contact breaker gap too wide	Check and reset.
	Incorrect valve clearances	Adjust.
	Incorrect spark plug gaps	Adjust.
	Tyres under inflated	Inflate.
	Dragging brakes	Check for air in system or faulty wheel or master cylinder.
Insufficient fuel delivery or weak mixture	Fuel tank air vent or pipe blocked or flattened	Clear obstruction.
	Clogged fuel filter	Clean.
	Float chamber needle valve clogged	Clear with air pressure.
	Faulty fuel pump valves	Renew.
	Fuel pump diaphragm split	Renew.
	Fuel pipe unions loose	Tighten.
	Fuel pump lid not seating correctly	Renew gasket.
	Inlet manifold gasket or carburettor flange gasket leaking	Renew as necessary.
	Incorrect adjustment of carburettor	Adjust, see Section 14.

Chapter 4 Ignition system

Contents

General description 1
Contact breaker - adjustment 2
Contact breaker points - removal and refitting 3
Condenser (capacitor) - removal, testing and refitting ... 4
Distributor - removal and refitting 5
Ignition timing 6
Distributor - dismantling and inspection 7
Distributor - reassembly 8
Coil - description and polarity 9
Spark plugs and leads 10
Ignition system - fault finding 11
Ignition system - fault symptoms 12

Specifications

System ... ... 12V negative earth, - re. battery, coil and distributor

Firing order 1 3 4 2

Static ignition timing: ... ... 7º BTDC at 600 rpm
   except North America ... ... 5º BTDC at 700 rpm

Spark plugs (14 mm)
   Type (up to 1972) ... ... Hitachi L46 - P or NGK BP - 6E
      (1972 onwards) ... ... Hitachi L46 - PW or NGK BP - 5ES
   Gap ... ... 0.031 to 0.035 in.

Coil
   Make (1972 onwards) ... ... Hanskin or Hitachi oil-filled
   Type (up to 1972) ... ... HP5 - 13E or C6R - 200
   Type (1972 onwards) ... ... H5 - 15 - 2 or C6R - 601
   Resistor (matched with coil) ... ... RC15 or 556OR - 1510

Condenser
   Capacity ... ... 0.20 to 0.24 uf

Distributor
   Make ... ... Hitachi
   Type (up to 1971) ... ... D411 - 61
      (up to 1971 - North America) ... ... D412 - 63
      (after 1971) ... ... D412 - 80 (manual gearbox)
      (after 1971) ... ... D412 - 89 (automatic transmission)

   Direction of rotation of rotor ... ... anti-clockwise
   Contact breaker points gap ... ... 0.018 to 0.022 in.

Servicing data (all models)
   Lower shaft diameter ... ... 0.4902 in. wear limit 0.0008 in.
   Shaft to housing clearance ... ... 0.0004 to 0.0015 in.
   Shaft (upper section) diameter ... ... 0.3150 in. wear limit 0.0006 in.
   Shaft to cam clearance ... ... 0.0002 to 0.0011 in.
   Counterweight hole diameter ... ... 0.1969 in. wear limit 0.0007 in.
   Counterweight hole to pivot clearance ... ... 0.0002 to 0.0018 in.

Torque wrench settings

   Spark plugs ... ... 11 to 15 lb/ft   1.5 to 2.1 kg/m

1 General description

In order that the engine can run correctly it is necessary for an electrical spark to ignite the fuel/air mixture in the combustion chamber at exactly the right moment in relation to engine speed and load. The ignition system is based on feeding low tension (LT) voltage from the battery to the coil where it is converted to high tension (HT) voltage. The high tension voltage is powerful enough to jump the spark plug gap in the cylinders many times a second under high compression pressures, providing that the system is in good condition and that all adjustments are correct.

The ignition system is divided into two circuits. The low tension circuit and the high tension circuit.

The low tension (sometimes known as the primary) circuit consists of the battery lead to the control box, lead to the ignition switch, lead from the ignition switch to the low tension or primary coil windings (terminal SW), and the lead from the low tension coil windings (coil terminal CB) to the contact breaker points and condenser in the distributor.

The high tension circuit consists of the high tension or secondary coil windings, the heavy ignition lead from the centre of the coil to the centre of the distributor cap, the rotor arm, and the spark plug leads and spark plugs.

The system functions in the following manner. Low tension voltage is changed in the coil into high tension voltage by the opening and closing of the contact breaker points in the low tension circuit. High tension voltage is then fed via the carbon brush in the centre of the distributor cap to the rotor arm of the distributor cap, and each time it comes in line with one of the four metal segments in the cap, which are connected to the spark plug leads, the opening and closing of the contact breaker points causes the high tension voltage to build up, jump the gap from the rotor arm to the appropriate metal segement and so via the spark plug lead to the spark plug, where it finally jumps the spark plug gap before going to earth.

The ignition is advanced and retarded automatically, to ensure the spark occurs at just the right instant for the particular load at the prevailing engine speed.

The ignition advance is controlled both mechanically and by a vacuum operated system. The mechanical governor mechanism comprises two lead weights, which move out from the distributor shaft as the engine speed rises due to centrifugal force. As they move outwards they rotate the cam relative to the distributor shaft, and so advance the spark. The weights are held in position by two light springs and it is the tension of the springs which is largely responsible for correct spark advancement.

The vacuum control consists of a diaphragm, one side of which is connected via a small bore tube to the carburettor, and the other side to the contact breaker plate. Depression in the inlet manifold and carburettor, which varies with engine speed and throttle opening, causes the diaphragm to move, so moving the contact breaker plate, and advancing or retarding the spark. A fine degree of control is achieved by a spring in the vacuum assembly.

2 Contact breaker - adjustment

1 To adjust the contact breaker points to the correct gap, first pull off the two clips securing the distributor cap to the distributor body, and lift away the cap. Clean the cap inside and out with a dry cloth. It is unlikely that the four segments will be badly burned or scored, but if they are the cap will have to be renewed.
2 Inspect the carbon brush contact located in the top of the cap - see that it is unbroken and stands proud of the plastic surface.
3 Check the contact spring on the top of the rotor arm. It must be clean and have adequate tension to ensure good contact.
4 Gently prise the contact breaker points open to examine the

condition of their faces. If they are rough, pitted, or dirty, it will be necessary to remove them for resurfacing, or for replacement points to be fitted.
5 Presuming the points are satisfactory, or that they have been cleaned and replaced, measure the gap between the points by turning the engine over until the heel of the breaker arm is on the highest point of the cam.
6 A 0.18 to 0.22 in feeler gauge should now just fit between the points.
7 If the cap varies from this amount slacken the contact plate securing screw.
8 Adjust the contact gap by inserting a screwdriver in the notched hole, in the breaker plate. Turn clockwise to increase and anti-clockwise to decrease the gap. When the gap is correct tighten the securing screw and check the gap again.
9 Making sure the rotor is in position replace the distributor cap and clip the spring blade retainers into position.

3 Contact breaker points - removal and refitting

1 Slip back the spring clips which secure the distributor cap in position. Remove the distributor cap and lay it to one side, only removing one or two of the HT leads from the plugs if necessary to provide greater movement of the cap.
2 Pull the rotor from the distributor shaft.
3 Unscrew the contact breaker securing screws a turn or two and disconnect the LT lead from the contact breaker arm.
4 If necessary, unscrew the securing screws a turn or two more and slide the contact breaker arms sideways to remove them.
5 Inspect the faces of the contact points. If they are only lightly burned or pitted then they may be ground square on an oilstone or by rubbing a carborundum strip between them. Where the points are found to be severely burned or pitted, then they must be renewed and at the same time the cause of the erosion of the points established. This is most likely to be due to poor earth connections from the battery negative lead to body earth or the engine to earth strap. Remove the connecting bolts at these points, scrape the surfaces free from rust and corrosion and tighten the bolts using a star type lock washer. Other screws to check for security are: the baseplate to distributor body securing screws, the condenser securing screw and the distributor body to lockplate bolt. Looseness in any of these could contribute to a poor earth connection. Check the condenser (Section 4).
6 Refitting the contact breaker assembly is a reversal of removal and when fitted, adjust the points gap as described in the preceding Section.

4 Condenser (capacitor) - removal, testing and refitting

1 The condenser ensures that with the contact breaker points open, the sparking between them is not excessive to cause severe pitting. The condenser is fitted in parallel and its failure will automatically cause failure of the ignition system as the points will be prevented from interrupting the low tension circuit.
2 Testing for an unserviceable condenser may be effected by switching on the ignition and separating the contact points by hand. If this action is accompanied by a blue flash then condenser failure is indicated. Difficult starting, missing of the engine after several miles running or badly pitted points are other indications of a faulty condenser.
3 The surest test is by substitution of a new unit.
4 Removal of the condenser is by means of withdrawing the screw which retains it to the distributor. Replacement is a reversal of this procedure.

5 Distributor - removal and refitting

1 To remove the distributor complete with cap from the engine, begin by pulling the plug lead terminals off the four

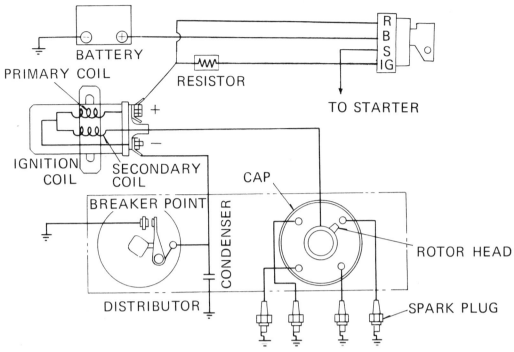

Fig. 4.1. Ignition circuit

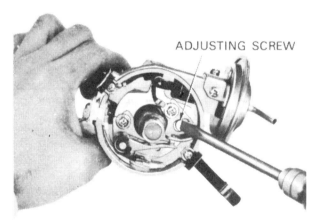

Fig. 4.2. Adjusting the contact breaker gap (Section 2)

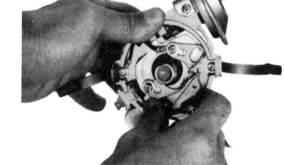

Fig. 4.3. Sliding the contact breaker arms from beneath their securing screws (Section 3)

spark plugs. Free the HT lead from the centre of the coil to the centre of the distributor by undoing the lead retaining cap from the coil.

2 Pull off the rubber pipe holding the vacuum tube to the distributor vacuum advance and retard take off pipe.

3 Disconnect the low tension wire from the coil.

4 Undo and remove the bolt which holds the distributor clamp plate to the crankcase and lift out the distributor.

5 Loosen the bolt which secures the clamp plate to the distributor body.

6 To refit the distributor, turn the engine by hand using a spanner on the crankshaft pulley securing bolt until number one piston is at TDC. This position is indicated when the 0° mark on the crankshaft pulley is in alignment with the pointer on the timing cover (compression stroke, both number one cylinder valves closed).

7 When correctly installed, the distributor rotor should take up the position shown in Fig.04.00. Due to the meshing action of the distributor and camshaft drive gears however, the distributor drive shaft must be turned back (clockwise) by about 60° from the position it will finally take up. Insert the distributor into its

crankcase location and when fully inserted, check the rotor alignment. the tip of which should be opposite number 2 contact in the distributor cap.

8 Reconnect the HT and LT leads and then time the ignition as described in the following Section.

6 Ignition - timing

1 This operation should be required only if the distributor has been removed and refitted or adjustment is necessary due to a change of fuel or engine condition.

2 Connect a timing light (stroboscope) between number one spark plug and number one HT lead terminal.

3 Mark the timing cover pointer and the specified BTDC mark (5° or 7° according to vehicle - see Specifications Sections) on the crankshaft pulley. Loosen the distributor to clamp plate bolt.

4 Start the engine which should be at normal operating temperature and let it run at the specified idling speed (600 rpm).

5 By directing the timing light onto the chalked marks, the

mark on the crankshaft pulley will appear to be stationary. Having previously loosened the distributor body clamp plate bolt, the distributor may be rotated slightly until the timing marks are in alignment. Where the limited adjustment provided by the oval clamp plate bolt hole is found to be sufficient to attain the correct alignment, then the distributor must be removed and re-meshed with the camshaft as described in the preceding Section.

6 When the timing is correct, tighten the distributor body to clamp plate bolt.

7 Distributor - dismantling amd inspection

1 Remove the distributor cap, rotor and contact breaker points as described in Section 3 of this Chapter, also the vacuum capsule.

2 Remove the two securing screws from the baseplate and remove the baseplate.

3 Unscrew and remove the screw from the centre of the cam. Should this be very tight, hold the cam using a close fitting spanner and take care not to damage the high-point surfaces.

4 Using a suitable drift, drive out the pin from the drive pinion end of the shaft.

5 Withdraw the distributor drive shaft complete with the mechanical advance assembly.

6 If it is necessary to dismantle this assembly, take care not to stretch the springs during removal and to mark their respective positions; also the counter weights in relation to their pivots so that they may be refitted in their original locations.

7 With the distributor dismantled, clean all the components in paraffin and inspect for wear. Renewal of components should be limited to the advance mechanism springs. Should wear in the shaft, bushes, the counter weight pivots or holes be outside the tolerances given in Specifications, then the distributor should be renewed on an exchange basis.

8 Finally check that the distributor index number aligns with the type of transmission fitted as is listed in Specifications.

8 Distributor - reassembly

1 Reassembly is a reversal of dismantling but high melting point grease must be applied sparingly at the positions indicated in Fig. 4.10.

2 Always use a new pin to secure the pinion to the driveshaft.

3 If the mechanical advance mechanism has been dismantled then it should be reassembled in accordance with the diagrams, (Fig. 4.11) using the one appropriate to the index number of the distributor.

9 Coil - description and polarity

1 High tension current should be negative at the spark plug terminals. To ensure this, check the LT connections to the coil are correctly made.

2 The LT wire from the distributor must connect with the (—) negative terminal on the coil.

3 The coil (+) positive terminal is connected to the ignition/starter switch.

4 An incorrect connection can cause as much as a 60% loss of spark efficiency and can cause rough idling and misfiring at speed.

10 Spark plugs and leads

1 The correct functioning of the spark plugs is vital for the correct running and efficiency of the engine. The plugs fitted as standard are listed on the Specification page.

2 At intervals of 5000 miles the plugs should be removed, examined, cleaned and, if worn excessively, renewed. The

Fig. 4.4. Distributor vacuum capsule and securing screws

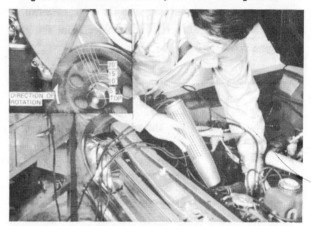
Fig. 4.5. Timing the ignition using a stroboscope (Section 6)

Fig. 4.6. Removing the cam to shaft securing screw (Section 7)

Fig. 4.7. Driving out the shaft securing pin to drive gear (Section 7)

Measuring plug gap. A feeler gauge of the correct size (see ignition system specifications) should have a slight 'drag' when slid between the electrodes. Adjust gap if necessary

Adjusting plug gap. The plug gap is adjusted by bending the earth electrode inwards, or outwards, as necessary until the correct clearance is obtained. Note the use of the correct tool

Normal. Grey-brown deposits lightly coated core nose. Gap increasing by around 0.001 in (0.025 mm) per 1000 miles (1600 km). Plugs ideally suited to engine and engine in good condition

Carbon fouling. Dry, black, sooty deposits. Will cause weak spark and eventually misfire. Fault: over-rich fuel mixture. Check: carburettor mixture settings, float level and jet sizes; choke operation and cleanliness of air filter. Plugs can be re-used after cleaning

Oil fouling. Wet, oily deposits. Will cause weak spark and eventually misfire. Fault: worn bores/piston rings or valve guides; sometimes occurs (temporarily) during running-in period. Plugs can be re-used after thorough cleaning

Overheating. Electrodes have glazed appearance, core nose very white - few deposits. Fault: plug overheating. Check: plug value, ignition timing, fuel octane rating (too low) and fuel mixture (too weak). Discard plugs and cure fault immediately

Electrode damage. Electrodes burned away; core nose has burned, glazed appearance. Fault: initial pre-ignition. Check: as for 'Overheating' but may be more severe. Discard plugs and remedy fault before piston or valve damage occurs

Split core nose (may appear initially as a crack). Damage is self-evident, but cracks will only show after cleaning. Fault: pre-ignition or wrong gap-setting technique. Check: ignition timing, cooling system, fuel octane rating (too low) and fuel mixture (too weak). Discard plugs, rectify fault immediately

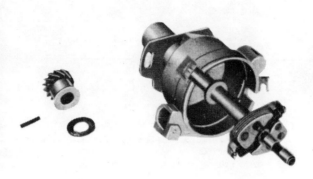

Fig. 4.8. Withdrawal of the distributor drive shaft (Section 7)

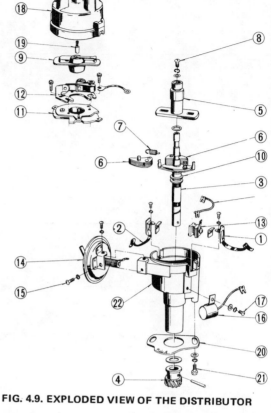

FIG. 4.9. EXPLODED VIEW OF THE DISTRIBUTOR

1 cap clip	12 contact breaker arm
2 cap clip	assembly
3 drive shaft	13 LT terminal and insulator
4 pinion	14 vacuum capsule
5 cam assembly	15 capsule securing screw
6 counterweight	16 condenser (capacitor)
7 spring	17 condenser securing screw
8 cam to shaft securing	18 distributor cap
screw	19 carbon brush
9 rotor	20 distributor lock plate
10 thrust washer	21 lockplate bolt
11 baseplate	22 distributor body

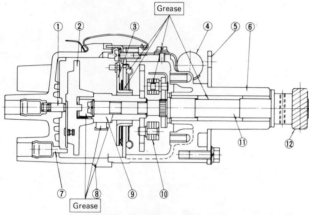

FIG. 4.10. SECTIONAL VIEW OF DISTRIBUTOR INDICATING GREASE APPLICATION POINTS DURING REASSEMBLY (SECTION 8)

1 carbon brush	7 cap contact segment
2 rotor	8 cap
3 baseplate	9 cam
4 condenser (capacitor)	10 counterweight
5 lock plate	11 shaft
6 body	12 pinion

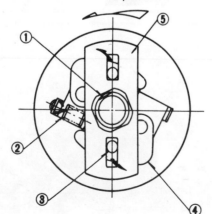

FIG. 4.11. REASSEMBLY DIAGRAM FOR CAM, SPRINGS AND COUNTERWEIGHTS LEFT HAND TYPE D412 DISTRIBUTOR, RIGHT HAND TYPE D411 (SECTION 8)

1 rotor/cam positioning flat	2 spring	4 counterweight	6 spring
	3 counterweight	5 cam assembly	

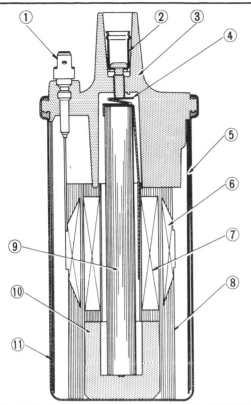

FIG. 4.12. SECTIONAL VIEW OF THE COIL (SECTION 9)

1 primary terminal (two)
2 secondary terminal
3 cap
4 coil spring
5 side core
6 primary winding
7 secondary winding
8 insulating oil
9 centre core
10 insulator
11 casing

condition of the spark plug will also tell much about the overall condition of the engine.

3 If the insulator nose of the spark plug is clean and white, with no deposits, this is indicative of a weak mixture, or too hot a plug. (A hot plug transfers heat away from the electrode slowly - a cold plug transfers it away quickly).

4 If the top and insulator nose is covered with hard black looking deposits, then this is indicative that the mixture is too rich. Should the plug be black and oily, then it is likely that the engine is fairly worn, as well as the mixture being too rich.

5 If the insulator nose is covered with light tan to greyish brown deposits, then the mixture is correct and it is likely that the engine is in good condition.

6 If there are any traces of long brown tapering stains on the outside of the white portion of the plug, then the plug will have to be renewed, as this shows that there is a faulty joint between the plug body and the insulator, and compression is being allowed to leak away.

7 Plugs should be cleaned by a sand blasting machine, which will free them from carbon more thoroughly than cleaning by hand. The machine will also test the condition of the plugs under compression. Any plug that fails to spark at the recommended pressure should be renewed.

8 The spark plug gap is of considerable importance, as, if it is too large or too small the size of the spark and its efficiency will be seriously impaired. The spark plug gap should be set to between 0.031 and 0.035 in for the best results.

9 To set it, measure the gap with a feeler gauge, and then bend open, or close, the outer plug electrode until the correct gap is achieved. The centre electrode should never be bent as this may crack the insulation and cause plug failure, if nothing worse.

10 When replacing the plugs, remember to use new plug washers and replace the leads from the distributor in the correct firing order 1,3,4,2, No 1 cylinder being the one nearest the radiator.

11 The plug leads require no routine attention other than being kept clean and wiped over regularly.

11 Ignition system - fault finding

Failures of the ignition system will either be due to faults in the HT or LT circuits. Initial checks should be made by observing the security of spark plug terminals, Lucar type terminals, coil and battery connection. More detailed investigation and the explanation and remedial action in respect of symptoms of ignition malfunction are described in the next Section.

12 Ignition system - fault symptoms

Engine fails to start
1 If the engine fails to start and the car was running normally when it was last used, first check there is fuel in the fuel tank. If the engine turns over normally on the starter motor and the battery is evidently well charged, then the fault may be in either the high or low tension circuits. First check the HT circuit. Note: If the battery is known to be fully charged; the ignition light comes on, and the starter motor fails to turn the engine **check the tightness of the leads on the battery terminals** and also the secureness of the earth lead to its **connection to the body**. It is quite common for the leads to have worked loose, even if they look and feel secure. If one of the battery terminal posts gets very hot when trying to work the starter motor this is a sure indication of a faulty connection to that terminal.

2 One of the commonest reasons for bad starting is wet or damp spark plug leads and distributor. Remove the distributor cap. If condensation is visible internally, dry the cap with a rag and also wipe over the leads. Replace the cap.

3 If the engine still fails to start, check that current is reaching the plugs, by disconnecting each plug lead in turn at the spark plug end, and hold the end of the cable about 3/16th inch away from the cylinder block. Spin the engine on the starter motor.

4 Sparking between the end of the cable and the block should be fairly strong with a regular blue spark. (Hold the lead with rubber to avoid electric shocks). If current is reaching the plugs, then remove them and clean and regap them. The engine should now start.

5 If there is no spark at the plug leads take off the HT lead from the centre of the distributor cap and hold it to the block as before. Spin the engine on the starter once more. A rapid succession of blue sparks between the end of the lead and the block indicate that the coil is in order and that the distributor cap is cracked, the rotor arm faulty, or the carbon brush in the top of the distributor cap is not making good contact with the spring on the rotor arm. Possibly the points are in bad condition. Clean and reset them as described in this Chapter.

6 If there are no sparks from the end of the lead from the coil, check the connections at the coil end of the lead. If it is in order start checking the low tension circuit.

7 Use a 12 v voltmeter or a 12 v bulb and two lengths of wire. With the ignition switch on and the points open test between the low tension wire to the coil (it is marked SW or +) and earth. No reading indicates a break in the supply from the ignition switch. Check the connections at the switch to see if any are loose. Refit them and the engine should run. A reading shows a faulty coil or condenser, or broken lead between the coil and the distributor.

8 Take the condenser wire off the points assembly and with the points open, test between the moving point and earth. If there now is a reading, then the fault is in the condenser. Fit a new one and the fault is cleared.

9 With no reading from the moving point to earth, take a reading between earth and the CB or - terminal of the coil. A reading here shows a broken wire which will need to be replaced between the coil and distributor. No reading confirms that the coil has failed and must be replaced, after which the engine will

run once more. Remember to refit the condenser wire to the points assembly. For these tests it is sufficient to separate the points with a piece of dry paper while testing with the points open.

Engine misfires

10 If the engine misfires regularly run it at a fast idling speed. Pull off each of the plug caps in turn and listen to the note of the engine. Hold the plug cap in a dry cloth or with a rubber glove as additional protection against a shock from the HT supply.

11 No difference in engine running will be noticed when the lead from the defective circuit is removed. Removing the lead from one of the good cylinders will accentuate the misfire.

12 Remove the plug lead from the end of the defective plug and hold it about 3/16th inch away from the block. Restart the engine. If the sparking is fairly strong and regular the fault must lie in the spark plug.

13 The plug may be loose, the insulation may be cracked, or the points may have burnt away giving too wide a gap for the spark to jump. Worse still, one of the points may have broken off. Either renew the plug, or clean it, reset the gap, and then test it.

14 If there is no spark at the end of the plug lead, or if it is weak and intermittent, check the ignition lead from the distributor to the plug. If the insulation is cracked or perished, renew the lead. Check the connections at the distributor cap.

15 If there is still no spark, examine the distributor cap carefully for tracking. This can be recognised by a very thin black line running between two or more electrodes, or between an electrode and some other part of the distributor. These lines are paths which now conduct electricity across the cap thus letting it run to earth. The only answer is a new distributor cap.

16 Apart from the ignition timing being incorrect, other causes of misfiring have already been dealt with under the section dealing with the failure of the engine to start. To recap - these are that:

a) The coil may be faulty giving an intermittent misfire
b) There may be a damaged wire or loose connection in the low tension circuit
c) The condenser may be short circuiting
d) There may be a mechanical fault in the distributor (broken driving spindle or contact breaker spring).

17 If the ignition timing is too far retarded, it should be noted that the engine will tend to overheat, and there will be a quite noticeable drop in power. If the engine is overheating and the power is down, and the ignition timing is correct, then the carburettor should be checked, as it is likely that this is where the fault lies.

Chapter 5 Clutch

Contents

General description 1	Master cylinder - removal, dismantling, servicing, reassembly 8
Clutch adjustment - hydraulically operated 2	Slave (operating) cylinder - removal, dismantling, servicing,
Clutch adjustment - mechanically (cable) operated 3	reassembly 9
Clutch pedal (hydraulic) - removal and	Clutch assembly - removal 10
refitting 4	Clutch - inspection and renovation 11
Clutch pedal (mechanical) - removal and refitting 5	Release bearing - removal and refitting 12
Clutch operating cable - renewal 6	Clutch - refitting 13
Hydraulic system - bleeding 7	Fault diagnosis 14

Specifications

Type	single dry plate with diaphragm spring pressure plate

Driven plate

Friction disc diameter	7.09 in.
thickness	0.140 in.
Total friction area	40.92 in.
Number of cushion springs	6

Adjustment data (hydraulic operation)

Pedal height from inclined toe-board	5.57 in.
Pedal free movement	1.181 in.
Release bearing/diaphragm spring clearance, see Section 2 ...	0.0276 to 0.0551 in.

Adjustment data (mechanical operation)

Pedal height from inclined toe-board	5.4 to 5.8 in.
Pedal free movement	0.433 to 0.591 in.
Release bearing/diaphragm spring clearance, see Section 3 ...	0.0354 to 0.0472 in.
Master cylinder diameter	5/8 in.
Master cylinder mounting shim availability	0.0630 in. 0.0315 in. 0.0197 in.
Slave cylinder diameter	3/4 in.

Torque wrench settings

	lb/ft	kg/m
Clutch assembly to flywheel bolts	16	2.2
Bellhousing to crankcase bolts	12 to 16	1.6 to 2.2

1 General description

1 All vehicles are fitted with a 7 inch diameter diaphragm spring, single plate clutch. The unit comprises a pressed steel cover which is dowelled to the rear face of the flywheel and bolted to it and contains the pressure plate, pressure plate diaphragm spring and the fulcrum rings.

2 The clutch disc is free to slide along the splined first motion shaft and is held in position between the flywheel and the pressure plate by the pressure of the pressure plate spring. Friction lining material is riveted to the clutch disc and it has a spring cushioned hub to absorb transmission shocks and to help ensure a smooth take-off.

3 The circular diaphragm spring is mounted on shouldered pins held in place in the cover by two fulcrum rings. The spring is also held to the pressure plate by three spring steel clips which are riveted in position.

4 The clutch is either actuated hydraulically (LHD vehicles) or mechanically by a cable (RHD vehicles). Where the clutch is actuated hydraulically, the pendant clutch pedal is connected to the clutch master cylinder and hydraulic fluid reservoir by a short pushrod. The master cylinder and hydraulic reservoir are mounted on the engine side of the bulkhead in front of the driver.

5 Depressing the clutch pedal moves the piston in the master cylinder fowards, so forcing hydraulic fluid through the clutch hydraulic pipe to the slave cylinder.

6 The piston in the slave cylinder moves forward on the entry of the fluid and actuates the clutch release arm by means of a short pushrod.

7 The release arm pushes the release bearing forwards to bear against the release plate, so moving the centre of the diaphragm spring inwards. The spring is sandwiched between two annular rings which act as fulcrum points. As the centre of the spring is pushed in, the outside of the spring is pushed out, so moving the pressure plate backwards and disengaging the pressure plate from the clutch disc.

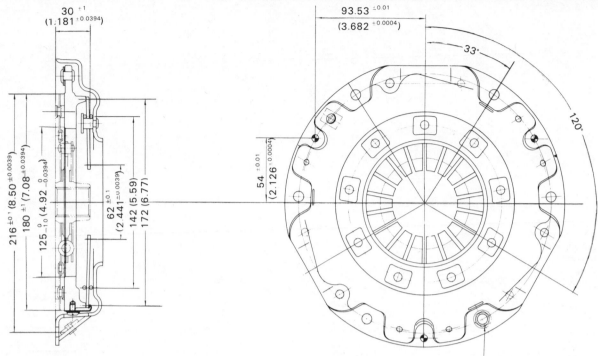

Fig. 5.1. Sectional and dimensional diagrams of the clutch assembly

Fig. 5.2. The clutch pressure plate assembly (1) and the driven plate (2)

8   When the clutch pedal is released the diaphragm spring forces the pressure plate into contact with the high friction linings on the clutch disc and at the same time pushes the clutch disc a fraction of an inch forwards on its splines so engaging the clutch disc with the flywheel. The clutch disc is now firmly sandwiched between the pressure plate and the flywheel so the drive is taken up.

9   As the friction linings on the clutch disc wear the pressure plate automatically moves closer to the disc to compensate. There is therfore no need to periodically adjust the clutch.

10 Where a cable type clutch actuating mechanism is fitted, the principle of operation is similar to that already described for the hydraulic type but correct adjustment must at all times be maintained as described in Section 3 of this Chapter.

2   Clutch adjustment - hydraulically operated

1   This adjustment or setting is normally carried out when the vehicle is built and will not be required unless new components have been fitted.

2   Shims are fitted between the engine rear bulkhead and the mounting face of the master cylinder so that the distance between the inclined floor and the top surface of the clutch Pedal pad is 5.65 in (without the pedal arm stop fitted). Shims of three different thicknesses are available and ones should be selected to provide the specified dimension.

3   Fit the pedal arm stop and adjust it to give a floor to clutch pedal top surface dimension of 5.57 in, see Fig.5.3. Secure the pedal stop locknut. Now check the adjustment of the slave cylinder rod.

4   Refer to Fig. 5.5 and release the locknut (1).

5   Turn the adjusting nut so that it becomes further from the slave cylinder. Continue rotating the nut until the release lever is pressed against the release bearing and any free movement has been eliminated.

6   Now turn the adjusting nut back 1¼ turns and secure it in position with the locknut. This adjustment will give the correct clearance between the diaphragm spring fingers and the thrust surface of the clutch release bearing which is between 0.0276 and 0.0551 in.

3   Clutch adjustment - mechanically (cable) operated

1   Adjust the clutch pedal arm stop to provide a floor to top surface of the pedal pad dimension of between 5.4 and 5.8 in. Secure the stop locknut.

2   Loosen the clutch cable locknut and turn the adjuster nut to give a free movement of between 0.43 and 0.59 in at the centre of the pedal pad.

3   If this adjustment is correctly made, then the total free movement at the connecting point of the cable clevis and release lever will be between 0.1181 and 0.1575 in. This in turn will ensure a clearance between the diaphragm spring fingers and the clutch release bearing thrust face of between 0.0354 and 0.0472 in. (Fig. 5.6).

4   Tighten the cable locknut making sure that the position of the adjuster nut does not alter.

4   Clutch pedal (hydraulic) - removal and refitting

1   Detach the return spring from the pedal arm.

2   Loosen the lock nut on the master cylinder push-rod and screw the rod out of the clevis fork on the pedal arm.

3   Unscrew and remove the nut and lock washer from the pedal cross shaft and then slide the pedal arm from the shaft.

4   Refitting is a reversal of removal but always check the adjustment as described in Section 2.

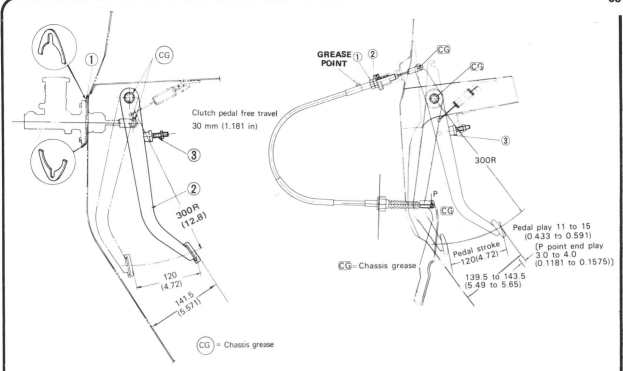

Clutch pedal free travel
30 mm (1.181 in)

300R
(12,8)

120
(4.72)

141.5
(5.571)

CG = Chassis grease

GREASE POINT

CG = Chassis grease

300R

P

Pedal play 11 to 15
(0.433 to 0.591)
(P point end play
3.0 to 4.0
(0.1181 to 0.1575))

Pedal stroke
120(4.72)

139.5 to 143.5
(5.49 to 5.65)

FIG. 5.3. CLUTCH PEDAL HEIGHT ADJUSTMENT DIAGRAM FOR HYDRAULIC TYPE OPERATION (SECTION 2)

1 Shim 2 pedal arm 3 pedal stop

FIG. 5.4. CLUTCH PEDAL HEIGHT ADJUSTMENT DIAGRAM FOR MECHANICAL (CABLE) TYPE OPERATION (SECTIONS 2 AND 6)

1 locknut 3 pedal stop
2 adjustment nut

0.7 to 1.4
(0.0276 to 0.0551)

1.0 to 2.0
(0.0394 to 0.0787)

3.0 to 4.0
(0.1181 to 0.1575)

0.9 to 1.2
(0.0354 to 0.0472)

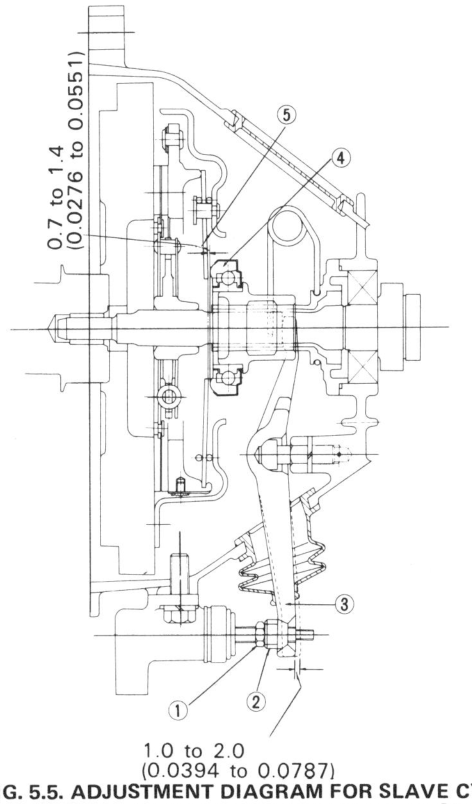

FIG. 5.5. ADJUSTMENT DIAGRAM FOR SLAVE CYLINDER OPERATING ROD TO GIVE CORRECT RELEASE BEARING TO DIAPHRAGM SPRING CLEARANCE (SECTION 2)

1 locknut 4 release bearing
2 adjusting nut 5 diaphragm spring
3 release lever

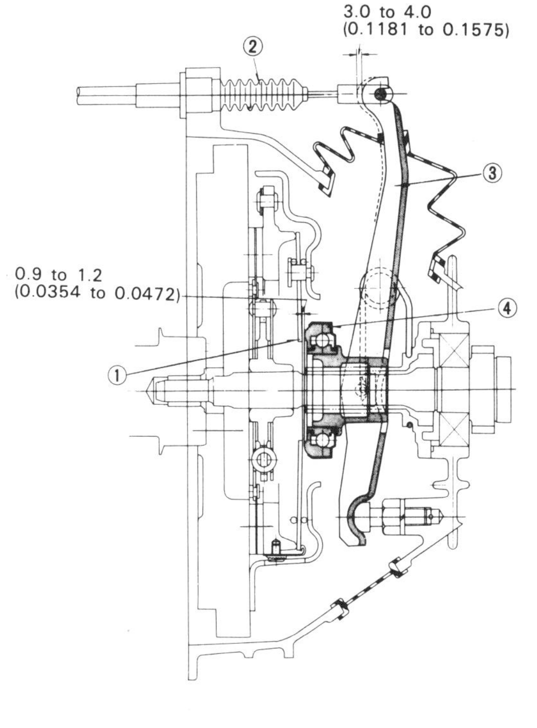

FIG. 5.6. ADJUSTMENT DIAGRAM FOR CABLE OPERATED CLUTCH TO GIVE CORRECT RELEASE BEARING TO DIAPHRAGM SPRING CLEARANCE (SECTION 3)

1 diaphragm spring 3 release lever
2 clutch cable 4 release bearing

FIG. 5.7. CLUTCH CABLE ADJUSTMENT NUTS (SECTION 3)

1 adjusting nut   2 lock nut

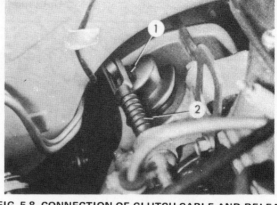

FIG. 5.8. CONNECTION OF CLUTCH CABLE AND RELEASE LEVER (SECTION 3)

1 release lever   2 cable

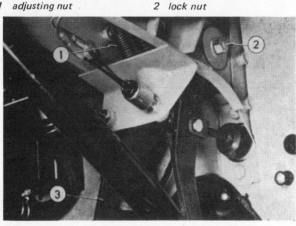

FIG. 5.9. CLUTCH AND BRAKE PEDAL FIXING (SECTION 4)

1 clutch pedal return spring   3 clutch pedal arm
2 shaft

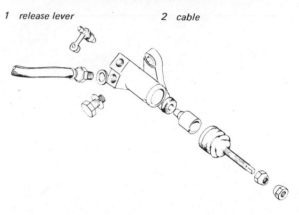

Fig. 5.10. Exploded view of the slave (operating) cylinder (Section 8)

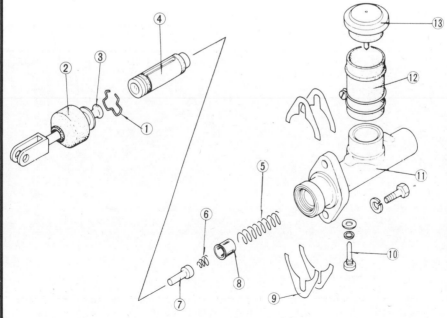

FIG. 5.11. EXPLODED VIEW OF THE CLUTCH MASTER CYLINDER (SECTION 9)

1 circlip
2 rubber dust cover
3 push rod
4 piston/seal assembly
5 return spring
6 inlet valve spring
7 inlet valve
8 spring retainer
9 shim
10 inlet valve stop
11 body
12 fluid reservoir
13 reservoir cap

5 Clutch pedal (mechanical) - removal and refitting

1 Loosen the locknut on the threaded section of the clutch outer cable at the engine bulkhead.
2 Disconnect the cable clevis fork from the clutch release lever by removing the split pin and clevis.
3 Unhook the return spring from the clutch pedal arm.
4 Unscrew and remove the nut and lock washer from the pedal cross shaft and then slide the pedal arm from the shaft. Detach the cable from the pedal arm.
5 Refitting is a reversal of removal but always check the adjustment as described in Section 3.

6 Clutch operating cable - renewal

1 Cable renewal will be required in the event of breakage, fraying or stretching so much that the specified adjustment cannot be carried out.
2 Carry out the operations described in paragraphs 1 to 4 of the preceding Section.
3 Connect the new cable so that the locating mark is at the bulkhead end and is visible when viewed from above (Fig. 5.4).
4 Apply grease at the points indicated and carry out the adjustment described in Section 3.

7 Hydraulic system - bleeding

1 The need for bleeding the cylinders and fluid line arises when air gets into it. Air gets in whenever a joint or seal leaks or part has to be dismantled. Bleeding is simply the process of venting the air out again.
2 Make sure the reservoir is filled and obtain a piece of 3/16 inch bore diameter rubber tube about 2 to 3 feet long and a clean glass jar. A small quantity of fresh, clean hydraulic fluid is also necessary.
3 Detach the cap (if fitted) on the bleed nipple at the clutch slave cylinder and clean up the nipple and surrounding area. Unscrew the nipple ¾ turn and fit the tube over it. Put about ½ inch of fluid in the jar and put the other end of the pipe in it. The jar can be placed on the ground under the car.
4 The clutch pedal should then be depressed quickly and released slowly until no more air bubbles come from the pipe. Quick pedal action carries the air along rather than leave it behind. Keep the reservoir topped up.
5 When the air bubbles stop tighten the nipple at the end of a down stroke.
6 Check that the operation of the clutch is satisfactory. Even though there may be no exterior leaks it is possible that the movement of the pushrod from the clutch cylinder is inadequate because fluid is leaking internally past the seals in the master cylinder. If this is the case, it is best to replace all seals in both cylinders.
7 Always use clean hydraulic fluid which has been stored in an airtight container and has remained unshaken for the preceding 24 hours.

8 Master cylinder - removal, dismantling, servicing, reassembly

1 The master cylinder and fluid reservoir are a single unit and indications of something wrong with it are if the pedal travels down without operating the clutch efficiently (assuming, of course, that the system has been bled and there are no leaks).
2 To remove the unit from the car first seal the cap with a piece of film to reduce fluid wastage whilst dismantling the pipes. Alternatively, the fluid may be pumped out from the clutch cylinder bleed nipple by opening the nipple and depressing the pedal several times.
3 From inside the car remove the split pin and clevis pin which attaches the pushrod assembly to the clutch pedal.

4 Disconnect the fluid line which runs between the master cylinder and the slave (operating) cylinder.
5 Unscrew and remove the two bolts which secure the master cylinder to the engine rear bulkhead.
6 Withdraw the master cylinder from the bulkhead, retaining the two shims which are fitted between the cylinder face and the bulkhead.
7 Peel back the rubber dust cover from the end of the master cylinder, remove the circlip and inlet valve stop pin.
8 The internal components may then be ejected, either by tapping the end of the cylinder on a piece of wood or by applying air pressure from a tyre pump at the fluid outlet pipe.
9 Clean all components in clean hydraulic fluid or methylated spirit. Examine the internal surfaces of the master cylinder for scoring or bright areas; also the surface of the piston. Where these are apparent, renew the complete master cylinder assembly.
10 Discard all rubber seals, making sketches if necessary before removing them from the piston so that the new seals will be fitted with their lips and chamfers the correct way round.
11 Obtain a repair kit and examine all the items supplied for damage, particularly the seals for cuts or deterioration in storage.
12 Commence reassembling by dipping the new seals in clean hydraulic fluid and fitting them to the piston, using only the fingers to manipulate them into their grooves. Ensure that they are correctly located with regard contour as originally fitted.
13 Use all the new items supplied in the repair kit and reassemble in the reverse order to dismantling, lubricating each component in clean hydraulic fluid before it is fitted into the master cylinder.
14 When all the internal components have been installed, fit a new circlip and screw in the inlet valve stop pin.
15 Bolt the master cylinder to the engine rear bulkhead using the original shims if the original master cylinder is being refitted. Where a new master cylinder is being installed then shims of differing thicknesses should be on hand. In either case, once the master cylinder has been installed and the push-rod connected to the brake pedal arm then the adjustment described in Section 2 must be carried out.
16 Reconnect the fluid pipe between the master and slave cylinders, fill the reservoir with clean hydraulic fluid and bleed the system as described in Section 7. Probe the reservoir vent hole in the cap to ensure that it is not clogged.

9 Slave (operating) cylinder - removal, dismantling, servicing, reassembly

1 Disconnect the fluid pipe from the slave cylinder. To do this, uncouple the union at the master cylinder and plug the union outlet to prevent loss of fluid. Now unscrew the flexible pipe from the slave cylinder taking care not to twist the pipe and retaining the sealing washer.
2 Remove the adjuster nut and the locknut from the slave cylinder operating rod and then disconnect the operating rod from the clutch release lever.
3 Unscrew and remove the slave cylinder to clutch bellhousing securing bolts and lift the cylinder away.
4 Peel back the dust cover and remove the circlip.
5 Eject the internal components of the slave cylinder either by tapping the end of the unit on a piece of wood or by applying air pressure from a tyre pump at the fluid hose connection.
6 Wash all components in clean hydraulic fluid or methylated spirit. Discard the seals and examine the piston and cylinder bore surfaces for scoring or bright areas. Where these are evident, renew the complete assembly.
7 Obtain a repair kit and examine all the items supplied for damage, particularly the seals for cuts or deterioration in storage.
8 Commence reassembling by dipping the new seals in clean hydraulic fluid and fitting them to the piston, using the fingers only to manipulate them.
9 Use all the new items supplied in the repair kit and re-assemble in reverse order to dismantling, lubricating each

component in clean hydraulic fluid before it is fitted into the cylinder bore.

10 When all the internal components have been installed, fit a new circlip and the new rubber dust cover supplied with the repair kit.

11 Refit the slave cylinder to the clutch bellhousing, reconnect the fluid supply pipe and the operating push-rod to the clutch release lever.

12 Bleed the hydraulic system as described in Section 7.

13 Adjust the operating rod nut as described in Section 2.

10 Clutch assembly - removal

1 Remove the engine/gearbox as a unit as fully described in Chapter 1, or alternatively 'drop' the gearbox alone as described in Chapter 6.

2 Separate the gearbox from the engine by removing the clutch bellhousing to crankcase securing bolts.

3 Mark the position of the now exposed clutch pressure plate cover in relation to the flywheel on which it is mounted.

4 Unscrew the clutch assembly securing bolts a turn at a time in diametrically opposite sequence until the tension of the diaphragm spring is released. Remove the bolts and lift the pressure plate assembly away.

5 Lift the driven plate (friction disc) from the flywheel.

11 Clutch - inspection and renovation

1 Due to the self adjusting nature of the clutch it is not always easy to decide when to go to the trouble of removing the gearbox in order to check the wear on the friction lining. The only positive indication that something needs doing is when it starts to slip or when squealing noises on engagement indicate that the friction lining has worn down to the rivets. In such instances it can only be hoped that the friction surfaces on the flywheel and pressure plate have not been badly worn or scored. A clutch will wear according to the way in which it is used. Much intentional slipping of the clutch while driving - rather than the correct selection of gears - will accelerate wear. It is best to assume, however, that the friction disc will need renewal every 35,000 miles at least and that it will be WORTH replacing it after 25,000 miles. The maintenance history of the car is obviously very useful in such cases.

2 Examine the surfaces of the pressure plate and flywheel for signs of scoring. If this is only light it may be left, but if very deep the pressure plate unit will have to be renewed. If the flywheel is deeply scored it should be taken off and advice sought from an engineering firm. Providing it may be machined completely across the face the overall balance of engine and flywheel should not be too severely upset. If renewal of the flywheel is necessary the new one will have to be balanced to match the original.

3 The friction plate lining surfaces should be at least 1/32 in (0.8 mm) above the rivets, otherwise the disc is not worth putting back. If the lining material shows signs of breaking up or black areas where oil contamination has occurred it should also be renewed. If facilities are readily available for obtaining and fitting new friction pads to the existing disc this may be done but the saving is relatively small compared with obtaining a complete new disc assembly which ensures that the shock absorbing springs and the splined hub are renewed also. The same applies to the pressure plate assembly which cannot be readily dismantled and put back together without specialised riveting tools and balancing equipment. An allowance is usually given for exchange units.

12 Release bearing - removal and refitting

1 The release bearing is of ball bearing, grease sealed type and

although designed for long life it is worth renewing at the same time as the other clutch components are being renewed or serviced.

2 Deterioration of the bearing should be suspected when there are signs of grease leakage or the unit is noisy when spun with the fingers.

3 Remove the rubber dust excluder which surrounds the release lever at the bellhousing aperture.

4 Disconnect and remove the return spring (2) (Fig. 5.12).

5 Detach the release lever from the release bearing retainer hub.

6 Withdraw the release bearing/hub assembly from the input shaft.

7 If necessary remove the release lever from its ball pivot.

8 Remove the bearing from its retainer hub using a suitable puller.

9 Fit the new bearing to the retainer hub using a press and ensuring that the pressure is exerted on the inner race of the bearing only, (Fig. 5.13).

10 Apply a dab of wheel bearing grease to the tip of the release lever pivot ball and pack the internal recess of the bearing retainer hub with the same type of lubricant, (Fig. 5.14).

11 Fit the hub/bearing assembly over the input shaft.

12 Refit the return spring and the rubber dust excluder.

13 Check that the release bearing turns freely and actuate the release lever only fractionally and check that the return spring is operating correctly.

13 Clutch - refitting

1 Before the drive plate and clutch pressure plate assembly can be refitted to the flywheel, a guide tool must be obtained. This may be either an old input shaft from a dismantled gearbox or a stepped mandrel similar to the one shown in Fig. 5.15.

2 Examine the spigot bush located in the centre of the flywheel. If it is worn or damaged, the bush must be renewed as described in Chapter 1. If the bush is in good condition insert a quantity of high melting point grease into it.

3 Locate the driven plate against the face of the flywheel, ensuring that the projecting side of the centre splined hub faces towards the gearbox.

4 Offer up the pressure plate assembly to the flywheel aligning the marks made prior to dismantling and insert the retaining bolts finger tight. Where a new pressure plate assembly is being fitted, locate it to the flywheel in a similar relative position to the original by reference to the index marking and dowel positions.

5 Insert the guide tool through the splined hub of the driven plate so that the end of the tool locates in the flywheel spigot bush. This action of the guide tool will centralise the driven plate by causing it to move in a sideways direction.

6 Insert and remove the guide tool two or three times to ensure that the driven plate is fully centralised and then tighten the pressure plate securing bolts a turn at a time and in a diametrically opposite sequence, to a torque of 16 lb/ft to prevent distortion of the pressure plate cover.

7 Reconnect the gearbox to the engine. Do this by supporting the gearbox and engaging the input shaft with the driven plate hub splines and the flywheel spigot bush. Keep the input shaft and gearbox perfectly square during the refitting operation and do not allow the weight of the gearbox to hang, even momentarily, upon the input shaft while it is only partially engaged with the driven plate otherwise damage to the clutch components may result.

8 Insert the clutch bellhousing to engine crankcase securing bolts and tighten them to a torque of 12-16 lb/ft.

9 Refit the engine/gearbox unit to the vehicle as described in Chapter 1.

10 Adjust the clutch free movement according to type as described in Section 2 or 3.

FIG. 5.12. THE CLUTCH RELEASE BEARING AND RELEASE LEVER (SECTION 12)

1 release lever
2 return spring

3 grease sealed release
bearing

Fig. 5.13. Pressing the release bearing onto its retainer hub
(Section 12)

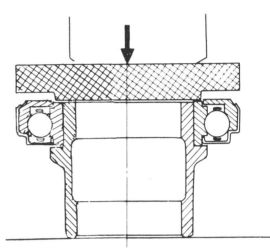

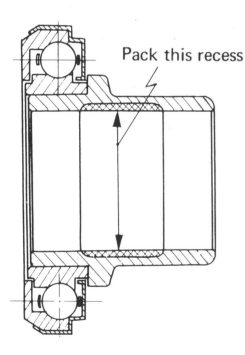

Pack this recess

Fig. 5.14. Release bearing retainer hub greasing diagram
(Section 12)

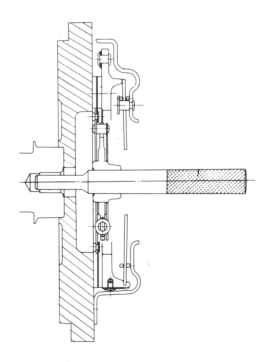

Fig. 5.15. Centralising the driven plate with the aid of a
stepped mandrel (Section 13)

Fault finding - Clutch

Symptom	Reason/s	Remedy
Judder when taking up drive	Loose engine or gearbox mountings	Tighten and inspect rubber insulators for deterioration.
	Badly worn friction surfaces or contaminated with oil	Renew driven plate and rectify oil leakage, probably crankshaft rear oil seal or input shaft oil seal.
	Worn splines on gearbox input shaft or driven plate hub	Renew component.
	Worn input shaft spigot bush in flywheel	Extract old and fit new bush.
Clutch spin (failure to disengage) so that gears cannot be meshed	Incorrect release bearing to diaphragm spring finger clearance	Adjust according to type, see Sections 2 or 3.
	Driven plate sticking on input shaft splines due to rust. May occur after vehicle standing idle for long period	As temporary remedy, engage top gear, apply handbrake, depress clutch and start engine. If driven plate badly stuck, engine will not turn. When engine running, rev up and slip clutch until normal clutch disengagement is possible. Renew driven plate at earliest opportunity.
	Damaged or misaligned pressure plate assembly	Renew pressure plate assembly.
Clutch slip (increase in engine speed does not result in increase in vehicle road speed - particularly on gradients)	Incorrect release bearing to diaphragm spring finger clearance	Adjust clearance according to type, see Sections 2 or 3.
	Friction surfaces worn out or oil contaminated	Renew driven plate and rectify oil leakage.
Noise evident on depressing clutch pedal	Dry, worn or damaged release bearing	Renew bearing.
	Insufficient pedal free travel	Adjust according to type see Sections 2 or 3.
	Weak or broken pedal return spring	Renew.
	Weak or broken clutch release lever return spring.	Renew.
	Excessive play between driven plate hub splines and input shaft splines	Renew both components.
Noise evident as clutch pedal released	Distorted driven plate	Renew.
	Broken or weak driven plate cushion coil springs	Renew driven plate as an assembly.
	Insufficient pedal free travel	Adjust according to type, see Section 2 or 3.
	Weak or broken clutch pedal return spring	Renew.
	Weak or broken release lever return spring	Renew.
	Distorted or worn input shaft	Renew input shaft (see Chapter 6) and driven plate if necessary.
	Release bearing loose on retainer hub	Renew hub and bearing.

Chapter 6 Gearbox

Contents

General description 1
Gearbox - removal and refitting 2
Gearbox - dismantling 3
Gearbox - inspection 4
Gearbox - reassembly and adjustment 5
Steering column gearchange (3 speed manual gearbox) - removal, servicing, adjustment, refitting 6
Gearbox controlled vacuum advance 7
Fault diagnosis 8

Specifications

Manual gearbox

Type		R3W56 - three forward speeds and reverse (fitted only to RHD vehicles) synchromesh on all forward gears
Ratios:	1st	3.380 : 1
	2nd	1.734 : 1
	3rd	1.000 : 1
	reverse	3.640 : 1
Speedometer drive pinion		17/5
Type		R4W56 - four forward speeds and reverse, synchromesh on all forward gears
Ratios:	1st	3.757 : 1
	2nd	2.169 : 1
	3rd	1.404 : 1
	4th	1.000 : 1
	reverse	3.640 : 1
Speedometer drive pinion		17/5
Standard backlash (all gears)		0.0031 to 0.0059 in.
Standard end play (forward gears)		0.0059 to 0.0098 in.
Reverse idler gear end play		0.0020 to 0.0079 in.
Reverse gear (countershaft) end play		0.0020 to 0.0059 in.
Reverse gear (mainshaft) end play		0.0039 to 0.0098 in.
Synchromesh ring/cone clearance		0.0413 to 0.0551 in.
Countershaft adjusting shim availability thickness		0.0315 - 0.0354 - 0.0394 - 0.0433 - 0.0472 - 0.0512 in.
Front cover adjusting shim availability thickness		0.0197 - 0.0079 - 0.0039 in.
Oil capacity		2 Imp. pints

Torque wrench settings

	lb/ft
Engine to bellhousing bolts	12 to 16
Gearbox rear mounting (to bodyframe bolt)	23 to 29
Speedometer drive pinion assembly bolts	4 to 8
Front cover bolts	7 to 12
Extension to main housing bolts	12 to 16
Oil drain plug	30 to 43
Filler drain plug	30 to 43
Reverse lamp switch	15 to 18

For Automatic Transmission see page 83.

MANUAL GEARBOX

1 General description

The Datsun 1200 has been supplied with either a four speed manually operated gearbox (floor shift control) or a three speed with steering column control. The latter is only to be found on right hand drive vehicles and in view of the availability of the four speed box it is not to be encountered very frequently.

Both types of manual gearbox have synchromesh on all forward gears. Each gearbox includes a reverse gear.

The three and four speed gearboxes are of similar construction; and the four speed version only is dealt with in this Chapter. However, reference should be made to Specifications Section as there are considerable differences in the gear ratios between the two types.

The steering column control fitted with three speed gearboxes is fully described in Section 6.

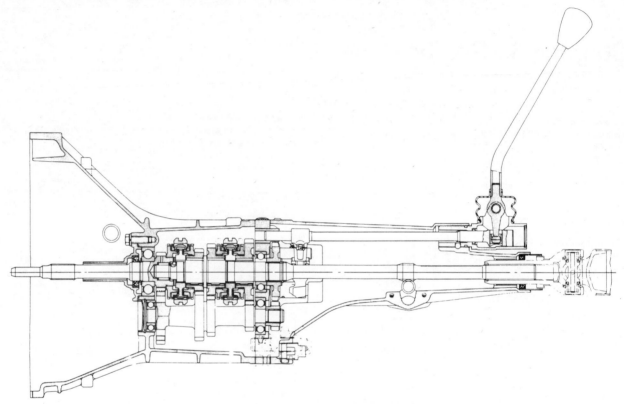

Fig. 6.1. Sectional view of the four speed gearbox

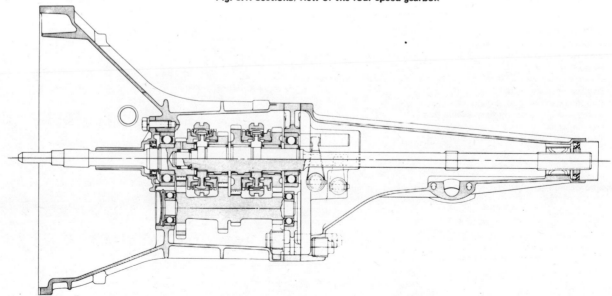

Fig. 6.2. Sectional view of the three speed gearbox

2 Gearbox - removal and refitting

1 If possible, obtain the use of a pit or hydraulic vehicle hoist. Failing this, jack the vehicle up sufficiently high so that the underbody clearance is slightly greater than the depth of the clutch bellhousing. Support the vehicle adequately on blocks or axle stands.

2 Refer to Fig. 6.3 and disconnect the exhaust downpipe (1) from the manifold.

3 Drain the gearbox oil.

4 Mark the edges of the propeller shaft rear driving flange and the rear axle pinion flange for exact refitting. Unscrew and remove the four flange securing bolts, pull the propeller shaft forward slightly and then move it rearwards to disengage the propeller shaft splined component from the gearbox rear extension housing.

5 Disconnect the speedometer drive cable and the reversing lamp switch cable from the gearbox extension housing.

6 Disconnect the gearshift control rods by removing the split pins (steering column change) or circlips (floor shift).

7 If the clutch mechanism is of hydraulic type, remove the slave cylinder from the bellhousing and disconnect its operating rod from the clutch release lever.

8 With a mechanically operated clutch control, disconnect the clutch cable from the release lever.

9 Place a jack under the sump, taking care that it does not foul the drain plug, using a piece of wood between the jack and the sump.

10 Unscrew the two gearbox rear mounting bolts (5) place a supporting jack under the gearbox and remove the two securing bolts from the mounting/body attachments (6).

11 Unscrew the starter motor cable connection and the two starter motor securing bolts and remove the starter.

12 Unscrew and remove the bellhousing to engine securing bolts.

13 Lower both jacks progressively until the gearbox can be withdrawn rearwards from beneath the vehicle. Do not allow the weight of the gearbox to hang even momentarily upon the clutch driven plate while the input shaft is still engaged with it or the clutch assembly may be damaged. Do not lower the jacks more than is necessary for the gearbox to clear the underside of the body floor otherwise undue strain will be caused to the engine mountings, the radiator hoses, the fuel inlet line and other components.

14 Refitting is a reversal of removal. If the clutch driven plate is inadvertently displaced during removal it will have to be centred as described in Chapter 5. When the gearbox is installed, check the clutch adjustment (Chapter 5) and refill the gearbox with the correct grade and quantity of oil. Reconnect the steering column or floor mounted gearchange lever as appropriate.

3 Gearbox - dismantling

1 Support the gearbox on a stand or on a bench. Remember that the gearbox housing is of aluminium alloy which should be handled with reasonable care. Where the exterior of the unit is only lightly covered with oil or road dirt then it should be cleaned with paraffin. Heavy deposits of oil and dirt should be removed using a proprietary solvent such as 'Gunk'.

2 Detach the flexible dust cover from the release lever aperture in the clutch bellhousing, detach the return spring and withdraw the release lever and the release bearing and its retainer hub.

3 Unscrew and remove the three securing bolts from the front cover away.

4 Unscrew and remove the two bolts which secure the speedometer pinion assembly to the extension housing and remove the pinion assembly.

5 Remove the screwed plug which is located above and slightly to the rear of the speedometer pinion aperture. Carefully remove the plunger, return spring and bush.

6 Drift out the remote gearshift rod stop from the extension housing and then separate the control rod from the control

FIG. 6.3. GEARBOX REMOVAL POINTS (SECTION 2)

1 exhaust pipe
2 propeller shaft
3 speedometer cable
4 gear selector
5 inner mounting bolts
6 mounting to body frame
   shaft mechanism
   bolts

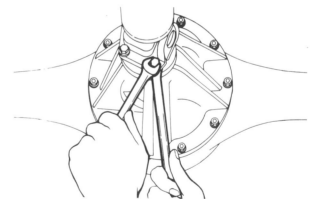

Fig. 6.4. Removing the propeller shaft/axle pinion bolts (Section 2)

Fig. 6.5. Speedometer cable (1) and gear selector linkage retaining clevis pins and split pins (2) (Section 2)

FIG. 6.6. GEARBOX REAR MOUNTING BOLTS (SECTION 2)

1   to extension housing   2   to body frame

FIG. 6.7. CLUTCH RELEASE COMPONENTS (SECTION 3)

1   release lever   3   release bearing
2   return spring

**Fig. 6.8. Gearbox front cover (1) and securing bolts (2)
(Section 3)**

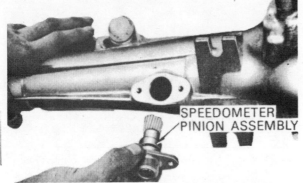

**Fig. 6.9. Removing the speedometer pinion drive assembly
(Section 3)**

bracket on the rear of the housing.

7   Unscrew and remove the eight bolts which secure the extension housing to the main gearbox casting. Tap the edges of the mating flanges with a wooden or plastic faced mallet and then withdraw the extension housing by pulling it straight off and over the remote control rod and the mainshaft.

8   Carefully separate the adaptor plate from the rear end of the gearbox main housing. Withdraw the adaptor plate to which are attached the mainshaft and countershaft assemblies, taking care not to lose the thrust washer located on the front end of the countershaft.

9   Make up a suitable support plate which can be bolted to the adaptor plate and will then be secured in the vice jaws for the following operations to be carried out.

10   Drive the retaining pin from the reverse gear shift fork using a suitable drift. Remove the fork and reverse idler gear.

11   Using a pair of circlip pliers, extract the circlip and then remove the thrust washer and reverse gear, (Fig. 6.14).

12   Drive out the retaining pins from the remaining gear selector forks.

13   Unscrew the selector shaft detent ball plugs and retain carefully each of the balls and return springs. Withdraw all the selector rods from the adaptor plate.

14   Tap the end of the mainshaft assembly with a wooden or plastic faced mallet to extract the mainshaft and countershaft gear assemblies.

15   Pull the input shaft from its connection with the mainshaft. The following operations should only be carried out if the necessary bearing extractors and a press are available.

16   From the input shaft, detach the circlip, the thrust washer and the bearing using a suitable puller.

17   From the front end of the mainshaft remove, in sequence, the needle roller bearing, the synchronizer hub thrust washer, the steel ball, the 3rd/4th synchronizer unit, the baulk ring, third gear and the mainshaft needle bearing.

18   Support the mainshaft bearing adequately and press the mainshaft out of the bearing centre race.

19   With the bearing removed, withdraw the thrust washer, first gear, the needle bearing, the baulk ring, 1st/2nd synchronizer unit, second baulk ring, second gear and needle bearing in the sequence shown in Fig. 6.20.

20   From the countershaft assembly, remove the circlips, one from each end.

21   Pull off the 13 toothed reverse gear followed by the ball bearing using a suitable extractor.

22   From the other end of the countershaft remove the thrust washer and ball bearing. The countershaft cannot be further dismantled.

4   Gearbox - inspection

1   Clean all the internal components in paraffin.

2   Examine closely the interior and exterior surfaces of the gearbox main and extension housings for cracks or porosity.

3   Check the mating faces of the housings and remove any burrs or pieces of old gasket or jointing compound.

4   Check the bush in the rear end of the extension housing and renew if worn. Extract the rear oil seal and fit a new one, using a tubular drift to locate it. Renew the remote control selector rod retaining pin if necessary.

5   Check all ball bearings for cracks in the races and for noisy or slack movement when rotated by hand.

6   Renew the needle roller bearings if worn or damaged.

7   Inspect the mainshaft for twist or spline wear and renew if necessary.

8   Examine the synchronizer units for wear or damage. If there has been a history of noisy or slow gear selection, renew the synchronizer unit complete. If there is slight wear on any component (sleeve, hub, thrust washer etc), this should be renewed individually.

9   Examine each of the baulk rings for wear or damage. Place each baulk ring on its appropriate gear cone and measure the dimension A shown in Fig.6.21 which should be between the

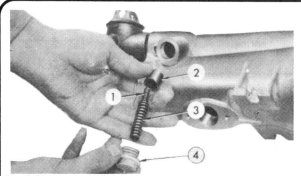

Fig. 6.10. Removing the threaded plug (4) return spring (3) plunger (1) and bush (2) from the extension housing (Section 3)

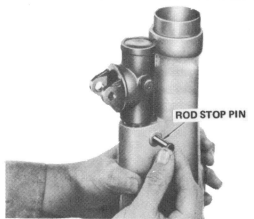

Fig. 6.11. Removing the gear selector remote control rod stop pin (Section 3)

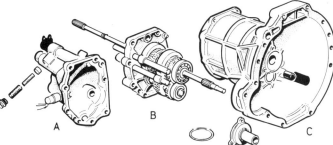

FIG. 6.12. THE MAJOR COMPONENTS OF THE GEARBOX (SECTION 3)

A   extension housing
B   adaptor plate and mainshaft and countershaft assemblies
C   gearbox housing and front cover

Fig. 6.13. Removing reverse selector fork (1) and reverse idler gear (2) (Section 3)

FIG. 6.14. REMOVING REVERSE GEAR CIRCLIP AND THRUST WASHER (SECTION 3)

1   circlip   3   thrust washer
2   reverse gear

Fig. 6.15. Removing a selector fork retaining pin (Section 3)

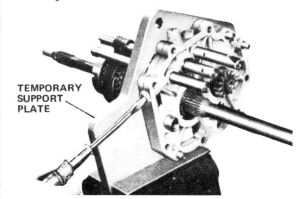

Fig. 6.16. Unscrewing a selector fork detent ball plug (Section 3)

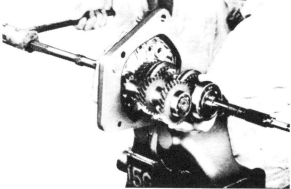

Fig. 6.17. Extracting the mainshaft and countershaft assemblies from the adaptor plate (Section 3)

76

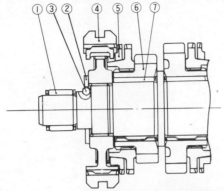

FIG. 6.18. SECTIONAL VIEW OF FRONT END OF MAIN-SHAFT (SECTION 3)

1 needle bearing
2 thrust washer
3 ball
4 synchro sleeve

5 baulk ring
6 3rd gear wheel
7 needle bearing

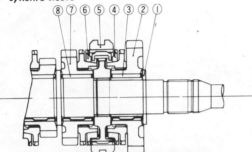

FIG. 6.20. SECTIONAL VIEW OF 1ST/2ND GEAR COMPON-ENTS ON THE MAINSHAFT (SECTION 3)

1 thrust washer
2 first gear
3 needle bearing
4 baulk ring

5 synchro sleeve
6 baulk ring
7 second gear
8 needle bearing

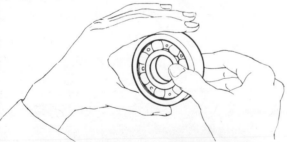

Fig. 6.22. Testing a bearing for wear (Section 4)

Fig. 6.24. Checking end-float (Section 4)

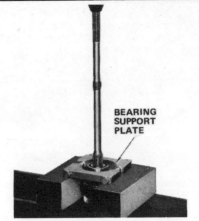

BEARING SUPPORT PLATE

Fig. 6.19. Pressing off a mainshaft bearing (Section 3)

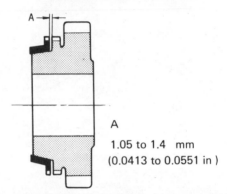

A

A

1.05 to 1.4 mm
(0.0413 to 0.0551 in)

Fig. 6.21. Synchro baulk ring to cone clearance diagram (Section 4)

STEP WEAR

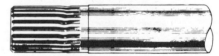

TWIST

Fig. 6.23. Visual indications of shaft wear (Section 4)

COUNTER BEARING SHIM

Fig. 6.25. Location of the countershaft bearing seat (Section 5)

tolerances specified. Where the gap is less than 0.020 in, renew the baulk ring.

10 Check all the gears for wear, damaged or chipped teeth. Where such damage is evident, the driven and driving gears should be renewed as a set. Where the gearbox has covered a substantial period of service it will be appropriate to test for backlash and end float with the gear train assembled on the mainshaft and countershaft and installed in the adaptor plate. Use a dial gauge to check for backlash, turning each gearwheel as far as it will go whilst holding the mainshaft perfectly still. The permitted backlash tolerance is between 0,0031 to 0.0059 in. Use a feeler gauge to check for end play. The correct tolerance for 1st and 2nd gears is between 0.0059 and 0.0098 in and 3rd gear between 0.0059 and 0.0138 in. Where the backlash or end play is greater than that specified, consideration should be given to purchasing a reconditional gearbox as the cost of a complete set of gears and other internal components will probably prove uneconomical by comparison.

11 The gearbox is now fully dismantled but before reassembly commences, check, in the case of three speed units the condition of the steering column gear change mechanism as described in Section 6.

12 Check the condition of the gearbox rear mounting rubber insulator and renew it if it has deteriorated.

5 Gearbox - reassembly and adjustment

1 Press the front and rear bearings onto the countershaft. Use suitable tubular supporting plates under the centre races while pressing on the ends of the countershaft.

2 The thickness of the countershaft bearing shim must now be established. To do this, insert the countershaft assembly into the gearbox housing so that the bearing seats fully into its seat, Fig.6.25.

3 A height gauge (ST 23040000 for three speed or ST 23050000 for 4 speed box) must now be borrowed from a Datsun dealer. Place the tool in position on the end of the gearbox as shown in Fig.6.26. Place feeler gauges on the upper surface of the bearing and adjust their thickness until the tool will just locate on the end surface of the gearbox housing. Move the feelers to two or three different points of the bearing periphery to establish the average thickness of the feelers. Remove the tool and from the total thickness of the feeler gauges subtract 0.008 in. Select a shim to match this final dimension from the sizes available from your Datsun dealer's parts department (0.0315 - 0.0354 - 0.0394 - 0.0433 - 0.0472 - 0.0512 in). When correctly carried out, the fitting of this selected shim will provide a countershaft end float (when finally installed) of between 0 and 0.0079 in.

4 Remove the countershaft assembly from the gearbox housing.

5 Dip all components in clean gear oil before assembling.

6 Fit the 13 toothed reverse gear to the splined end of the countershaft, ensuring that the conical side of the gear faces the bearing. Secure the gear in position with a new circlip.

7 Commence reassembly of the mainshaft by pushing on the needle bearing from the rear end of the shaft.

8 Fit the second gear followed by the baulk ring.

9 Fit the 1st/2nd synchronizer unit. If the synchronizer unit has been dismantled, assemble the sleeve, inserts and spring onto their respective hub, spacing the inserts 120° apart. **It is essential that both ends of the spring are not engaged in the same insert. (Fig6.29).**

10 As the synchronizer unit is fitted, align the inserts with the notches in the baulk ring.

11 Fit the first gear needle bearing, the baulk ring and the first gear, noting the relative positions of the gear cone (facing towards forward end of the mainshaft).

12 Locate the thrust washer and then press on the mainshaft bearing.

13 Fit the third gear needle bearing, the third gear, the baulking and the 3rd/4th synchronizer unit all from the front end of the mainshaft.

Fig. 6.26. Countershaft front bearing shim fitting diagram (Section 5)

Fig. 6.27. Fitting 2nd gear (27 teeth) to the mainshaft (Section 5)

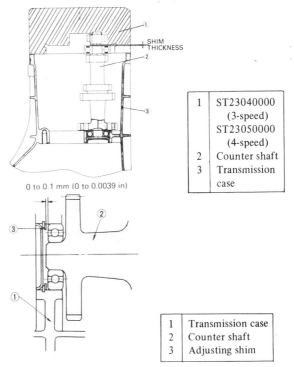

1	ST23040000 (3-speed) ST23050000 (4-speed)
2	Counter shaft
3	Transmission case

1	Transmission case
2	Counter shaft
3	Adjusting shim

Fig. 6.28. Fitting the synchro unit to 2nd gear which has already been fitted with the baulk ring (Section 5)

14 Locate the synchronizer hub thrust washer (oil grooves to rear) and stick a new steel ball in position in the cut-out in the washer using thick grease.

15 Fit the main bearing to the input shaft, locate the thrust washer against it (flat side to bearing) and fit a new circlip.

16 Fit the baulk ring onto the input shaft gear and then fit the input shaft assembly to the mainshaft.

17 With the adaptor plate/temporary support plate, still gripped in the vice; mesh and align the mainshaft and countershaft and by tapping the end of the input shaft with a wooden or plastic faced mallet install them into the adaptor plate. (Fig.6.33).

18 Fit the selector forks to their respective selector rods, noting carefully their location and orientation as shown in Fig.6.34. Do not pin the forks to the rods at this stage.

19 Fit the detent plungers, balls and springs (new ones if the originals have lost their tension) together with the selector rods to the adaptor plate. Use a short piece of rod of equivalent diameter to a selector rod to facilitate this operation. Ensure that the balls line up correctly with the grooves in the selector rods and having coated the threaded plugs with Loctite, screw them into position until their heads are flush with the surface of the adaptor plate.

20 Retain the gear selector forks to their shafts using new retaining pins.

21 Fit the reverse gear to the rear end of the mainshaft, followed by the thrust washer (flat side to bearing) and a new circlip.

22 Fit the reverse idler gear and reverse selector fork using a new retaining pin for the latter.

23 Pin the remote control rod fork in position. (Fig.6.36).

24 Release the adaptor plate from the support plate which has been secured in the vice.

25 Using heavy grease, stick the shim (selected as described in paragraph 3 of this Section) into position in the gearbox housing. (Fig.6.25).

26 Coat a new gasket on both sides with jointing compound and fit the adaptor plate assembly to the gearbox housing. Tap it into position making sure that the dowels align with the holes.

27 Engage the remote control gearshift rod with the bracket and engage the forward end of the rod in its hole in the adaptor plate. Align the remote control rod ready to receive the gearshift hand control lever.

28 Locate a new gasket covered both sides with a thin film of gasket cement and slide the extension housing carefully into position over the mainshaft and remote control rod. Take care not to damage the oil seal located in the rear end of the extension housing.

29 Insert the extension housing securing bolts and tighten to a torque of between 12 and 16 lb/ft.

30 Install the plunger/bush/spring assembly to the rear extension housing and apply jointing compound to the plug threads.

31 Fit the remote control stop pin to the rear extension housing.

32 Refit the speedometer pinion assembly.

33 Using a vernier type depth gauge, measure the difference in height between the front cover mating surface and the top surface of the outer race of the input shaft bearing. Fit shims which will reduce this measurement to between 0.1969 and 0.2028 in. The shims are available in the following thickness: 0.0197 - 0.0079 - 0.0039 in.

34 Renew the front cover oil seal and 'O' ring. Fit the shim pack previously determined, followed by the front cover and securing bolts. Tighten the bolts to between 7 and 12 lb/ft. torque.

35 Fit the clutch release bearing and hub, the release lever and return springs within the clutch bellhousing as described in Chapter 5.

36 When reassembly is complete, test by setting the remote gearshift control rod to the neutral position and turning the input shaft. The mainshaft should not rotate. Check for smooth operation of the gearshift mechanism by temporarily connecting the hand controlled gearchange lever. Install the gearbox as described in Section 2.

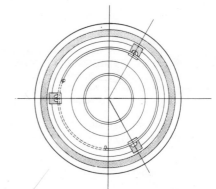

Fig. 6.29. Synchromesh unit showing correct location of spring ends (Section 5)

Fig. 6.30. Fitting 1st gear (32 teeth) to the mainshaft (Section 5)

Fig. 6.31. Fitting 3rd gear to the mainshaft (Section 5)

Fig. 6.32. Synchro hub thrust washer showing oil groove and ball recess (Section 5)

79

Fig. 6.33. Fitting the mainshaft and countershaft assemblies (meshed together) to the adaptor plate (Section 5)

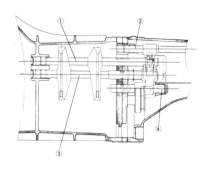

Fig. 6.36. Pinning the remote control rod fork to the selector rod (Section 5)

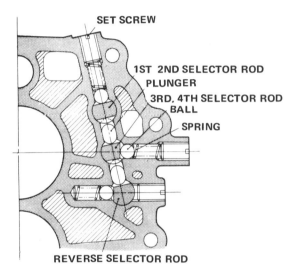

SET SCREW

1ST 2ND SELECTOR ROD

PLUNGER

3RD, 4TH SELECTOR ROD

BALL

SPRING

REVERSE SELECTOR ROD

FIG. 6.34. FITTING DIAGRAM FOR SELECTOR FORKS AND RODS (SECTION 5)

1 1st/2nd selector rod
2 remote control rod
3 3rd/4th selector rod
4 reverse selector rod

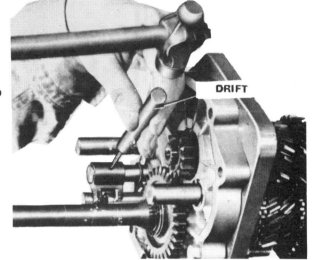

DRIFT

Fig. 6.37. Fitting the extension housing securing bolts (Section 5)

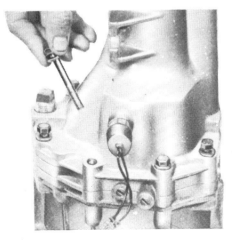

Fig. 6.35. Diagram showing location of detent balls and plungers in selector mechanism (Section 5)

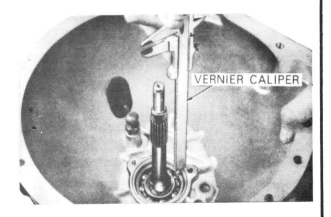

VERNIER CALIPER

Fig. 6.38. Calculating the thickness of the input shaft bearing shim (Section 5)

6 Steering column gearchange (3 speed manual gearbox) - removal, servicing, adjustment, refitting

1 Components of this type of control (available only on RHD vehicle) are shown in Fig.6.39.
2 Turn the steering wheel to the straight ahead position and remove the two horn ring or dual button securing screws from the back of the steering wheel.
3 Raise the horn ring or bar enough to disconnect the wires and remove the ring or horn button support bar.
4 Holding the steering wheel quite still, unscrew and remove the securing nut. Pull the wheel from its splined shaft. If it is stuck, use a wheel puller suitably insulated to prevent marking the plastic coating of the steering wheel hub.
5 Remove the two halves of the shroud which surrounds the top of the steering column and lighting switch unit.
6 Loosen the switch clamp screws after marking the position of the switch on the column.
7 Remove the circlip from the end of the hand control pivot pin, remove the pivot pin and withdraw the hand control.
8 Remove the 'C' washer from the end of the gear selector control rod, the retainer bolt and retainer, the 2nd/3rd gear change lever and bush.
9 Lower the control rod sufficiently to permit removal of the control lever pin from the lower bracket.
10 Withdraw the steering column gear selector rod from inside the vehicle.
11 The cross shaft and connecting rods may be removed from the gearbox and the vehicle body side member simply by withdrawing the split pins which secure them to the operating levers.
12 Examine all the dismantled components for wear, damage or distortion and renew as necessary.
13 Refitting is a reversal of removal but grease all sliding surfaces with heavy grease before installation.

14 Always use new split pins.
15 When the mechanism has been reconnected, set the hand control to the neutral position.
16 Adjust the nuts on each of the rods which connect to the two change levers so that the grooves on the lower support bracket and the upper edges of the levers are in alignment. (Fig.6.43).
17 Check for all positions of gear selection which should be smooth and positive. Further minor adjustments may be made to the control rods if necessary, to improve selection but any major lengthening or shortening of the control rods will probably be due to wear in the gearbox operating lever holes, in this event they must be renewed.

7 Gearbox controlled vacuum advance

1 An additional component of the fume emission control system fitted to models built after 1972 (manual gearbox only) is an ignition advance controller. The system restricts the vacuum advance of the distributor by admitting air to the capsule, until top gear is obtained to ensure complete combustion with minimal fume pollution. The restriction is adjusted automatically however during the initial warming up period particulary in cold weather, to ensure satisfactory road performance.
2 Operation and servicing of the control valve assembly is described in Chapter 3, also the part played by the automatic temperature controlled air cleaner.
3 The cut-out switch is located on the right hand side of the gearbox housing and interrupts the system electrical circuit when top gear is selected. Testing for serviceability of the switch should be carried out with an ohmmeter (indicates infinity when top gear selected, zero in all other positions) connected to the switch terminals. Renew if the readings are not as specified.
4 The thermo-switch is located on the right hand side panel of

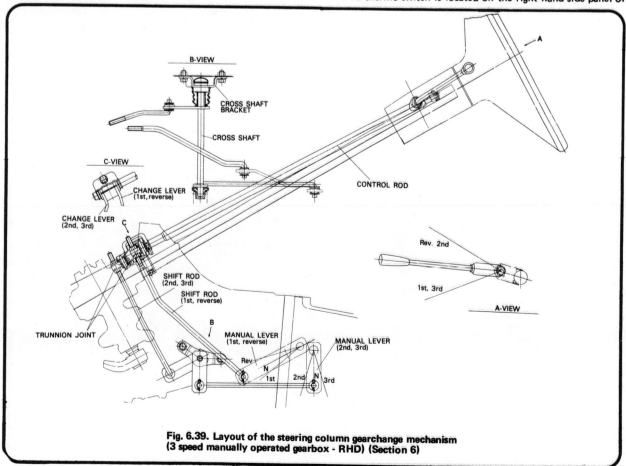

Fig. 6.39. Layout of the steering column gearchange mechanism (3 speed manually operated gearbox - RHD) (Section 6)

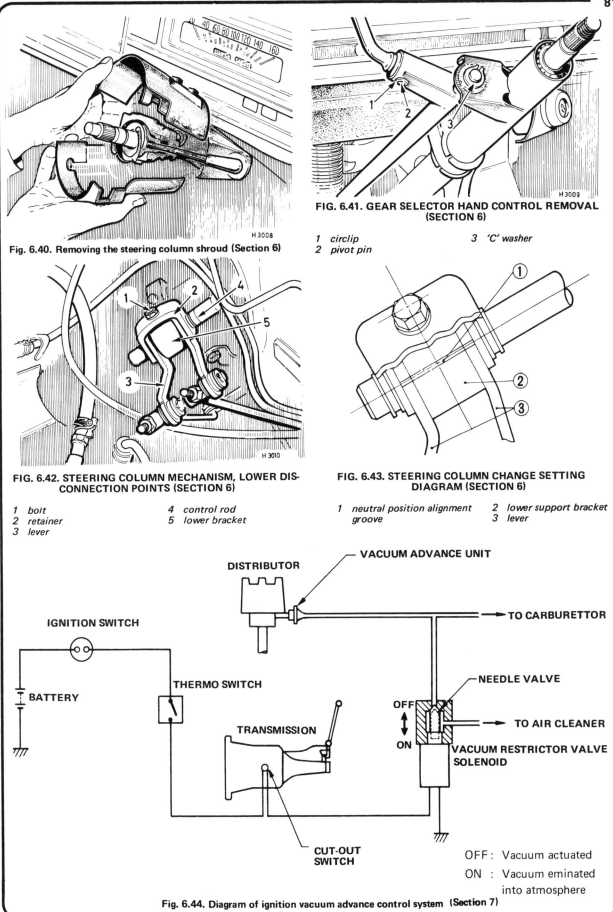

Fig. 6.40. Removing the steering column shroud (Section 6)

FIG. 6.41. GEAR SELECTOR HAND CONTROL REMOVAL (SECTION 6)

1 circlip   3 'C' washer
2 pivot pin

FIG. 6.42. STEERING COLUMN MECHANISM, LOWER DIS-CONNECTION POINTS (SECTION 6)

1 bolt   4 control rod
2 retainer   5 lower bracket
3 lever

FIG. 6.43. STEERING COLUMN CHANGE SETTING DIAGRAM (SECTION 6)

1 neutral position alignment   2 lower support bracket
   groove   3 lever

DISTRIBUTOR — VACUUM ADVANCE UNIT

TO CARBURETTOR

IGNITION SWITCH

BATTERY

THERMO SWITCH

TRANSMISSION

NEEDLE VALVE

OFF

ON

TO AIR CLEANER

VACUUM RESTRICTOR VALVE SOLENOID

CUT-OUT SWITCH

OFF: Vacuum actuated
ON : Vacuum eminated into atmosphere

Fig. 6.44. Diagram of ignition vacuum advance control system (Section 7)

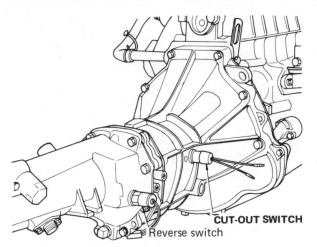

Fig. 6.45. Location of gear cut-out switch (Section 7)

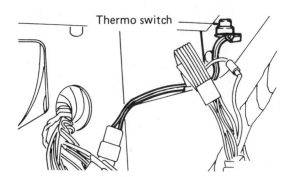

Fig. 6.46. Location of thermo-switch (Section 7)

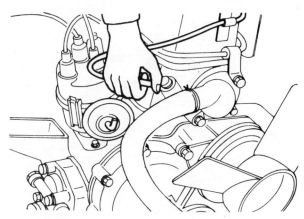

Fig. 6.47. Checking for vacuum (suction) at the end of the distributor to carburettor vacuum pipe (Section 7)

the facia and its function is to interrupt the electric current flow within the system when the temperature is below 55°F during the engine warming up period. To test this component, disconnect the electrical leads from it and connect an ohmmeter in their place. The ohmmeter should indicate zero when the ambient temperature is above 55°F. If this is not the case, renew the switch.

5   A simple test for the system as a whole may be carried out with the help of an assistant. With the engine at normal running temperature, disconnect the vacuum pipe from the carburettor. Place your thumb over the end of the pipe and with the engine running and clutch depressed by an assistant feel the vacuum (suction) as the gear selector lever is moved to all positions. A suction on the thumb should only be apparent when fourth gear is selected. When this test is performed with the engine cold (below 55°F) a suction should be felt at all gear selector positions.

Fault diagnosis

Symptom	Reason/s	Remedy
Ineffective synchromesh	Worn baulk rings or synchro hubs	Dismantle and renew.
Jumps out of one or more gears (on drive or over-run)	Weak detent springs or worn selector forks or worn gears	Dismantle and renew.
Noisy, rough, whining and vibration	Worn bearings and/or thrust washers (initially) resulting in extended wear generally due to play and backlash	Dismantle and renew.
Noisy and difficult engagement of gears	Clutch fault	Examine clutch operation.

NOTE: It is sometimes difficult to decide whether it is worthwhile removing and dismantling the gearbox for a fault which may be nothing more than a minor irritant. Gearboxes which howl, or where the synchromesh can be 'beaten' by a quick gear change, may continue to perform for a long time in this state. A worn gearbox usually needs a complete rebuild to eliminate noise because the various gears, if re-aligned on new bearings will continue to howl when different wearing surfaces are presented to each other.

    The decision to overhaul therefore, must be considered with regard to time and money available, relative to the degree of noise or malfunction that the driver has to suffer.

Automatic transmission

Contents

General description 1
Removal and refitting 2
Selector linkage - removal and refitting 3
Selector linkage - adjustment 4

Kickdown switch and downshift solenoid - checking ... 5
Starter inhibitor and reverse lamp switch - checking ... 6
Rear extension oil seal - renewal 7
Fault diagnosis 8

Specifications

Type	3N71B (3 forward speeds and reverse)
Ratios: 1st	2.458 : 1
2nd	1.458 : 1
3rd	1.000 : 1
reverse	2.182 : 1
Lubrication system	by internal pump
Cooling	air flow
Fluid capacity (excluding sealed torque converter)	9¾ Imp. pints
torque converter	4¾ Imp. pints
Engine idling speed (fume emission control fitted)	
selector in 'N'	800 rev/min
'D'	650 rev/min

Torque wrench settings

	lb/ft
Drive plate to torque converter bolts	6 to 7
Converter housing to engine bolts	30 to 36
Transmission housing to converter housing bolts	30 to 36
Rear extension to transmission housing bolts	15 to 18
Oil pan securing bolts	4 to 5
Inhibitor switch	4 to 5
Selector range lever to manual shaft	22 to 29
Lower selector rod lock nuts	15 to 21

1 General description

1 The automatic transmission which is fitted as an option to the Datsun 1200 range is the type 3N71B and is very similar in design to the Borg Warner model 35.

2 The unit provides three forward ratios and one reverse. Changing of the forward gear ratios is completely automatic in relation to the vehicle speed and engine torque input and is dependent upon the vacuum pressure in the manifold and the vehicle road speed to actuate the gear change mechanism at the precise time.

3 The transmission has six selector positions:

P - parking position which locks the output shaft to the interior wall of the transmission housing. This is a safety device for use when the vehicle is parked on an incline. The engine may be started with P selected and this position should always be selected when adjusting the engine while it is running. Never attempt to select P when the vehicle is in motion.

R - reverse gear.

N - neutral. Select this position to start the engine or when idling in traffic for long periods.

D - drive, for all normal motoring conditions.

2 - locks the transmission in second gear for wet road conditions or steep hill climbing or descents. The engine can be over revved in this position.

1 - the selection of this ratio above road speeds of approximately 25 mph will engage second gear and as the speed drops below 25 mph the transmission will lock into first gear. Provides maximum retardation on steep descents.

4 Due to the complexity of the automatic transmission unit, any internal adjustment or servicing should be left to a main Datsun agent. The information given in this Chapter is therefore confined to those operations which are considered within the scope of the home mechanic. An automatic transmission should give many tens of thousands of miles service provided normal maintenance and adjustment is carried out. When the unit finally requires major overhaul, consideration should be given to exchanging the old transmission for a factory reconditioned one, the removal and installation being well within the capabilities of the home mechanic as described later in this Chapter. The hydraulic fluid does not require periodic draining or refilling but

84

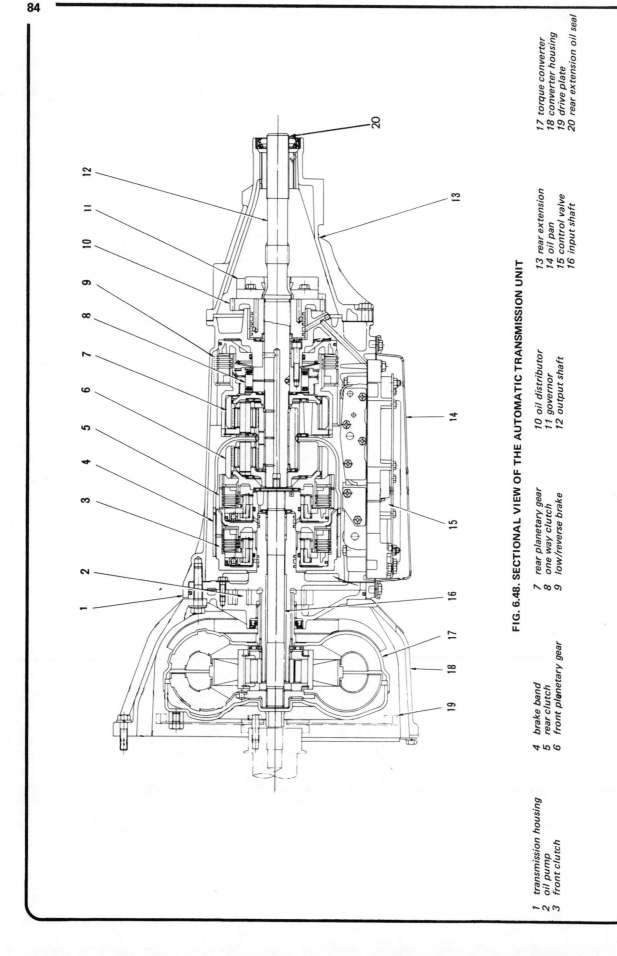

FIG. 6.48. SECTIONAL VIEW OF THE AUTOMATIC TRANSMISSION UNIT

1 transmission housing
2 oil pump
3 front clutch

4 brake band
5 rear clutch
6 front planetary gear

7 rear planetary gear
8 one way clutch
9 low/reverse brake

10 oil distributor
11 governor
12 output shaft

13 rear extension
14 oil pan
15 control valve
16 input shaft

17 torque converter
18 converter housing
19 drive plate
20 rear extension oil seal

the fluid level must be regularly checked and maintained as described in the Routine Maintenance Section at the front of this manual.

5 Periodically clean the outside of the transmission housing as the accumulation of dirt and oil is liable to cause overheating of the unit under extreme conditions.

6 Adjust the engine slow running as specified, 650 rpm in 'D'.

2 Removal and refitting

1 Removal of the engine and automatic transmission as a combined unit is described and illustrated in Chapter 1 of this manual. Where it is decided to remove the transmission leaving the engine in position in the vehicle, proceed as follows.

2 Disconnect the battery negative lead.

3 Drain the fluid from the transmission unit, retaining it in a clean container if required for further use.

4 Jack the car to an adequate working height and support on stands or blocks.

5 Disconnect the exhaust down pipe bracket.

6 Disconnect the wires from the starter inhibitor switch.

7 Disconnect the wires from the downshift solenoid.

8 Disconnect the vacuum pipe from the vacuum capsule which is located just forward of the downshift solenoid.

9 Separate the selector lever from the selector linkage.

10 Disconnect the speedometer drive cable from the rear extension housing.

11 Mark the edges of the propeller shaft rear driving flange and the pinion flange (for exact refitting) remove the four retaining bolts and withdraw the propeller shaft from its connection with the transmission rear extension housing.

12 Support the engine sump with a jack and use a block of wood to prevent damage to the surface of the sump.

13 Remove the cover from the lower half of the torque converter housing. Mark the torque converter housing and drive plate in relation to each other for exact replacement.

14 Unscrew and remove the four bolts which secure the torque converter to the drive plate. Access to each of these bolts, in turn, is obtained by rotating the engine slowly, using a spanner on the crankshaft pulley bolt.

15 Unbolt and withdraw the starter motor.

16 Support the transmission with a jack (preferably a trolley type).

17 Detach the rear transmission mounting from the transmission housing and the vehicle body frame.

18 Unscrew and remove the transmission to engine securing bolts.

19 Lower the two jacks sufficiently to allow the transmission unit to be withdrawn from below and to the rear of the vehicle. The help of an assistant will probably be required due to the weight of the unit.

20 Refitting is a reversal of removal but should the torque converter have been separated from the main assembly, ensure that the notch on the converter is correctly aligned with the corresponding one on the oil pump. (Fig.6.49). To check that the

torque converter has been correctly installed, the dimensions A in Fig.6.50 should be more than 0.650 in.

21 Tighten all bolts to the correct torques as specified in Specifications and refill the unit with the correct grade and quantity of fluid.

3 Selector linkage - removal and refitting

1 The transmission selector linkage layout is shown in Fig.6.51.

2 Remove the screw which secures the knob to the lever (1) and after removal of the self-tapping screws, withdraw the console box.

3 Disconnect the selector rod from the cross shaft.

4 Dismantle the hand operating lever, the shaft, the selector rod and bracket.

5 Refitting is a reversal of removal but adjust the linkage as described in the next Section.

4 Selector linkage - adjustment

1 The importance of correct adjustment of the gear selector linkage cannot be over emphasised. Incorrect selection can cause damage, overheating and breakdown of the unit.

2 Refer to Fig.6.51 and loosen the adjustment nuts (5).

3 Set the hand control to 'N'. Adjust the nuts so that the lever (10) is also located in the 'N' position without any tension from the rod (9).

4 Select all other positions and from beneath the vehicle check that a definite click can be heard in each position. The linkage must never be adjusted so that it overrides the transmission detent when the hand lever is moved from either direction to a new gear position.

5 Kick down switch and downshift solenoid - checking

1 If the kick-down facility fails to operate or operates at an incorrect change point, first check the security of the switch on the accelerator pedal arm and the wiring between the switch and the solenoid.

2 Turn the ignition key so that the ignition and oil pressure lamps illuminate but without operating the starter motor. Depress the accelerator pedal fully and as the switch actuates, a distinct click should be heard from the solenoid. Where this is absent, drain 2½ Imp. pints of fluid from the transmission unit unscrew the solenoid and fit a new one. Replenish the transmission fluid.

6 Starter inhibitor and reverse lamp switch - checking

1 Check that the starter motor operates only in N and P and the reversing lamps illuminate only with the selector lever in R.

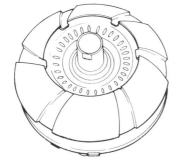

Fig. 6.49. Alignment notch on torque converter (Section 2)

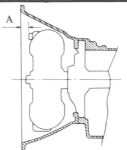

FIG. 6.50. CORRECT INSTALLATION OF TORQUE CONVERTER IN HOUSING (SECTION 2)

A = 0.650 in. or more

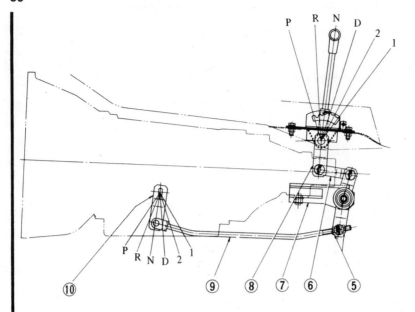

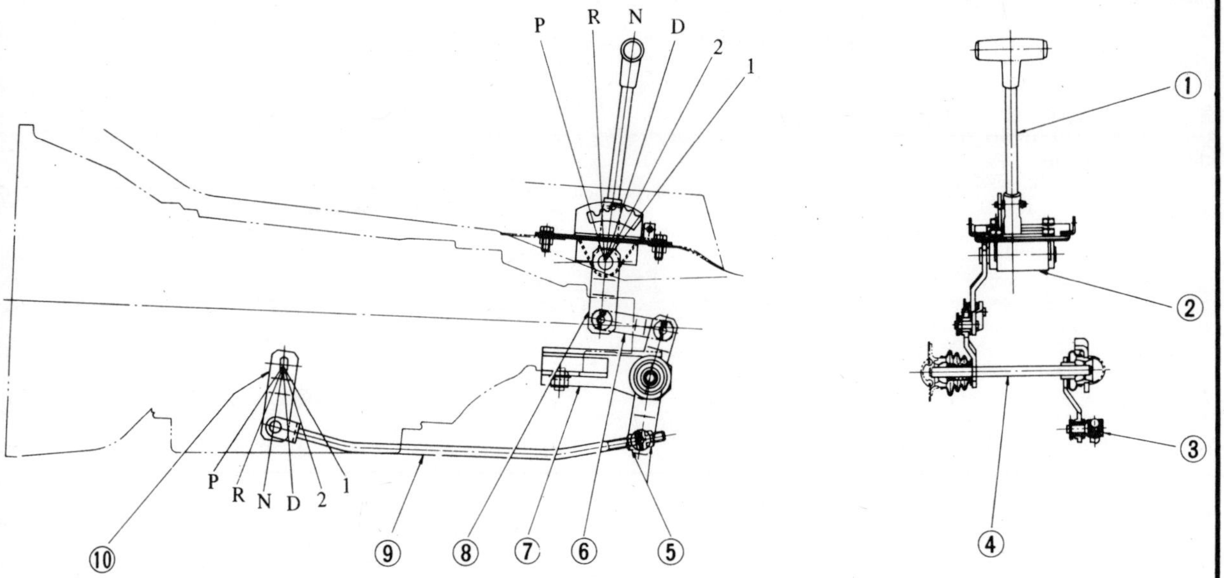

FIG. 6.51. SELECTOR CONTROL LINKAGE (SECTIONS 3 AND 4)

1	hand control lever	3	trunion	5	adjusting nut	8	hand control pivot
2	lever bracket	4	cross shaft	6	upper selector rod	9	lower selector rod
				7	cross shaft support	10	selector range lever

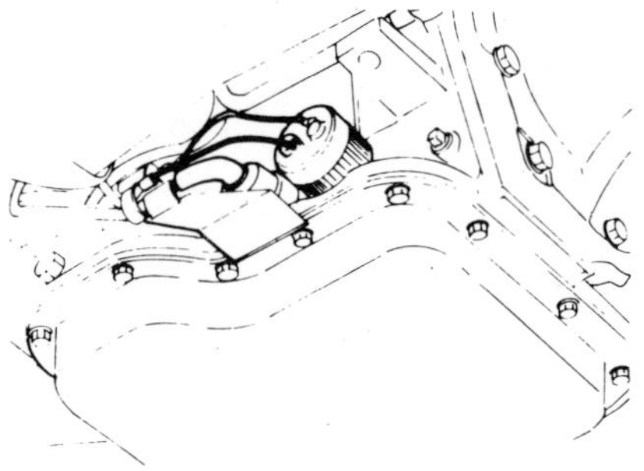

Fig. 6.52. Location of the downshift solenoid (Section 5)

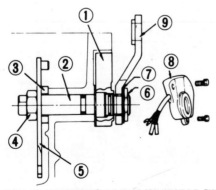

FIG. 6.53. COMPONENTS OF THE INHIBITOR SWITCH ASSEMBLY (SECTION 6)

1	switch	6	washer
2	shaft	7	securing nut
3	spacer	8	switch body (removed)
4	nut	9	range select lever
5	plate		

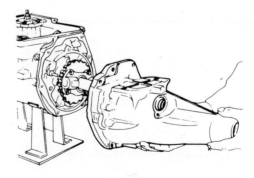

Fig. 6.54. Removing the rear extension housing (Section 7)

2 Any deviation from this arrangement should be rectified by adjustment, first having checked the correct setting of the selector linkage.

3 Refer to Fig.6.53 and detach the range selector lever (9) from the selector rod which connects it to the hand control. Now move the range selector lever to the N position.

4 Connect an ohmmeter to the black and yellow wires of the inhibitor switch. With the ignition switch on, the meter should indicate continuity of circuit when the range select lever is within 3 degrees (either side) of the N and P positions.

5 Repeat the test with the meter connected to the red and black wires and the range lever in R.

6 Where the switch requires adjusting to provide the correct moment of contact in the three selector positions, move the range lever to N and then remove the retaining nut (6), the two inhibitor switch securing bolts and the screw located below the switch.

7 Align the hole, from which the screw was removed, with the pinhole in the manual shaft (2). A thin rod or piece of wire may be used to do this. Holding this alignment, fit the inhibitor switch securing bolts and tighten them. Remove the alignment rod and refit the screw.

8 Refit the remaining switch components and test for correct operation as previously described. If the test procedure does not prove positive, renew the switch.

7 Rear extension oil seal - renewal

1 After a considerable mileage, leakage may occur from the seal which surrounds the shaft at the rear end of the automatic transmission extension housing. This leakage will be evident from the state of the underbody and from the reduction in the level of the hydraulic fluid.

2 Remove the propeller shaft as described in Section 2 of this Chapter.

3 Taking care not to damage the spined output shaft and the alloy housing, prise the old oil seal from its location. Drive in the new one using a tubular drift.

4 Should the seal be very tight in its recess, then support the transmission unit under the oil pan, remove the rear mounting, the speedometer drive cable and the rear extension to main transmission housing securing bolts.

5 Pull the extension housing straight off over the output shaft and governor assembly.

6 Using a suitable drift applied from the interior of the rear extension housing, remove the old oil seal. At the same time check the bush and renew it if it is scored or worn.

7 Refitting is a reversal of removal, but always use a new gasket between the rear extension and main housing and tighten the securing bolts to between 15 and 18 lb/ft.

Fault Diagnosis appears on next page.

Fault diagnosis

1   In addition to the information given in this Chapter reference should be made to Chapter 3 for the servicing and maintenance of the emission control equipment fitted to automatic transmission vehicles.
2   The most likely causes of faulty operation are incorrect oil level and linkage adjustment.

Symptom	Reason/s	Remedy
Engine will not start in N or P	Faulty starter or ignition circuit Incorrect linkage adjustment Incorrectly installed inhibitor switch	Check and repair. Adjust. Adjust.
Engine starts in selector positions other than N or P	Incorrect linkage adjustment Incorrectly installed inhibitor switch	Adjust. Adjust.
Severe bump when selecting D or R and excessive creep when hand brake released	Idling speed too high Vacuum circuit leaking	Check and adjust. Trace and repair.
Poor acceleration and low maximum speed	Incorrect oil level Incorrect linkage adjustment	Check and fill Adjust.

   Any other faults or mal-operation of the automatic transmission unit must be due to internal faults and should be rectified by your Datsun dealer. An indication of a major internal fault may be gained from the colour of the oil which under normal conditions should be transparent red. If it becomes discoloured or black then burned clutch or brake bands must be suspected.

Chapter 7 Propeller shaft

Contents

General description 1
Universal joints - testing for wear 2
Propeller shaft - removal and refitting 3
Universal joints - inspection, removal and
refitting 4
Fault diagnosis 5

Specifications

Propeller shaft type	tubular steel with two universal joints and sliding sleeve at front end
Distance between joints	46.8 in.
Outside diameter	2.713 in.
Maximum out of balance at 4,000 rev/min	0.2 oz/in.
Maximum shaft run out	0.024 in.

Torque wrench setting	lb/ft
Propeller shaft flange to rear axle pinion flange bolts	14 to 20

1 General description

1 The propeller shaft is of one piece tubular steel construction having a universal joint at each end to allow for vertical movement of the rear axle.
2 At the front end of the shaft is a sliding sleeve which engages with the transmission unit splined output shaft.
3 The propeller shaft is finely balanced during manufacture and it is recommended that an exchange unit is obtained rather than dismantle the universal joints when wear is evident. However, this is not always possible and provided care is taken to mark each individual yoke in relation to the one opposite then the balance will usually be maintained. Do not drop the assembly during servicing operations.

2 Universal joints - testing for wear

1 Wear in the needle roller bearings is characterized by vibration in the transmission, 'clonks' on taking up the drive, and in extreme cases lack of lubrication, metallic squeaking and ultimately grating and shrieking sounds as the bearings break up.
2 It is easy to check if the needle roller bearings are worn with the propeller shaft in position, by trying to turn the shaft with one hand, the other hand holding the rear axle flange when the rear universal joint is being checked, and the front half coupling when the front universal joint is being checked. Any movement between the propeller shaft and the front half couplings, and round the rear half couplings, is indicative of considerable wear.
3 If wear is evident, either fit a new propeller shaft assembly complete or renew the universal joints as described later in this Chapter.
4 A final test for wear is to attempt to lift the shaft and note any movement between the yokes of the joints.

3 Propeller shaft - removal and refitting

1 Jack up the rear of the car, or position the rear of the car over a pit.

2 If the rear of the car is jacked up, supplement the jack with support blocks so that danger is minimized should the jack collapse.
3 If the rear wheels are off the ground, place the car in gear and apply the handbrake to ensure that the propeller shaft does not turn when an attempt is made to loosen the four bolts securing the propeller shaft to the rear axle.
4 The propeller shaft is carefully balanced to fine limits and it is important that it is replaced in exactly the same position it was in prior to removal. Scratch marks on the propeller shaft and rear axle flanges to ensure accurate mating when the time comes for reassembly.
5 Unscrew and remove the four bolts and spring washers which hold the flange on the propeller shaft to the flange on the rear axle.
6 Slightly push the shaft forward to separate the two flanges, then lower the end of the shaft and pull it rearwards to disengage the gearbox mainshaft splines.
7 Place a large can or tray under the rear of the gearbox extension to catch any oil which is likely to leak past the oil seal when the propeller shaft is removed.
8 Replacement of the propeller shaft is a reversal of the above procedure. Ensure that the mating marks scratched on the propeller shaft and rear axle flanges line up, and always use new spring washers. Check the oil level in the gearbox and top up if necessary.

4 Universal joints - inspection, removal and refitting

1 Clean away all dirt from the ends of the bearings on the yokes so that the circlips may be removed using a pair of contracting circlip pliers. If they are very tight, tap the end of the bearing race (inside the circlip) with a drift and hammer to relieve the pressure.
2 Once the circlips are removed, tap the universal joints at the yoke with a soft hammer and the bearings and race will come out of the housing and can be removed easily.
3 If they are obstinate they can be gripped in a self-locking wrench for final removal provided they are to be renewed.
4 Once the bearings are removed from each opposite journal

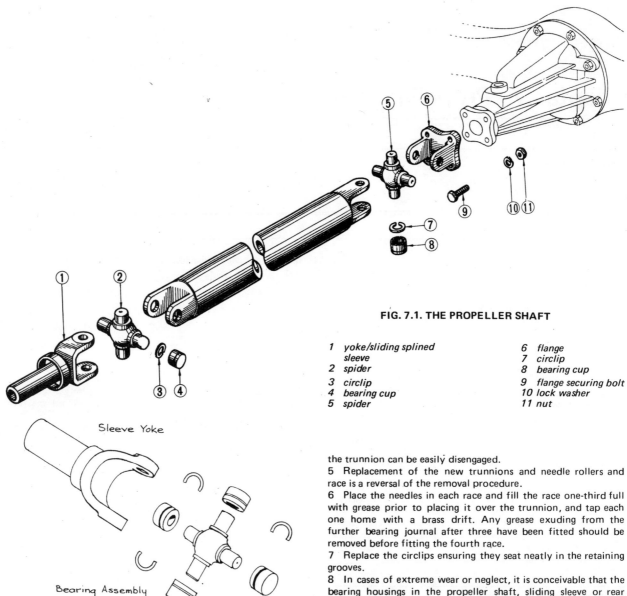

FIG. 7.1. THE PROPELLER SHAFT

1 yoke/sliding splined   6 flange
   sleeve   7 circlip
2 spider   8 bearing cup
3 circlip   9 flange securing bolt
4 bearing cup   10 lock washer
5 spider   11 nut

Sleeve Yoke

Bearing Assembly
Journal

Fig. 7.2. Universal joint assembly

the trunnion can be easily disengaged.
5 Replacement of the new trunnions and needle rollers and
race is a reversal of the removal procedure.
6 Place the needles in each race and fill the race one-third full
with grease prior to placing it over the trunnion, and tap each
one home with a brass drift. Any grease exuding from the
further bearing journal after three have been fitted should be
removed before fitting the fourth race.
7 Replace the circlips ensuring they seat neatly in the retaining
grooves.
8 In cases of extreme wear or neglect, it is conceivable that the
bearing housings in the propeller shaft, sliding sleeve or rear
flange have worn so much that the bearing races are a slack fit in
them. In such cases it will be necessary to replace the item
affected as well. Check also that the sliding sleeve splines are in
good condition and not a sloppy fit in the gearbox mainshaft.

Fault diagnosis

Symptom	Reason/s	Remedy
Vibration when vehicle running on road	Out of balance or distorted propeller shaft	Renew.
	Backlash in splined shaft	Renew components.
	Loose flange securing bolts	Tighten nuts.
	Worn universal joint bearings	Renew joints or complete propeller shaft assembly.

Chapter 8 Rear axle

Contents

General description 1
Routine maintenance 2
Rear axle - removal and refitting 3
Axle half shafts - removal and refitting 4

Axle shaft oil seal - renewal 5
Axle shaft bearings - removal and refitting 6
Pinion oil seal - renewal 7
Differential carrier - removal and refitting 8

Specifications

Type	semi-floating, rigid with hypoid gear
Construction	main axle casing - pressed steel differential carrier housing - light alloy
Ratio	3.90 : 1
Pinion bearing pre-load (with oil seal)	6 to 8 lb/in.
Axle shaft end play	less than 0.0039 in.
Oil capacity	1 3/8 Imp. pints

Torque wrench settings

	lb/ft
Differential housing to axle casing nuts	12 to 18
Brake backplate to axle casing bolts	11 to 14
Road spring U bolt nuts	23 to 29
Damper lower mounting bolts (saloon and van)	26 to 33
(coupe)	7 to 9
Pinion nut	87 to 123
Propeller shaft/pinion flange bolts	15 to 20
Oil filler and drain plugs	43 to 72

1 General description

The rear axle is of the semi-floating type and is held in place by two semi-elliptic springs. These provide the necessary lateral and longitudinal support for the axle.

The banjo type/casing carries the differential assembly which consists of a hypoid crown wheel and pinion and the two star pinion differential bolted in a carrier to the alloy casing nose piece.

All repairs can be carried out to the component parts of the rear axle without removing the axle casing from the car. It will be found simpler in practice to fit a guaranteed second hand axle from a car breakers yard rather than dismantle the differential unit which calls for special tools which very few garages will have.

As an alternative a replacement differential carrier assembly can be fitted which means that the axle can be left in position and dismantling is reduced to a minimum.

All nuts and bolts on the rear axle are to metric sizes.

2 Routine maintenance

1 At least every 30,000 miles, drain the oil (warm) from the rear axle and refill with the correct grade and quantity. It is preferable not to mix different brands of oil in the rear axle.
2 Regularly wipe accumulated oil and dirt from the breather outlet located on the top of the axle casing.

3 Rear axle - removal and refitting

1 Remove the hub caps from the road wheels and loosen the wheel nuts.
2 Jack up the bodyframe at the rear of the vehicle and support it on stands or blocks.
3 Place a jack under the centre of the rear axle casing and raise it sufficiently to take its weight but without raising the vehicle any higher.
4 Disconnect the rear damper lower mountings.
5 Loosen the locknut on the handbrake turnbuckle located above the propeller shaft, unscrew the turnbuckle to disconnect the cable.
6 Disconnect the flexible brake pipe from the three way connector which is bolted to the top of the axle casing. Plug both open ends of the fluid pipe to prevent loss of fluid and ingress of dirt.
7 Unscrew and remove the four bolts which secure the propeller shaft and rear axle pinion driving flange together. Mark the edge of the flange and then remove the propeller shaft.
8 Unscrew the nuts from the rear road spring U bolts. Remove the U bolts, spring seat location plates and seat pads.
9 The rear axle complete is now supported solely by the jack and may be withdrawn sideways through the space between the rear road spring and the bodyframe side member.
10 Refitting is a reversal of removal but the following points must be observed.
11 Tighten the rear spring U bolt nuts to a torque of between 23

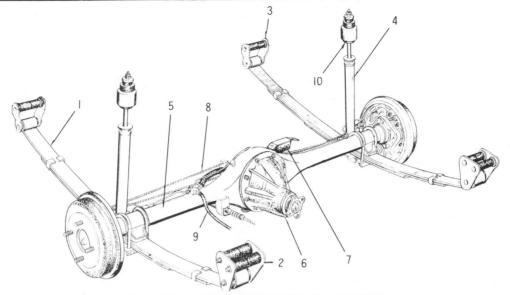

FIG. 8.1. THE REAR AXLE AND SUSPENSION LAYOUT

1 road spring	3 shackle
2 road spring mounting	4 damper

5 axle casing	8 handbrake cable
6 differential carrier housing	9 flexible brake hose
7 bump rubber	10 bump rubber

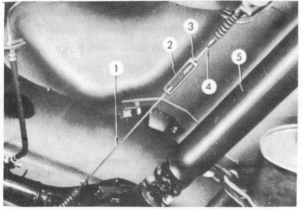

FIG. 8.2. LOCATION OF HANDBRAKE CABLE TURN-BUCKLE (SECTION 3)

1 rear cable	4 front cable
2 turnbuckle	5 propeller shaft
3 locknut	

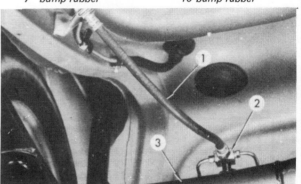

FIG. 8.3. LOCATION OF THREE-WAY BRAKE LINE CONNECTOR (SECTION 3)

1 flexible brake pipe	3 axle casing
2 three way connector	

Fig. 8.4. Location of U bolt nuts and damper lower mounting bolt (Section 3)

FIG. 8.5. BRAKE DISCONNECTION POINTS PRIOR TO AXLE SHAFT REMOVAL (SECTION 4)

1 fluid line union	3 return spring
2 handbrake link	

and 29 lb/ft.

12 Align the mating marks on the propeller shaft and pinion driving flange edges and tighten the securing bolts to a torque of between 15 and 20 lb/ft.

13 Reconnect the hydraulic brake hose and bleed the brakes as described in Chapter 9.

14 Reconnect and adjust the handbrake cable also as described in Chapter 9.

4 Axle half shafts - removal and refitting

1 Jack up the rear of the vehicle and support the rear axle on stands.

2 Remove the road wheels and brake drums.

3 Refer to Fig.8.5 and disconnect the handbrake linkage and the hydraulic pipe union, Plug the fluid line to prevent loss.

4 Unscrew and remove the four bolts which secure the brake backplate to the axle casing.

5 Using a sliding hammer remove the half shaft.

6 Before refitting a half shaft, it is recommended that the oil seal is always renewed as described in Section 5 of this Chapter.

7 Pass the half shaft carefully through the oil seal, keeping the shaft quite parallel with the axle casing tube. When the splines on the end of the shaft engage with those in the differential unit carefully tap the shaft right home. Using a straight edge and feeler gauge, check that the front face of the bearing does not project more than 0.0039 in above the end face of the axle casing. If it does then a bearing adjusting shim must be obtained and fitted.

8 Tighten the brake back plate bolts to a torque of between 11 and 16 lb/ft.

9 Disconnect the handbrake linkage and the hydraulic brake pipe. Bleed the brakes as described in Chapter 9.

10 Refit the road wheel and lower the jacks.

5 Axle shaft oil seal - renewal

1 Oil seepage into the rear brake drums is an indication of failure of the axle housing oil seals. Where oil contamination is observed, always check that this is not, in fact, hydraulic brake fluid leaking from a faulty wheel operating cylinder.

2 Remove the axle half shaft as described in the preceding Section.

3 Using a screwdriver as a lever prise the oil seal from the recess in the end of the axle casing.

4 Tap the new oil seal squarely into position using a piece of tube as a drift. Fill the space between the lips of the seal with grease.

5 Refit the axle half shaft as described in Section 4.

6 Axle shaft bearings - removal and refitting

1 The removal and fitting of half shaft bearings and spacer/collars is best left to a service station having suitable extracting and pressing equipment. Where the home mechanic has such facilities available, proceed as follows.

2 With the half shaft removed as described in Section 4 secure it in a vice fitted with jaw protectors.

3 Using a sharp cold chisel, make several deep cuts in the collar at equidistant points. The collar can then be easily withdrawn from the axle shaft. Take great care not to damage or distort the axle shaft during this operation.

4 Using a suitable extractor, remove the bearing from the axle shaft and finally the bearing spacer.

5 Press wheel bearing grease into the bearing and then locate the spacer, new bearing and new collar in position on the shaft. Press the components into position on the axle shaft using a suitable press to bear on the end of the collar.

6 Refit the axle half shaft (now reassembled) to the rear axle casing as described in Section 4.

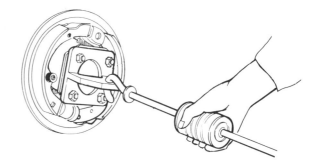

Fig. 8.6. Using a slide hammer to withdraw a half shaft (Section 4)

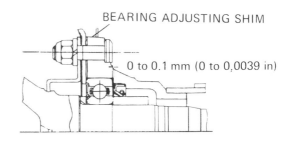

Fig. 8.7. Bearing surface to axle casing surface projection and location of adjusting shim (Section 4)

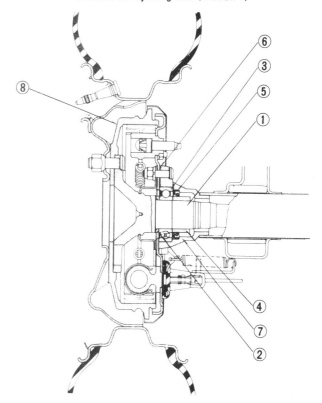

FIG. 8.8. SECTIONAL VIEW OF REAR AXLE HUB ASSEMBLY

1 Half shaft	5 oil seal
2 bearing spacer	6 adjustment shim
3 wheel bearing	7 axle casing
4 bearing collar	8 brake drum

94

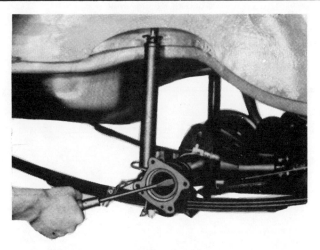

Fig. 8.9. Prising an axle shaft oil seal from the axle casing
(Section 5)

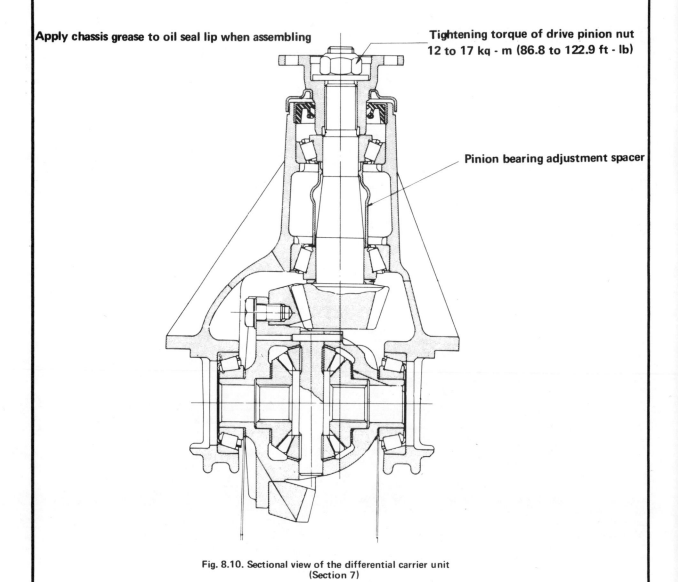

Apply chassis grease to oil seal lip when assembling

**Tightening torque of drive pinion nut
12 to 17 kq - m (86.8 to 122.9 ft - lb)**

Pinion bearing adjustment spacer

Fig. 8.10. Sectional view of the differential carrier unit
(Section 7)

7 Pinion oil seal - renewal

The pinion oil seal can be renewed with the axle in position in the car provided the following operations are carefully followed.

1 Jack up the rear of the car and support the axle on stands.

2 Mark the edges of the propeller shaft and pinion coupling flanges to ensure exact replacement.

3 Remove the four coupling bolts, detach the propeller shaft at the axle pinion flange and tie the propeller shaft to one side.

4 Remove both rear road wheels and brake drums to eliminate any drag.

5 Wind a cord round the pinion flange coupling and exerting a steady pull note the reading on a spring balance, this should be between 6 and 8 lb/in. The spring balance reading indicates the pinion bearing pre-load.

6 Mark the coupling in relation to the pinion splines for exact replacement.

7 Hold the pinion coupling flange by placing two 2 inch long bolts through two opposite holes, bolting them up tight, undo the self-locking nut whilst holding a large screwdriver or tyre lever between the two bolts as a lever.

8 Remove the defective oil seal by drifting in one side of the seal as far as it will go to force the opposite side of the seal from the housing.

9 Refit the new oil seal first having greased the mating surfaces of the seal and the axle housing. The flanges of the oil seal must face inwards. Using a piece of brass or copper tubing of suitable diameter, carefully drive the new oil seal into the axle housing recess until the face of the seal is flush with the housing. Make sure that the end of the pinion is not knocked during this operation.

10 Refit the coupling to its original position on the pinion splines after first having located the dust cover.

11 Fit a new pinion nut and holding the coupling still with the screwdriver or tyre lever, tighten the nut until the pinion end float only just disappears. Do not overtighten.

12 Rotate the pinion to settle the bearing and then check the pre-load using the cord and spring balance method previously described and by slight adjustment of the nut and rotation of the pinion obtain a spring balance pre-load figure to match that which applied before dismantling.

13 On no account overtighten the pinion nut as it cannot be slackened without introducing end-float caused by over compressing the collapsible spacer shown in Fig.8.10. Should this happen, withdraw the pinion nut, coupling, taper roller bearing and the collapsible spacer. Fit a new spacer and reassemble the other components and tighten the pinion nut to a torque of between 87 and 123 lb/ft. Tighten the nut only a fraction of a turn at a time once the lower specified torque setting has been reached and check the pre-load as previously described.

14 Remove the two holding bolts and refit the propeller shaft making sure to align the mating marks. Refit the brake drums and road wheels and lower the car.

8 Differential carrier - removal and refitting

1 The overhaul of the rear axle differential unit is not within the scope of the home mechanic due to the specialized gauges and tools which are required. Where the unit requires servicing or repair due to wear or excessive noise it is most economical to exchange it for a factory reconditioned assembly and this Section is limited to a description of the removal and refitting procedure.

2 Drain the oil from the rear axle.

3 Jack up the axle and partially withdraw the axle half shafts as described in Section 4 of this Chapter.

4 Disconnect and remove the propeller shaft as previously described.

5 Unscrew, evenly and in opposite sequence, the nuts from the ten differential unit securing studs. Pull the differential unit

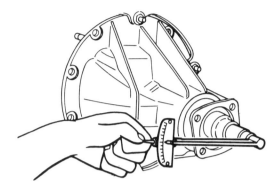

Fig. 8.11. Tightening the pinion nut using a torque wrench (Section 7)

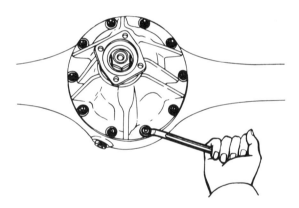

Fig. 8.12. Unscrewing a differential flange securing nut (Section 8)

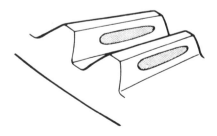

Fig. 8.13. Correct pinion tooth contact pattern on crownwheel teeth (Section 8)

from the main axle casing. Do not attempt to lever it from its location or the alloy mating flange may be damaged or broken.

6   Although only of academic interest, the now exposed crown wheel teeth should show a pinion tooth contact area as shown in Fig.8.13 provided the differential unit was correctly set up originally.

7   Scrape all trace of old gasket from the mating surface of the axle casing. Locate a new gasket in position having first lightly coated it with jointing compound.

8   Clean the mating surface of the differential carrier and remove any burrs. Install the carrier so that the pinion is at the lowest point.

9   Tighten the securing nuts to a torque of between 12 and 18 lb/ft.

10 Refit the half shafts and the propeller shaft.

11 Refit the road wheels and lower the jack.

12 Fill the differential unit to the correct level with the specified grade of oil.

Chapter 9 Braking system

Contents

General description 1
Routine maintenance 2
Bleeding the hydraulic system 3
Drum brakes - adjustment 4
Front brake shoes - inspection, removal and refitting ... 5
Rear brake shoes - inspection, removal and refitting ... 6
Flexible hoses - inspection, removal and refitting ... 7
Rigid brake lines - inspection, removal and refitting ... 8
Drum brake wheel cylinder seals - renewal 9
Front wheel cylinders - removal and refitting 10
Rear wheel cylinders - removal and refitting 11
Front disc brake friction pads - inspection, removal and refitting 12
Caliper unit - removal and refitting 13

Caliper unit - dismantling, servicing and reassembly 14
Front brake disc - removal and refitting 15
Master cylinder - single braking circuit - removal and refitting 16
Master cylinder - dual braking circuit - removal and refitting 17
Master cylinders - dismantling, servicing, reassembly ... 18
Dual circuit pressure differential switch 19
Foot brake pedal and stop lamp switch - adjustment 20
Handbrake - adjustment 21
Handbrake mechanism - removal and refitting 22
Fault diagnosis 23

Specifications

System type	hydraulically operated on all four wheels, mechanically operated handbrake on rear wheels only. Drum brakes all round or discs on front and drums on rear. Single or dual hydraulic circuit according to date of manufacture and operating territory.

Master cylinder
Type	single or tandem according to circuit
Make	NABCO or TOKICO
Cylinder bore internal diameter	11/16 in.

Front wheel caliper
Cylinder bore (internal diameter)	1.894 in.

Front wheel operating cylinder
Cylinder bore (internal diameter)	13/16 in.

Rear wheel operating cylinder
Cylinder bore (internal diameter)	13/16 in.

Front disc
Outside diameter	8.37 in.
Thickness	0.3740 in. (minimum 0.3307 in.)
Maximum run-out	less than 0.0012
Friction pad dimensions	1.673 in. wide x 2.091 in. long x 0.406 in. thick
Total friction pad area	14 in^2

Drums
Inside diameter	8 in. (maximum 8.051 in.)
Maximum ovality	0.0008 in.
Friction lining dimensions	7.68 in. long x 1.378 in. wide x 0.1890 in. thick
Total friction lining area	42.3 in^2

Brake foot pedal
Floor to pedal pad top surface dimension	5.57 in.
Pedal free movement	¼ to ½ in.
Hydraulic fluid	Castrol Girling Universal Brake and Clutch Fluid

Torque wrench settings   lb/ft

Brake pedal cross shaft nuts	...	...	...	...	...	12 to 22
Master cylinder securing nuts	...	...	...	...	...	15 to 21
Front wheel cylinder nuts	...	...	...	...	...	5 to 7
Front disc to hub bolt	...	...	...	...	...	20 to 27
Caliper securing bolts	...	...	...	...	...	33 to 44
Drum brake adjuster to backplate bolts	...	...	...	...	...	12 to 16
Handbrake lever to floor securing bolt	...	...	...	...	...	7 to 10
Transverse link to lower suspension strut bolts	...	...	...	...	...	33 to 44

1 General description

According to model either disc or drum brakes are fitted to the front wheels while all models have single leading shoe drum brakes at the rear. The mechanically operated handbrake works on the rear wheels only.

Where front drum brakes are fitted these are of the two leading shoe type with a separate cylinder for each shoe. Two adjusters are provided on each front wheel so that wear can be taken up on the brake linings. One adjuster is provided on each rear wheel for the same purpose. It is unusual to have to adjust the handbrake system as the efficiency of this system is largely dependent on the condition of the rear brake linings and the adjustment of the brake shoes. The handbrake can however be adjusted separately to the footbrake operated hydraulic system.

The hydraulic brake system on drum brakes operates in the following manner:- On application of the brake pedal, hydraulic fluid under pressure is pushed from the master cylinder to the brake operating cylinders in each wheel by means of a union, steel pipe lines and flexible hoses.

The hydraulic fluid moves the pistons out of the wheel cylinders so pushing the brake shoes into contact with the brake drums. This provides an equal degree of retardation on all four wheels in direct proportion to the brake pedal pressure. Return springs draw the shoes together again when the brake pedal is released.

The front disc brakes fitted to certain models (see specifications) are of the rotating disc and floating caliper type, with one caliper per disc. The caliper is positioned to act on the trailing edge of the disc. Each caliper contains two piston operated friction pads, which on application of the footbrake pinch the disc between them.

Application of the footbrake creates hydraulic pressure in the master cylinder and fluid from the cylinder travels via steel and flexible pipes to the cylinder in each caliper, thus pushing the pistons, to which are attached the friction pads, into contact with either side of the disc.

Two seals are fitted to the operating cylinder the outer seal prevents moisture and dirt entering the cylinder, while the inner seal which is retained in a groove inside the cylinder, prevents fluid leakage.

As the friction pads wear so the pistons move further out of the cylinder due to the elasticity of the seals and the level of the fluid in the hydraulic reservoir drops. Disc pads wear is therefore taken up automatically and eliminates the need for periodic adjustment by the owner.

The handbrake lever on all models is located between the front seats. A single cable runs from the lever to an equaliser bracket on the left of the rear axle. The cable runs through the equaliser bracket and operates the left hand rear brake. At the same time the bracket is deflected and twin cables attached to it running across the rear of the axle casing operate the right hand rear brake.

On certain models, in particular those cars for export to the USA a dual braking system is fitted providing separate hydraulic circuits for the front and rear brakes. Should one circuit fail the other circuit is unaffected and the car can still be stopped. A warning light is fitted on the facia which illuminates should either circuit fail.

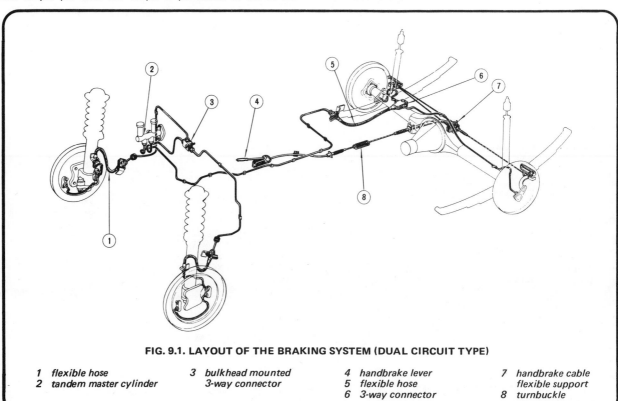

FIG. 9.1. LAYOUT OF THE BRAKING SYSTEM (DUAL CIRCUIT TYPE)

1 flexible hose	3 bulkhead mounted	4 handbrake lever	7 handbrake cable
2 tandem master cylinder	3-way connector	5 flexible hose	flexible support
		6 3-way connector	8 turnbuckle

2 Routine maintenance

1 Every 3,000 miles or more frequently if necessary, carefully clean the top of the brake master cylinder reservoir, remove the cap, and inspect the level of the fluid which should be ¼ in below the bottom of the filler neck. Check that the breathing holes in the cap are clear.

2 If the fluid is below this level, top up the reservoir with any hydraulic fluid conforming to specification. It is vital that no other type of brake fluid is used. Use of a non-standard fluid will result in brake failure caused by the perishing of special seals in the master and brake cylinders. If topping up becomes frequent then check the metal piping and flexible hoses for leaks, and check for worn brake or master cylinders which will also cause loss of fluid.

3 At intervals of 3,000 miles, or more frequently if pedal travel becomes excessive, adjust the brake shoes to compensate for wear of the brake linings. On models with disc brakes on the front it will only be necessary to adjust the rear brakes.

4 Every 6,000 miles in the case of drum brakes, remove the drums, inspect the linings for wear and renew them as necessary. At the same time thoroughly clean out all dust from the drums. With disc brakes, remove the pads and examine them for wear. If they are worn down to 1/8 inch or less (the distance being measured between the contact face of the pad and the face of the brake pad support plate) then they should be renewed.

5 Every 36,000 miles or three years whichever comes sooner, it is advisable to change the fluid in the braking system and at the same time renew all hydraulic seals and flexible hoses.

3 Bleeding the hydraulic system

1 Removal of all the air from the hydraulic system is essential to the correct working of the braking system, and before undertaking this examine the fluid reservoir cap to ensure that both vent holes, one on top and the second underneath but not in line, are clear; check the level of fluid and top up if required.

2 Check all brake line unions and connections for possible seepage, and at the same time check the condition of the rubber hoses, which may be perished.

3 If the condition of the wheel cylinders is in doubt, check for possible signs of fluid leakage.

4 If there is any possibility of incorrect fluid having been put into the system, drain all the fluid out and flush through with methylated spirit. Renew all piston seals and cups since these will be affected and could possibly fail under pressure.

5 Gather together a clean jam jar, a 9 in length of tubing which fits tightly over the bleed nipples, and a tin of the correct brake fluid.

6 To bleed the system clean the areas around the bleed valves, and start on the front brakes first by removing the rubber cup over the bleed valve, if fitted, and fitting a rubber tube in position.

7 Place the end of the tube in a clean glass jar containing sufficient fluid to keep the end of the tube underneath during the operation.

8 Open the bleed valve with a spanner and quickly press down the brake pedal. After slowly releasing the pedal, pause for a moment to allow the fluid to recoup in the master cylinder and then depress again. This will force air from the system. Continue until no more air bubbles can be seen coming from the tube. At intervals make certain that the reservoir is kept topped up, otherwise air will enter at this point again.

9 The bleeding sequence should be carried out in the following order - left rear, right rear, left front, right front.

10 Tighten the bleed screws when the pedal is still in the fully depressed position.

11 Use only clean hydraulic fluid for topping up the fluid reservoir.

4 Drum brakes - adjustment

1 Jack up each wheel in turn, remove the road wheel.

2 Chock the other wheels and release the handbrake.

3 The brakes are taken up by turning the square headed adjusters located on the rear of each backplate. Use a special brake adjusting spanner if possible or a close tolerance open ended one to avoid burring the adjuster.

4 Two adjusters are fitted to the front brakes and one to each of the rear brakes.

5 To adjust a front brake, turn one adjuster clockwise until the drum is locked and will not rotate. Back off the adjuster just sufficiently for the drum to rotate freely when turned by hand without any rubbing or scraping of the brake shoe.

6 Repeat the adjustment on the other adjuster.

7 Apply the foot brake pedal sharply and re-check the adjustment.

8 To adjust a rear brake, turn the single adjuster clockwise until the drum locks and then back off the adjuster until the drum is free to rotate when turned by hand. Do not confuse transmission drag with a binding brake.

9 Apply the front brake pedal hard and re-check the adjustment.

5 Front brake shoes - inspection, removal and refitting

1 After high mileages it will be necessary to fit replacement brake shoes with new linings. Refitting new brake linings to old shoes is not always satisfactory, but if the services of a local garage or workshop with brake lining equipment is available, then there is no reason why your own shoes should not be successfully relined.

2 Remove the hub cap, slacken off the wheel nuts, securely jack up the car and remove the road wheel.

3 Slacken the shoe adjusters by about two or three turns and withdraw the brake drum.

4 Brush any accumulated dust from the brake shoes and internal components.

5 The brake linings should be renewed if they are so worn that the rivet heads are flush with the surface of the lining. If bonded linings are fitted they must be removed when the material has worn down to 1/32 inch at its thinnest point. If the shoes are being removed to give access to the wheel cylinders, then cover the linings with masking tape to prevent any possibility of their becoming contaminated with grease or oil.

6 Before removing the shoes, note and sketch if necessary the location of the shoes with regard to their leading and trailing edges and the position of the shoe return springs.

7 Using a pair of pliers, unhook the return springs from the elongated holes in the shoe webs.

8 Again using pliers, grip the edges of the shoe steady spring retaining plates. Depress the plates and turn them through 90° so that they can be released from the retaining tee posts. Withdraw the steady springs.

9 Remove the brake shoes and use rubber bands to retain the wheel cylinder pistons in their cylinders. **On no account depress the footbrake pedal while the drum and brake shoes are removed.**

10 Slacken the shoe adjusters completely and then fit the new shoes taking particular care to see that they are the correct way round and that the return springs are correctly located.

11 Check the condition of the friction surface of the drum. If it is scored, it must be skimmed professionally or renewed.

12 Re-fit the brake drum and adjust the brakes as described in Section 4 of this Chapter.

13 Refit the road wheel and lower the jack.

6 Rear brake shoes - inspection, removal and refitting

1 The servicing of the rear brake shoes is similar to that

FIG. 9.2. BLEEDING A REAR BRAKE (SECTION 3)

1   bleed nipple   2   bleed tube

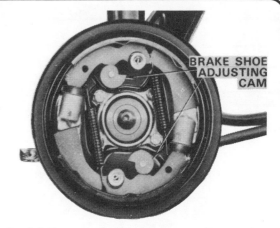

Fig. 9.3. Front wheel brake adjusting cams (Section 4)

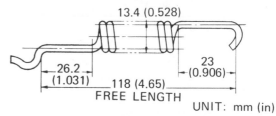

13.4 (0.528)

26.2 (1.031)

23 (0.906)

118 (4.65)

FREE LENGTH

UNIT: mm (in)

Fig. 9.5. Front shoe return spring dimensions (Section 5)

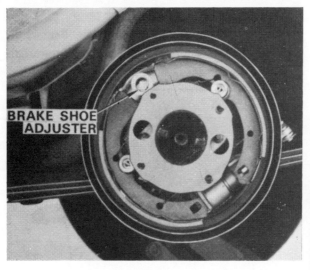

Fig. 9.4. A rear wheel brake adjuster (Section 4)

FIG. 9.7. A FRONT FLEXIBLE BRAKE HOSE (SECTION 7)

1   flexible hose   2   suspension strut

CYLINDER SIDE

12 (0.472)

30.6 (1.205)

58 (2.283)

119.2 (4.69)

FREE LENGTH

ADJUSTER SIDE

12 (0.472)

11 (0.433)

42 (1.654)

69.5 (2.736)

UNIT: mm (in)

FREE LENGTH

Fig. 9.6. Rear shoe return spring dimensions (Section 6)

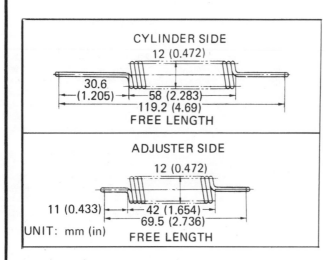

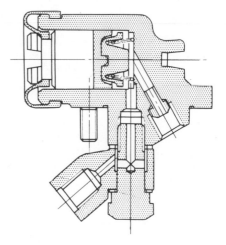

Fig. 9.8. Sectional view of a front wheel operating cylinder (Section 9)

described for the front shoes except that three shoe return springs are used and only one adjuster is fitted.

7 Flexible hoses - inspection, removal and refitting

1 Inspect the condition of the flexible hydraulic hoses leading from under the front wings to the brackets on the front suspension units, and also the single hose on the rear axle casing. If they are swollen, damaged or chafed, they must be renewed.
2 Undo the lock nuts at both ends of the flexible hoses and then holding the hexagon nut on the flexible hose steady undo the other union nut and remove the flexible hose and washer.
3 Replacement is a reversal of the removal procedure, but carefully check all the securing brackets are in a sound condition and that the lock nuts are tight. Bleed the hydraulic system (Section 3).

8 Rigid brake lines - inspection, removal and refitting

1 At regular intervals wipe the steel brake pipes clean and examine them for signs of rust or denting caused by flying stones.
2 Examine the securing clips which are plastic coated to prevent wear to the pipe surface. Bend the tongues of the clips if necessary to ensure that they hold the brake pipes securely without letting them rattle or vibrate.
3 Check that the pipes are not touching any adjacent components or rubbing against any part of the vehicle. Where this is observed, bend the pipe gently away to clear.
4 Any section of pipe which is rusty or chafed should be renewed. Brake pipes are available to the correct length and fitted with end unions from most Datsun dealers and can be made to pattern by many accessory suppliers. When installing the new pipes use the old pipes as a guide to bending and do not make any bends sharper than is necessary.
5 The system will of course have to be bled when the circuit has been reconnected.

9 Drum brake wheel cylinder seals - renewal

If hydraulic fluid is leaking from one of the brake cylinders it will be necessary to dismantle the cylinder and replace the dust cover and piston sealing rubber. If brake fluid is found running down the side of the wheel, or it is noticed that a pool of liquid forms alongside one wheel and the level in the master cylinder has dropped, and the hoses are in good order proceed as follows:
1 Remove the offending brake drum and shoes as described in Sections 5 or 6.
2 Gently pull off the rubber dust cover.
3 Take the piston complete with its seal out of the cylinder bore and then withdraw the spring from the bore as well. Should the piston and seal prove difficult to remove, gentle pressure on the brake pedal will push it out of the bore. If this method is used place a quantity of rag under the brake backplate to catch the hydraulic fluid as it pours out of the cylinder.
4 Inspect the cylinder bore for score marks caused by impurities in the hydraulic fluid. If any are found the cylinder and piston will require renewal together as an exchange unit.
5 If the cylinder bore is sound, thoroughly clean it out with fresh hydraulic fluid.
6 The old rubber seal will probably be visibly worn or swollen. Detach it from the piston, smear a new rubber seal with hydraulic fluid and assemble it to the piston with the flat face of the seal next to the piston rear shoulder. (Fig.9.8).
7 Reassembly is a direct reversal of the above procedure. If the rubber dust cap appears to be worn or damaged this should also be renewed.
8 Replenish the hydraulic fluid, replace the brake shoes and drum and bleed the braking system as described in Section 3.

10 Front wheel cylinders - removal and refitting

1 Remove the brake drum and shoes as described in Section 5.
2 Unscrew the rigid pipe union from the flexible hose. The flexible hose may be left undisturbed at the bracket/clip attached to the suspension leg. Plug the end of the flexible hose.
3 Unscrew the unions from the interconnecting pipe which joins the two wheel operating cylinders.
4 Unscrew and remove the two securing nuts from the wheel cylinders and withdraw the cylinder assemblies from the brake back plate.
5 Refitting the wheel cylinders is a reversal of removal but a smear of high melting grease must be applied to the brake back plate upon which the wheel cylinders slide and the raised shoe contact points. (Fig.9.10).
6 Tighten the wheel cylinder securing nuts to a torque of between 5 and 7 lb/ft. only.
7 When reassembly is complete, bleed the brakes (Section 3).

11 Rear wheel cylinders - removal and refitting

1 Remove the drum and shoes as described in Section 6.
2 Disconnect the handbrake cable link from the wheel cylinder operating arm and unscrew the brake pipe union from the wheel cylinder (refer to Fig.8.5 in the previous Chapter). Plug the brake pipe.
3 Peel back and remove the rubber dust cover from the wheel cylinder aperture and then slide out the adjustment shims and plates, noting carefully their sequence and exact location, Fig.9.11 .
4 Refitting is a reversal of removal but smear the raised sliding surfaces of the back plate with high melting point grease.
5 Smear the wheel cylinder shims and plate surfaces with grease and locate the cylinder assembly on the backplate. Using a spring balance check that the wheel cylinder will slide in its elongated aperture with a pull of between 5 and 15 lbs. If it moves too stiffly or too freely, check for rust or burrs or renew the forked shims.
6 When reassembly is complete, bleed the system (Section 3).

12 Front disc brake friction pads - inspection, removal and refitting

1 Remove the front wheels and inspect the amount of friction material left on the friction pads. The pads must be renewed when the thickness of the material has worn down to 1/8th inch.
2 With a pair of pliers pull out the small wire clip that holds the main retaining pins in place.
3 Remove the main retaining pins which run through the caliper, the metal backing of the pads and the shims. Remove the hanger springs and coil spring.
4 The friction pads and shims can now be removed from the caliper. If they prove difficult to move by hand a pair of long nosed pliers can be used.
5 Carefully clean the recesses in the caliper in which the friction pads and shims lie, and the exposed faces of each piston from all traces of dirt and rust.
6 Remove the cap(s) from the master cylinder reservoir and either suck or syphon out an inch or two of fluid to allow for the rise in fluid level when the caliper pistons are pressed into the caliper body. Alternatively, the reservoir may be allowed to overflow provided a rag or receptacle is placed underneath the master cylinder. Remember, hydraulic brake fluid acts as a very efficient paint and cellulose stripper!
7 Press in each piston into the caliper body. Use a flat piece of wood or tyre lever to do this and keep the pistons square during the operation. Alternatively, as the caliper is of the floating type, by first pushing the unit inwards and then pulling it outwards, the pistons can be pressed in using the disc itself as a pressure plate. **Whichever method is used, never press the pistons in**

Fig. 9.9. Location of front wheel cylinders (1 and 3) and inter-connecting hydraulic pipe (2) (Section 10)

Fig. 9.10. Grease smear points on front drum brake backplate (Section 10)

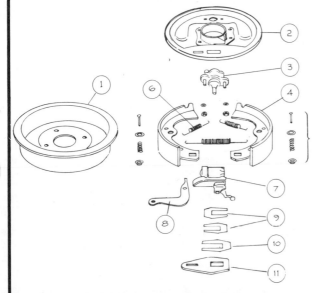

FIG. 9.11. COMPONENTS OF A REAR DRUM BRAKE ASSEMBLY (SECTION 11)

1 drum
2 backplate
3 adjuster
4 shoe
5 shoe steady
6 shoe return spring
7 wheel operating cylinder
8 handbrake lever
9 operating cylinder shims
10 operating cylinder plate
11 rubber dust excluder

FIG. 9.12. TESTING THE FORCE REQUIRED TO SLIDE A REAR WHEEL CYLINDER (SECTION 11)

1 spring balance   2 wheel cylinder

FIG. 9.13. DISC FRICTION PAD COMPONENTS (SECTION 12)

1 pad   3 pin securing clip
2 retaining pins

BRAKE PAD

Fig. 9.14. Removing a friction pad from a disc brake (Section 12)

Fig. 9.15. Anti-squeak shims in position on disc pads (Section 12)

Fig. 9.16. Location of the transverse link to suspension strut bolts (Section 13)

Fig. 9.17. Location of caliper unit retaining bolts (Section 13)

Fig. 9.18. Tapping the caliper yoke to release the cylinder assembly (Section 14)

beyond the dust excluding seals or the inner seals will be damaged and the caliper unit will have to be dismantled in order to renew them.

8 Fit the new friction pads complete with anti-squeak shims. These must be fitted so that the arrow points in the direction of rotation of the disc and positioned **against** the steel back of the pad.

9 Insert the retaining pins so that they trap the hanger springs as they pass through their locating holes. Note that the small coil spring fits on the pin which is furthest from the caliper bleed nipple.

10 Fit the securing clip to the retaining pins.

11 Press the brake pedal hard two or three times and top up the fluid reservoir to the correct level with clean non-aerated fluid of the specified type.

12 Refit the road wheels and lower the jack.

13 When renewing friction pads always renew them as sets of two.

13 Caliper unit - removal and refitting

1 Remove the friction pads as described in the preceding Section.

2 Unscrew the fluid pipe union at the caliper body, slightly loosen the rigid pipe union at the suspension strut bracket and swing the hydraulic pipe out of the way.

3 Ensure that the bodyframe is adequately supported and unscrew and remove the two bolts which secure the transverse link to the bottom of the suspension strut. (Fig.9.16).

4 Pull the suspension strut outwards just far enough to provide access to the caliper unit securing bolts. Unscrew and remove these and withdraw the caliper.

5 Refitting the caliper unit is a reversal of removal, tighten the caliper securing bolts to a torque of between 33 and 44 lb/ft and the transverse link to suspension strut bolts to a similar torque.

6 Bleed the hydraulic system when the caliper and friction pads have been refitted.

14 Caliper unit - dismantling, servicing and reassembly

1 Clean the outside of the unit thoroughly and observe strict cleanliness throughout the following operations.

2 Press the pistons into the caliper housing and expel the hydraulic fluid from the fluid inlet orifice.

3 Secure the yoke carefully in a vice and tap to release the cylinder body as shown in Fig.9.18. .

4 As the cylinder body is removed, take care that the pistons do not drop out and become damaged.

5 Remove the bias ring from the recess of piston A. (Fig.9.20).

6 The two pistons are not interchangeable and a mark should be made in their recessed surfaces, also on the rim of the respective cylinder so that they will be returned to their original positions on reassembly.

7 Remove the retaining rings and dust excluding seals from the exposed faces of both pistons.

8 Expel the pistons from the cylinders. This is best accomplished by applying air pressure from a tyre pump at the caliper fluid inlet orifice.

9 Extract the seals from cylinders using the fingers only to manipulate them from their grooves.

10 Clean all components in methylated spirit or clean hydraulic fluid. Inspect the cylinder walls for scoring, bright spots or corrosion. Where these are evident, renew the complete caliper assembly.

11 Obtain a repair kit which will contain all the necessary seals and replacement parts. Check that the rubber seals have not deteriorated or become deformed in storage.

12 Dip the new seals in hydraulic fluid and locate them in their grooves in the cylinder bores. Use only the fingers to manipulate them into position. Note the correct fitting of the seal chamfer, (Fig.9.22).

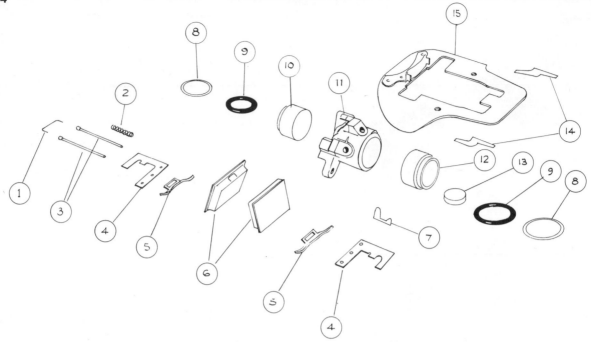

FIG. 9.19. EXPLODED VIEW OF A DISC BRAKE CALIPER UNIT (SECTION 14)

1 retaining pin clip	5 hanger spring	9 rubber dust excluder	13 bias ring
2 coil spring	6 friction pads	10 piston (B)	14 yoke spring
3 retaining pins	7 bleed screw	11 cylinder assembly	15 yoke
4 anti-squeak shim	8 retaining ring	12 piston (A)	

PISTON A   PISTON B

Fig. 9.20. Caliper piston identification. Piston A with dimple carries the bias ring (Section 14)

Fig. 9.21. The retaining ring (1) and dust excluding seal on a disc brake caliper (Section 14)

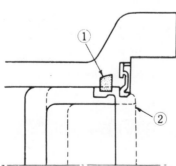

Fig. 9.22. Diagram showing correct location of caliper piston seal (1). Normal operating position of piston is shown at (2) (Section 14)

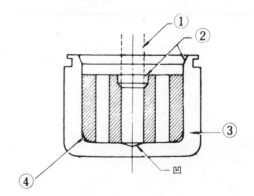

FIG. 9.23. BIAS RING FITTING DIAGRAM (PISTON A) (SECTION 14)

1 caliper yoke	3 piston
2 countersunk	4 radiused rim of bias ring

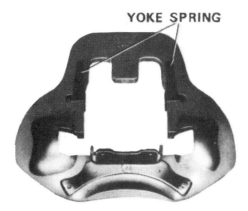

YOKE SPRING

YOKE SPRING

Fig. 9.24. Springs correctly fitted when viewed from both sides
of a disc caliper yoke (Section 14)

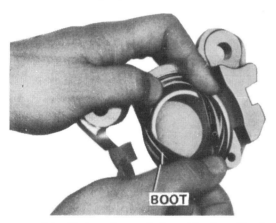

BOOT

Fig. 9.25. Fitting a dust excluding rubber boot (Section 15)

Fig. 9.26. Disc caliper yoke correctly mated with the cylinder
assembly (Section 15)

Fig. 9.27. Disc/hub securing bolts (Section 15)

13 Place the bias ring into the recess of piston A. Check that the
slightly rounded rim enters the piston recess first.
14 Dip the pistons in clean hydraulic fluid and insert them
carefully into their respective cylinders. Do not push them in too
far (see paragraph 7, Section 12).
15 Turn the bias ring so that it is correctly aligned when the
tongue of the yoke engages with it.
16 Fit the dust excluding seals and the retaining rings.
17 If new springs are to be fitted to the yoke, ensure that they
are installed as shown in Fig.9.24.
18 Lightly grease the yoke sliding grooves on the outside of the
cylinder body.
19 Locate the yoke with the cylinder body, checking that the
bias ring in the end of the piston is correctly aligned to receive
the tongue of the yoke. Note that the longer tapering side of the
yoke springs should be visible from the same side as the bleed
nipple and fluid inlet orifice.

15 Front brake disc - removal and refitting

1 When the friction pads are inspected also check the condition
of the discs themselves. If they are badly scored then they may
be skimmed professionally but the minimum disc thickness
which must be maintained is 0.3307 in. Where skimming will
produce a disc thinner than this, then the disc must be renewed.
2 The maximum run-out (out of true) is limited to a maximum
of 0.0012 in. Where this is exceeded, the disc must either be
true or renewed.
3 To remove the disc, first remove the pads (Section 12) and
the caliper unit (Section 13).
4 Tap off the cap from the end of the hub, remove the split pin
and castellated nut from the end of the stub axle (for full details
see Chapter 11).
5 Pull the hub/disc assembly forward slightly and extract the
thrust washer and the outer roller bearing. Remove the hub/disc
assembly.
6 The disc can be separated from the hub by removing the four
securing bolts.
7 Refitting is a reversal of removal. Tighten the hub/disc bolts
to a torque of 32 to 43 lb/ft. Adjust the front hub bearing as
described in Chapter 11.

16 Master cylinder - single braking circuit - removal and refitting

1 Disconnect the brake pedal arm from the master cylinder
operating push rod.
2 Unscrew the hydraulic fluid outlet pipe from the master
cylinder. Plug the pipe to prevent the ingress of dirt.
3 Unscrew and remove the two bolts which secure the master
cylinder to the engine rear bulkhead and withdraw the unit
complete with any adjustment shims.
4 Refitting is a reversal of removal. Always refit the shims
which were retained on removal and check the pedal adjustment

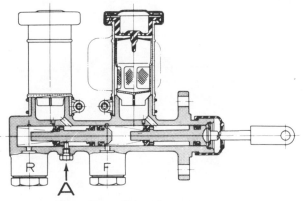

FIG. 9.28. SECTIONAL VIEW OF A TANDEM MASTER CYLINDER (SECTION 18)

R   rear circuit valve cap and pipe union
A   piston stop bolt
F   front circuit valve cap and pipe union

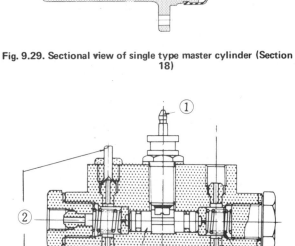

Fig. 9.29. Sectional view of single type master cylinder (Section 18)

FIG. 9.30. LOCATION AND CONNECTIONS – DUAL HYDRAULIC CIRCUIT PRESSURE DIFFERENTIAL SWITCH (SECTION 19)

1	Left hand front brake pipeline	3	from master cylinder (rear circuit)
2	from master cylinder (front circuit)	4	to rear brakes
		5	to right hand front brake

FIG. 9.31. SECTIONAL VIEW OF PRESSURE DIFFERENTIAL SWITCH (SECTION 19)

1	terminal	3	piston assembly
2	hydraulic pipe	4	spring

FIG. 9.32. BRAKE PEDAL AND STOP LAMP SWITCH CONNECTIONS (SECTION 20)

1	stop lamp switch	4	clevis pin
2	locknut	5	master cylinder pushrod
3	pedal arm	6	cross shaft nut

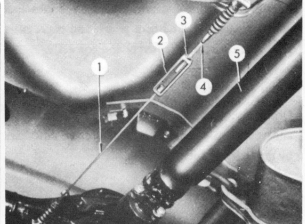

FIG. 9.33. LOCATION OF THE HANDBRAKE CABLE ADJUSTER (SECTION 21)

1	rear cable	4	front cable
2	turnbuckle	5	propeller shaft
3	locknut		

as described in Section 20. Bleed the hydraulic system as described in Section 3.

17 Master cylinder - dual braking circuit - removal and refitting

1 The removal and refitting of the tandem master cylinder used on dual braking circuits is similar to that described in the preceding Section for single master cylinders.
2 Note that there are two fluid outlet unions and pipes, one to supply the rear hydraulic circuit and one to supply the front circuit.

18 Master cylinders - dismantling, servicing, reassembly

1 The procedure for dismantling, servicing and reassembly of both the single and tandem type master cylinders is similar. Both types of unit will be described in this Section and the operations will generally apply if reference is made to the appropriate illustration for the location of internal seals and components.
2 Drain the hydraulic fluid from the reservoir and expel the fluid remaining in the cylinder bodies by actuating the push rod.
3 Unscrew and remove the stop bolt from the base of the cylinder body (tandem type only).
4 Peel back the rubber dust cover from the end of the cylinder body, extract the now exposed circlip and withdraw the stop washer and push rod assembly.
5 With tandem master cylinders, remove the primary piston assembly, the secondary piston assembly and the return spring. If these components are difficult to extract from the cylinder body, either tap the unit on a piece of wood or apply pressure from a tyre pump to one of the fluid outlet ports (holding the other closed with the finger).
6 Remove the valve caps and valve assemblies.
7 With single type master cylinders, removal of the internal components is similar to that described for tandem units but only one piston assembly is used.
8 Clean all components in methylated spirit or hydraulic fluid. Examine the cylinder bores for scoring or bright wear areas. If these are evident, renew the master cylinder complete.
9 Obtain the appropriate repair kit. It is essential that the correct kit for the make of cylinder is obtained, either NABCO or TOKICO. They are not interchangeable. If the piston seals have deteriorated, do not attempt to remove them but renew the piston as an assembly.
10 Do not remove the fluid reservoirs unless essential.
11 Assemble the internal components into the master cylinder body in the reverse order to dismantling. Dip each part in clean hydraulic fluid before assembly and use only the fingers to manipulate the rubber seals and cups into the cylinder bore. With tandem type master cylinders, tighten the valve caps to between 18 and 25 lb/ft tightening torque and the stop bolt to 2 lb/ft.

19 Dual circuit pressure differential switch

1 With dual circuit hydraulic braking systems, a switch is fitted to the engine rear bulkhead to monitor any drop in pressure in either of the circuits. It also serves as a handbrake 'ON' warning device.
2 The switch is essentially a piston which is kept in balance when the pressure in the front and rear hydraulic circuits is equal. Should a leak occur in either circuit then the piston is displaced by the greater pressure existing in the non-leaking circuit and makes an electrical contact to illuminate a warning lamp on the vehicle facia.
3 In the event of the warning lamp coming on, check immediately to establish the source of fluid leakage. This may be in the rigid or flexible pipes or more likely, at the wheel operating cylinders, master cylinder or caliper units.
4 When the faulty component has been repaired or renewed,

bleed the brakes as described in Section 3 of this Chapter when the pressure differential switch piston will automatically return to its 'in balance' position.
5 In the event of a fault developing in the switch itself, renew it as an assembly.

20 Foot brake pedal and stop lamp switch - adjustment

1 The foot brake pedal is attached to a common cross shaft with the clutch pedal. Removal and refitting of the pedal arm is described in Chapter 5.
2 The height of the brake pedal must be checked and adjusted if necessary whenever the master cylinder or pedal assembly have been removed and refitted.
3 Loosen the locknut on the pedal arm stop bolt and screw the bolt free from contact with the pedal arm.
4 Measure the distance between the inclined slope of the floorboard and the top surface of the pedal pad. This should be 5.65 in. If the dimension varies from this, add or remove shims between the master cylinder mounting face and the engine rear bulkhead. Ensure that the upper and lower half shim packs are of equal thickness (availability 0.0197 - 0.0315 - 0.0630 in).
5 When this basic setting is correct, screw the pedal arm stop bolt down to reduce the floorboard to pedal pad top surface dimension to 5.57 in. Tighten the locknut. Correct pedal free movement is between ¼ and ½ in.
6 The stop lamp switch is located on the reverse side of the pedal arm stop bolt bracket. It is operated by a spring loaded plunger operating immediately the foot brake pedal is depressed. Any fine adjustment which may be required is carried out by loosening the locknut and moving the switch body nearer or further from the bracket as necessary.

21 Handbrake - adjustment

1 The handbrake is adjusted automatically whenever the rear brake shoes are adjusted. However, due to cable stretch, additional adjustment may be required when the handbrake lever can be pulled more than six notches (clicks) to the full-on position.
2 Carry out the adjustment by slackening the locknut on the turnbuckle which is located above the propeller shaft and joins the handbrake cable sections together. Rotate the turnbuckle sufficiently to bring the handbrake lever movement within that specified and tighten the locknut.
3 Jack up the rear road wheels and check that the rear brake shoes do not bind when the handbrake is fully off.

22 Handbrake mechanism - removal and refitting

1 Separate the front and rear cables by unscrewing the turnbuckle which is located above the propeller shaft.
2 Detach the locking plate from beneath the vehicle at the point where the cable enters the interior.
3 From inside the vehicle remove the cable clip, the handbrake lever shroud and unbolt the lever from the floor. Withdraw the handbrake lever assembly complete with cable.
4 Detach the flexible cable support from its bracket on the rear axle, remove the lockplate and disconnect the cable.
5 Unscrew the locknut on the flexible support and slide the rubber dust excluder, nut washer and bracket plate down the cable. These may be removed once the cables are detached from the wheel cylinder operating levers at the rear wheel backplates.
6 Check the cables for chafing or corrosion and the handbrake lever ratchet for wear. Renew as necessary.
7 Reassembly is a reversal of dismantling. Apply a small quantity of grease to the handbrake lever ratchet and to the threads of the turnbuckle to prevent corrosion. Use new split pins in the clevises which connect the cable end fittings to the wheel cylinder operating levers and apply a drop of oil to the

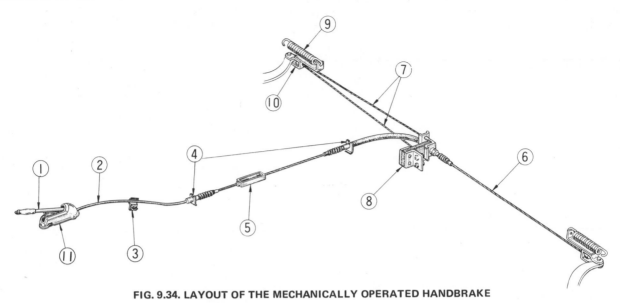

FIG. 9.34. LAYOUT OF THE MECHANICALLY OPERATED HANDBRAKE

1 handbrake lever	4 lock plate	6 cable	9 return spring
2 cable	5 turnbuckle (cable adjuster	7 cable	10 clevis fork
3 cable clip	and connector)	8 flexible cable support	11 shroud

23 Fault diagnosis

Brake grab
Brake shoe linings or pads not bedded-in
Contaminated with oil or grease
Scored drums or discs

Brake drag
Master cylinder faulty
Brake foot pedal return impeded
Blocked filler cap vent
Seized wheel caliper or cylinder
Incorrect adjustment of handbrake
Weak or broken shoe return springs
Crushed or blocked pipelines

Brake pedal feels hard
Friction surfaces contaminated with oil or grease
Glazed friction material surfaces
Rusty disc surfaces
Seized caliper or wheel cylinder

Excessive pedal travel
Low fluid level in reservoir
Excessive disc run-out
Worn front wheel bearings
System requires bleeding
Worn pads or linings

Pedal creep during sustained application
Fluid leak
Faulty master cylinder

Pedal spongy or springy
System requires bleeding
Perished flexible hose
Loose master cylinder
Cracked brake drum
Linings not bedded-in
Faulty master cylinder

Fall in master cylinder fluid level
Normal disc pad wear
Leak

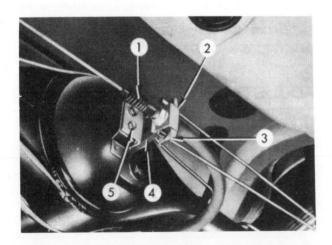

**FIG. 9.35. HANDBRAKE CABLE SUPPORT COMPONENTS
ON REAR AXLE (SECTION 22)**

1 convoluted dust cover	4 flexible support
2 washer	5 securing bolt
3 bracket	

clevis pins.
8 When installation is complete, adjust the handbrake as described in Section 21.

Chapter 10 Electrical system

Contents

General description 1
Battery - removal and refitting 2
Battery - maintenance and inspection 3
Electrolyte replenishment 4
Battery charging 5
Alternator - general description and maintenance 6
Alternator - removal and refitting 7
Alternator - servicing 8
Starter motor - general description 9
Starter motor - removal and refitting 10
Starter motor - dismantling, servicing, reassembly 11
Voltage regulator and cut-out - description, testing,
adjustment 12
Fuses 13
Flasher circuit - fault tracing and rectification 14
Hazard warning lamp circuit - description 15
Headlamp flasher circuit description 16
Headlamp units - removal and refitting 17

Headlamps - adjustment 18
Front indicator and parking lamps - bulb renewal 19
Rear lamp cluster - bulb renewal 20
Side flasher and license plate lamps - bulb
renewal 21
Lighting switch - removal and refitting 22
Direction indicator and headlamp flasher switch -
removal and refitting 23
Horns - description and adjustment 24
Combined ignition switch and steering column lock -
removal and refitting 25
Anti-theft device - removal and refitting 26
Windscreen wiper and washer - description and maintenance 27
Wiper mechanism - removal and refitting 28
Instrument panel - removal and refitting 29
Front seat belt switches 30
Heated rear window 31
Fault diagnosis 32

Specifications

Electrical system

Battery type	Hitachi
Voltage	12
Capacity at 20 hour rate	60 amp/hr
Earth	negative

Alternator

Type	Hitachi LT135 - 13B
Nominal rated output	35 amps
Maximum continuous speed	13500 rpm
Brush length (new)	0.571 in.
Minimum brush length	0.2756 in.
Brush spring tension	0.55 to 0.77 lb

Voltage regulator

Type	Hitachi TL1Z - 37 or TL1Z - 57
Regulating voltage	14.3 to 15.3 volts at 68°F
Core gap	0.024 to 0.040 in.
Point gap	0.012 to 0.016 in.

Cut-out

Release voltage	4.2 to 5.2 at 'N' terminal
Core gap	0.032 to 0.040 in.
Point gap	0.016 to 0.024 in.

Fuse box

Type	cartridge
Number of fuses	six
Rating	4 x 15 amp
	2 x 10 amp

Starter motor

	Manual gearbox	Automatic transmission
Make and type	Hitachi S114 - 87M	Hitachi S114 - 156
Type	pre-engaged	
Nominal output	1.0 kw	
Load torque	more than 6.5 lb/ft	more than 7.2 lb/ft
Number of pinion teeth		

Brush length (new) ...	...	...	...	...	...	...	0.630 in.		0.551 in.
Minimum brush length	...	...	...	...	...	...	0.256 in.		0.177 in.
Brush spring tension	...	...	...	...	...	...	3.5 lb		1.8 lb
Drive pinion to stop face gap	...	...	...	...	...		0.0118 to 0.0591 in.	
Solenoid end face to plunger nut dimension		...	...	...			1.248 to 1.272 in.	

Sealed beams and bulbs

							Wattage	Number
Headlamp ...	...	...	...	...	...	...	50/40	6012
Direction indicator and parking	...	...	...	...	...	23/8	1034
Direction indicator side repeater	...	...	...	...	...	8	67
License plate	...	...	...	...	...	...	7.5	89
Tail light and stop	...	...	...	...	...	...	23/8	1034
Direction indicator	...	...	...	...	...	...	23	1073
Reversing	...	...	...	...	...	...	23	1073
Instrument panel	...	...	...	...	...	...	1.7	161 (three)
Wiper/washer control	...	...	...	...	...	3.4	158
Heater control	...	...	...	...	...	...	3.4	57
Ignition warning	...	...	...	...	...	...	1.7	161
Direction indicator warning	...	...	...	...	...	1.7	161 (two)
Headlamp main beam indicator	...	...	...	...	...	1.7	161
Oil pressure warning	...	...	...	...	...	1.7	161
Brake warning	...	...	...	...	...	...	1.7	161
Interior lamp	...	...	...	...	...	...	10	festoon
Clock ...	...	...	...	...	...	...	1.7	161 (two)

Where square faced instruments are fitted, the following type bulbs are used:

							Wattage	Number of bulbs
Instrument panel	...	...	...	...	...	...	3.4	2
Direction indicator warning	...	...	...	...	...	3.4	2
Headlamp main beam indicator	...	...	...	...	...	3.4	1
Ignition warning	...	...	...	...	...	...	3.4	1
Oil pressure	...	...	...	...	...	...	3.4	1
Clock ...	...	...	...	...	...	...	3.4	1

1 General description

The electrical system is of 12 volts, negative earth. The major components comprise a lead acid type battery; an alternator; belt driven from the crankshaft pulley; and a pre-engaged starter motor.

The battery supplies a steady current to the ignition system and for all the electrical accessories. The alternator maintains the charge in the battery and the voltage regulator adjusts the charging rate according to the battery's demands. The cut-out prevents the battery discharging to earth through the alternator when the engine is switched off and current generation stops.

2 Battery - removal and refitting

1 The battery is located at the front on the right hand side of the engine compartment.
2 Disconnect the negative terminal first whenever servicing the battery.
3 Then remove the positive terminal, and remove the battery frame holding-down screws and lift the frame away.
4 Lift out the battery carefully to avoid spilling electrolyte on the paintwork.
5 Replacement is a reversal of removal procedure but when reconnecting the terminals, clean off any white deposits present and smear with petroleum jelly.

3 Battery - maintenance and inspection

1 Keep the top of the battery clean by wiping away dirt and moisture.
2 Remove the plugs or lid from the cells and check that the electrolyte level is just above the separator plates. If the level has fallen, add only distilled water until the electrolyte level is just above the separator plates.
3 As well as keeping the terminals clean and covered with petroleum jelly, the top of the battery, and especially the top of the cells, should be kept clean and dry. This helps prevent corrosion and ensures that the battery does not become partially discharged by leakage through dampness and dirt.
4 Once every three months, remove the battery and inspect the battery securing bolts, the battery clamp plate, tray and battery leads for corrosion (white fluffy deposits on the metal which are brittle to touch). If any corrosion is found, clean off the deposits with ammonia and paint over the clean metal with an anti-rust/anti-acid paint.
5 At the same time inspect the battery case for cracks. If a crack is found, clean and plug it with one of the proprietary compounds marketed by firms, such as Holts, for this purpose. If leakage through the crack has been excessive then it will be necessary to refill the appropriate cell with fresh electrolyte as detailed later. Cracks are frequently caused to the top of the battery cases by pouring in distilled water in the middle of winter AFTER instead of BEFORE a run. This gives the water no chance to mix with the electrolyte and so the former freezes and splits the battery case.
6 If topping up the battery becomes excessive and the case has been inspected for cracks that could cause leakage, but none are found, the battery is being over-charged and the voltage regulator will have to be checked and reset (Section 12).
7 With the battery on the bench at the three monthly interval check, measure its specific gravity with a hydrometer to determine the state of charge and condition of the electrolyte. There should be very little variation between the different cells and if a variation in excess of .025 is present it will be due to either:
a) Loss of electrolyte from the battery at some time caused by spillage or a leak, resulting in a drop in the specific gravity of the electrolyte when the deficiency was replaced with distilled water

instead of fresh electrolyte.

b) An internal short circuit caused by buckling of the plates or a similar malady pointing to the likelihood of total battery failure in the near future.

8   The specific gravity of the electrolyte for fully charged conditions at the electrolyte temperature indicated, is listed in Table A. The specific gravity of a fully charged battery at different temperatures of the electrolyte is given in Table B.

TABLE A

Specific Gravity - Battery Fully Charged

1.268 at 100°F or 38°C electrolyte temperature
1.272 at 90°F or 32°C electrolyte temperature
1.276 at 80°F or 27°C electrolyte temperature
1.280 at 70°F or 21°C electrolyte temperature
1.284 at 60°F or 16°C electrolyte temperature
1.288 at 50°F or 10°C electrolyte temperature
1.292 at 40°F or   4°C electrolyte temperature
1.296 at 30°F or -1.5°C electrolyte temperature

TABLE B

Specific Gravity - Battery Fully Discharged

1.098 at 100°F or 38°C electrolyte temperature
1.102 at 90°F or 32°C electrolyte temperature
1.106 at 80°F or 27°C electrolyte temperature
1.110 at 70°F or 21°C electrolyte temperature
1.114 at 60°F or 16°C electrolyte temperature
1.118 at 50°F or 10°C electrolyte temperature
1.122 at 40°F or   4°C electrolyte temperature
1.126 at 30°F or -1.5°C electrolyte temperature

4   Electrolyte replenishment

1   If the battery is in a fully charged state and one of the cells maintains a specific gravity reading which is .025 or more lower than the others, and a check of each cell has been made with a voltage meter to check for short circuits (a four to seven second test should give a steady reading of between 1.2 to 1.8 volts), then it is likely that electrolyte has been lost from the cell with the low reading at some time.

2   Top up the cell with a solution of 1 part sulphuric acid to 2.5 parts of water. If the cell is already fully topped up draw some electrolyte out of it with a pipette. The total capacity of each cell is ¾ pint.

3   When mixing the sulphuric acid and water NEVER ADD WATER TO SULPHURIC ACID - always pour the acid slowly onto the water in a glass container. IF WATER IS ADDED TO SULPHURIC ACID IT WILL EXPLODE.

4   Continue to top up the cell with the freshly made electrolyte and then recharge the battery and check the hydrometer readings.

5   Battery charging

1   In winter time when heavy demand is placed upon the battery, such as when starting from cold, and much electrical equipment is continually in use, it is a good idea to occasionally have the battery fully charged from an external source at the rate of 3.5 or 4 amps.

2   Continue to charge the battery at this rate until no further rise in specific gravity is noted over a four hour period.

3   Alternatively, a trickle charger charging at the rate of 1.5 amps can be safely used overnight.

4   Specially rapid 'boost' charges which are claimed to restore the power of the battery in 1 to 2 hours are most dangerous as they can cause serious damage to the battery plates.

6   Alternator - general description and maintenance

1   A HITACHI LT 135 - 13B type alternator is fitted.

2   Maintenance consists of occasionally wiping away any dirt or oil which may have collected on the unit.

3   Check the fan belt tension every 3000 miles and adjust as described in Chapter 2 by loosening the mounting bolts. Pull the alternator body away from the engine block, do not use a lever as it will distort the alternator casing.

4   No lubrication is required as the bearings are grease sealed for life.

5   Take extreme care when making circuit connections to a vehicle fitted with an alternator and observe the following. When making connections to the alternator from a battery always match correct polarity. Before using electric-arc welding equipment to repair any part of the vehicle, disconnect the connector from the alternator and disconnect the positive battery terminal. Never start the car with a battery charger connected. Always disconnect both battery leads before using a main charger. If boosting from another battery, always connect in parallel using heavy cable. It is not recommended that testing of an alternator should be undertaken at home due to the testing equipment required and the possibility of damage occurring during testing. It is best left to automotive electrical specialists.

7   Alternator - removal and refitting

1   Loosen the alternator mounting bracket bolts and strap, push the unit towards the engine block sufficiently far to enable the fan belt to be slipped off the alternator pulley.

2   Remove the cable connectors from the alternator and withdraw the mounting bracket bolts. Lift away the alternator.

3   Replacement is a reversal of removal procedure but ensure that the connections are correctly made and that the fan belt is adjusted as described in Chapter 2.

8   Alternator - servicing

1   Servicing operations should be limited to renewal of the brushes. The major components of the alternator should normally last the life of the unit and in the event of failure a factory exchange replacement should be obtained.

2   To renew the brushes, refer to Fig.10.1 and remove the cover securing screws and withdraw the cover. Draw the brush holder forward and withdraw the brushes. Disconnect the brush holder from the terminal only if essential for cleaning.

3   If the brushes are worn to the limit mark inscribed on them (minimum length 0.2756 in) they must be renewed. Insert the new brushes in the holder and check that they slide smoothly. If

Fig. 10.1. Alternator brushes removed (Section 8)

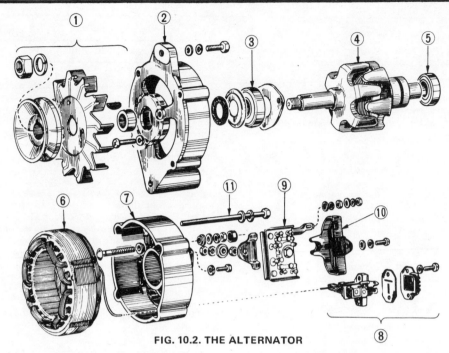

FIG. 10.2. THE ALTERNATOR

1 pulley assembly	4 rotor	7 rear cover	10 diode cover
2 front cover	5 rear bearing	8 brush assembly	11 tie bolt
3 front bearing	6 stator	9 diode plate	

Brush wear limiting line

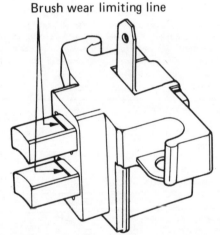

Fig. 10.3. Alternator brush wear limit indicating mark (Section 8)

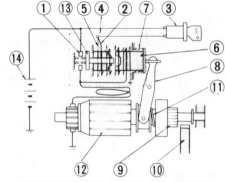

FIG. 10.4. STARTER MOTOR CIRCUIT

1 fixed contact	8 shift fork
2 coil	9 drive pinion
3 ignition switch	10 flywheel ring gear
4 solenoid	11 pinion sleeve spring
5 shunt coil	12 armature
6 plunger	13 moving contact
7 spring	14 battery

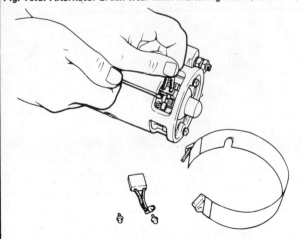

Fig. 10.5. Removing a starter brush (Section 11)

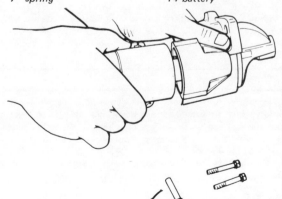

Fig. 10.6. Removing a starter solenoid (Section 11)

there is any tendency to stick clean them with a fuel moistened rag or rub them with a fine file.

4 Check that the brush coil spring contacts are straight and have not been compressed or extended.

5 Refit the brush holder, cover and retaining screws.

9 Starter motor - general description

1 This type of starter motor incorporates a solenoid mounted on top of the starter motor body. When the ignition switch is operated, the solenoid moves the starter drive pinion, through the medium of the shift lever, into engagement with the flywheel starter ring gear. As the solenoid reaches the end of its stroke and with the pinion by now fully engaged with the flywheel ring gear, the fixed and moving contacts close and engage the starter motor to rotate the engine.

This fractional pre-engagement of the starter drive does much to reduce the wear on the flywheel ring gear associated with inertia type starter motors.

10 Starter motor - removal and refitting

1 Disconnect the cable from the battery negative terminal.

2 Disconnect the black and yellow wire from the S terminal on the solenoid and the black cable from the B terminal also on the end cover of the solenoid.

3 Unscrew and remove the two starter motor securing bolts, pull the starter forward, tilt it slightly to clear the motor shaft support from the flywheel ring gear and withdraw it.

4 Refitting is a reversal of removal.

11 Starter motor - dismantling, servicing, reassembly

1 Servicing operations should be limited to renewal of brushes, renewal of the solenoid, the overhaul of the starter drive gear and cleaning the commutator.

2 The major components of the starter should normally last the life of the unit and in the event of failure, a factory exchange replacement should be obtained.

3 The starter fitted to vehicles with automatic transmission is of heavy duty type but the descriptions given in this Section apply to both types.

4 Access to the brushes is obtained by slipping back the cover band. Unscrew and remove the screws which retain the brush lead tags. With an 'L' shaped rod pull aside the brush tension springs and pull the brushes from their holders.

5 Measure the overall length of each of the two brushes and where they are worn below the minimum recommended (see Specifications) renew them.

6 Ensure that each brush slides freely in its holder. If necessary, rub with a fine file and clean any accumulated carbon dust or grease from the holder with a fuel moistened rag.

7 Disconnect the cable which runs from the starter motor to the 'M' terminal on the solenoid cover. Withdraw the split pin and cotter pin from the shift fork and the two solenoid securing bolts. Remove the solenoid rearwards from the starter motor front housing.

8 Refitting a solenoid is a reversal of removal but the length of the plunger must be checked and adjusted if necessary. To do this, depress the plunger fully against a hard surface and measure the distance between the end of the plunger and the face of the solenoid body ('L' in Fig.10.8).

9 Carry out any adjustment by slackening the nut (1) and rotating the pillar nut (2). Retighten the locknut when adjustment is complete.

10 Normally, the commutator may be cleaned by holding a piece of non-fluffy rag moistened with fuel against it as it is rotated by hand. If on inspection, the mica separators are level with the copper segments then they must be undercut by between 0.020 and 0.032 in.

11 Remove the brushes and solenoid as previously described.

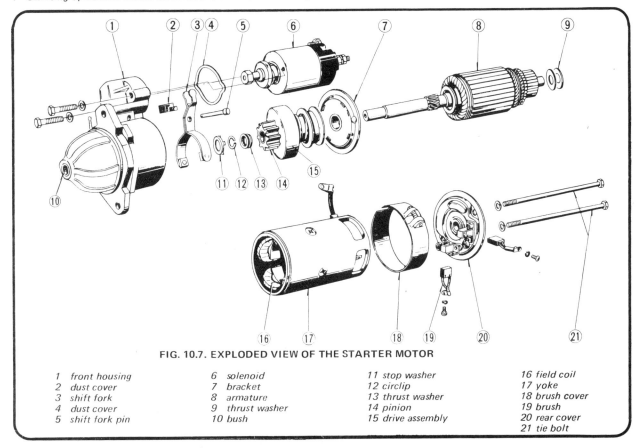

FIG. 10.7. EXPLODED VIEW OF THE STARTER MOTOR

1	front housing	6	solenoid	11	stop washer	16	field coil
2	dust cover	7	bracket	12	circlip	17	yoke
3	shift fork	8	armature	13	thrust washer	18	brush cover
4	dust cover	9	thrust washer	14	pinion	19	brush
5	shift fork pin	10	bush	15	drive assembly	20	rear cover
						21	tie bolt

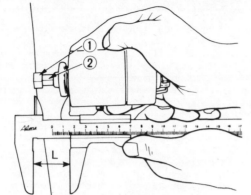

FIG. 10.8. MEASURING STARTER SOLENOID PLUNGER
PROJECTION (SECTION 11)

1 locknut   2 pillar bolt adjuster

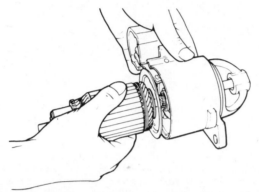

Fig. 10.10. Withdrawing the starter motor armature from the
front housing (Section 11)

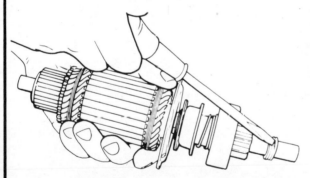

Fig. 10.12. Prising off the starter pinion drive stop washer
(Section 11)

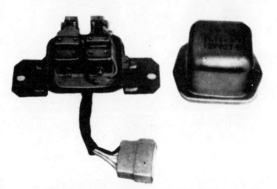

Fig. 10.14. Hitachi type TLIZ-37 voltage regulator (left) and
cut-out (right) (Section 12)

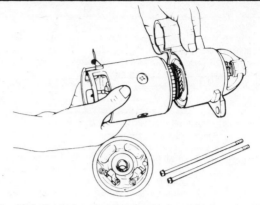

Fig. 10.9. Removing the starter yoke from the front housing
(Section 11)

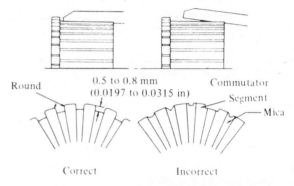

Fig. 10.11. Diagram for undercutting starter commutator
(Section 11)

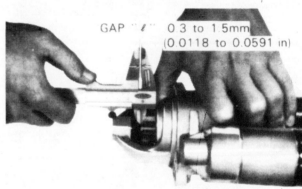

Fig. 10.13. Measuring starter pinion to thrust washer gap
(Section 11)

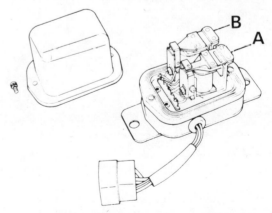

Fig. 10.15. Hitachi type TLIZ-57 voltage regulator (A) and
cut-out (B) (Section 12)

Unscrew and remove the two long bolts which secure the yoke to the front housing. Withdraw the yoke from the front housing, tapping it with a soft faced mallet if necessary to free it. Take great care not to damage the field coils of the yoke by catching them on the armature during removal.

12 Withdraw the armature with shift fork/pinion assembly attached.

13 Undercut the mica separators of the commutator using an old hacksaw blade ground to suit. The commutator may be polished with a piece of very fine glass paper-never use emery cloth as the carborundum particles will become embedded in the copper surfaces.

14 Refit the armature by reversing the removal procedure.

15 In the event of malfunction of pinion drive assembly, remove the armature as previously described in this Section. Prise the stop washer from the armature shaft using a screwdriver, detach the circlip from its groove and slide off the thrust washer, starter pinion and drive assembly.

16 Wash the components of the drive gear in paraffin and inspect for wear or damage, particularly to the pinion teeth and renew as appropriate. Refitting is a reversal of dismantling but stake a new stop washer in position and oil the sliding surfaces of the pinion assembly with a light oil, applied sparingly.

17 When the starter motor has been fully reassembled, actuate the solenoid which will throw the drive gear forward into its normal flywheel engagement position. Do this by connecting jumper leads between the battery negative terminal and the solenoid 'M' terminal and between the battery positive terminal and the soleniod 'S' terminal. Now check the gap between the end face of the drive pinion and the mating face of the thrust washer. This should be between 0.0118 and 0.0591 in measured either with a vernier gauge or feelers.

12 Voltage regulator and cut-out - description, testing, adjustment

1 The regulator and cut-out are located as a combined unit on the forward face of the left hand suspension strut mounting within the engine compartment. Alternative types of unit may be encountered, the Hitachi TL1Z-37 or TL1Z-57 and reference should be made to Figs.10.14, 10.15 to observe the respective positions of the voltage regulator and the cut-out.

2 The voltage regulator controls the output from the alternator depending upon the state of the battery and the demands of the vehicle electrical equipment and it ensures that the battery is not overcharged. The cut-out is virtually an automatic switch which completes the charging circuit as soon as the alternator starts to rotate and isolates it when the engine stops so that the battery cannot be discharged to earth through the alternator. One visual indication of the correct functioning of the cut-out is the ignition warning lamp. When the lamp is out, the system is charging.

3 **Before testing, check that the alternator drive belt is not broken or slack and that all electrical leads are secure.**

4 Test the regulator voltage with the unit still installed in the vehicle. If it has been removed make sure it is positioned with the connector plug hanging downward. Carry out the testing with the engine compartment cold and complete the test within one minute to prevent the regulator heating up and affecting the specified voltage readings.

5 Establish the ambient temperature within the engine compartment, turn off all vehicle electrical equipment and ensure that the battery is in a fully charged state. Connect a good quality ammeter, voltmeter and resistor as shown in Fig.10.16.

6 Start the engine and immediately detach the short circuit wire. Increase the engine speed to 2500 rpm and check the voltmeter reading according to the pre-determined ambient temperature (table Fig.10.17).

7 If the voltage does not conform to that specified, continue to run the engine at 2500 rpm for several minutes and then with the engine idling check that the ammeter reads below 5 amps. If

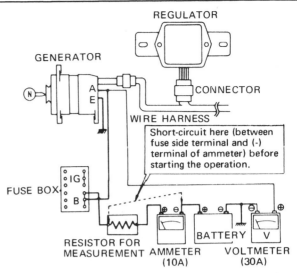

Fig. 10.16. Test circuit for voltage regulator (Section 12)

Ambient temperature [°C (°F)]	Rated regulating voltage (V)
-10 (14)	14.6 to 15.6
0 (32)	14.45 to 15.45
10 (50)	14.3 to 15.3
20 (68)	14.15 to 15.15
30 (86)	14.0 to 15.0
40 (104)	13.85 to 14.85

Fig. 10.17. Voltage regulator temperature/rated voltage table (Section 12)

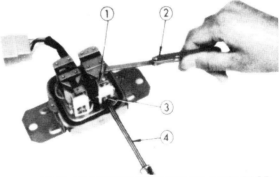

FIG. 10.18. ADJUSTING CORE GAP ON A VOLTAGE REGULATOR (SECTION 12)

1 contacts   *3 adjusting screw*
2 feeler gauge   *4 screwdriver*

the reading is above this, the battery is not fully charged and must be removed for charging as otherwise accurate testing cannot be carried out.

8 Switch off the engine, remove the cover from the voltage regulator and inspect the surfaces of the contacts. If these are rough or pitted, clean them by drawing a strip of fine emery cloth between them.

9 Using feeler gauges, check and adjust the core gap if necessary, to between 0.024 and 0.040 in.

10 Check and adjust the contact point gap if necessary, to between 0.012 and 0.016 in.
11 By now the voltage regulator will have cooled down so that the previous test may be repeated. If the voltage/temperature is still not compatible, switch off the engine and adjust the regulator screw. Do this by loosening the locknut and turning the screw clockwise to increase the voltage reading and anti-clockwise to reduce it.
12 Turn the adjuster screw only fractionally before retesting the voltage charging rate again with the unit cold. Finally tighten the locknut.
13 If the cut-out is operating incorrectly, first check the fan belt and the ignition warning lamp bulb. Connect the positive terminal of a moving coil voltmeter to the 'N' socket of the regulator connecting plug and the voltmeter terminal to earth as shown in Figs.10.21 and 10.22.
14 Start the engine and let it idle. Check the voltmeter reading. If the reading is O volts check for continuity between the N terminals of the regulator unit and the alternator. If the reading is below 5.2 volts and the ignition warning lamp remains on, check and adjust the core gap to between 0.032 and 0.040 in and the points gap to 0.016 and 0.024 in. Remember that this time the adjustments are carried out to the cut-out **not** the voltage regulator although the procedure is similar.
15 If the reading is over 5.2 volts with the ignition warning lamp on and the core and points gap are correctly set, the complete regulator unit must be renewed.
16 The cut-out is operating correctly if the voltmeter shows a reading of more than 5.2 volts (ignition lamp out).

13 Fuses

1 The main fuse box is located under the facia panel to the right of the steering column. It contains four 15 amp cartridge type fuses and two 10 amp. The accessories and circuits protected by the individual fuses are indicated on the fuse box cover.
2 A fusible link is incorporated in the battery to alternator cable as an additional protection for the starting and charging circuits.
3 In the event of a fuse or fusible link blowing, always establish the cause before fitting a new one. This is most likely to be due to faulty insulation somewhere in the wiring circuit. Always carry a spare fuse for each rating and never be tempted to substitute a piece of wire or a nail for the correct fuse or a fire may be caused or, at least, the electrical component ruined.

14 Flasher circuit - fault tracing and rectification

1 The flasher unit is a small metal container located under the dashboard and next to the steering column. The unit is actuated by the direction indicator switch.
2 If the flasher unit fails to operate, or works very slowly or rapidly, check out the flasher indicator circuit as detailed below, before assuming that there is a fault in the unit.
a) Examine the direction indicator bulbs both front and rear for broken filaments.
b) If the external flashers are working but either of the internal flasher warning lights have ceased to function, check the filaments in the warning light bulbs and replace with a new bulb if necessary.
c) If a flasher bulb is sound but does not work check all the flasher circuit connections with the aid of the wiring diagram found at the end of this Chapter.
d) With the ignition switched on check that the current is reaching the flasher unit by connecting a voltmeter between the 'plus' terminal and earth. If it is found that current is reaching the unit connect the two flasher unit terminals together and operate the direction indicator switch. If one of the flasher warning lights comes on this proves that the flasher unit itself is at fault and must be replaced as it is not possible to dismantle

and repair it.

15 Hazard warning lamp circuits - description

1 This system comprises a switch and independent flasher unit. When the switch is actuated, all the direction indicator flashers illuminate simultaneously as a warning to other drivers that the vehicle is stationary due to breakdown.

16 Headlamp flasher circuit - description

1 Irrespective of whether the headlamp switch is off or on, the headlamps may be flashed for signalling purposes by depressing the tapered knob on the end of the direction indicator switch.
2 The circuit for this facility is shown in Fig.10.28.

17 Headlamp units - removal and refitting

1 Sealed beam, double filament units are fitted which in the event of failure must be renewed as units.
2 With coupe models only, remove the grille attachment screws and remove the grille. With all other models unscrew and remove the three headlamp rim screws only and withdraw the rim.
3 Loosen the three screws which secure the retaining ring to the headlamp body, rotate the ring slightly to disengage it from the screw heads and withdraw the ring.
4 Pull the sealed beam unit forward far enough to detach the connecting plug and remove it.
5 Refitting is a reversal of removal but ensure that the word 'TOP' is correctly located.

18 Headlamps - adjustment

1 Although it is preferable to have the headlamps correctly set on modern optical setting equipment, the following procedure will provide a reasonable alternative, carried out in conditions of darkness.
2 Place the vehicle on level ground, (unloaded and with the tyres correctly inflated), square to and 33 ft from a wall or garage door.
3 Make two marks on the wall, each 22 inches either side of the vehicle centre line and 26 inches above the ground.
4 Remove the rims from the headlamps to expose the lateral and vertical adjustment screws.
5 Switch the headlamps to full (main) beam and mask one of the lamps. Adjust the screws of the unmasked lamp until the maximum intensity of the light pattern is centred on the mark on the wall.
6 Mask the lamp which has been adjusted and repeat the operations on the other headlamp. Finally switch off and refit the rims.

19 Front indicator and parking lamps - bulb renewal

1 Remove the two screws which secure the lens and remove the bulbs which are of normal bayonet type.

20 Rear lamp cluster - bulb removal

1 Tail, stop and flasher indicator bulbs are removed from the rear of the lamp cluster without the necessity of withdrawing the lens or lamp unit.
2 Remove the bulb holder by turning it in an anti-clockwise direction and pulling it from the lamp housing. The bulb is fitted by the normal bayonet method.

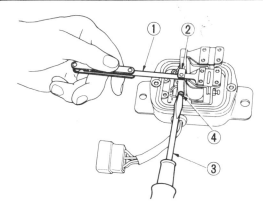

FIG. 10.19. ADJUSTING POINTS GAP ON A VOLTAGE REGULATOR (SECTION 12)

1 feeler gauge   3 screwdriver
2 adjusting screw   4 contact

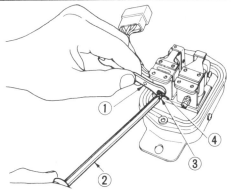

FIG. 10.20. REGULATING THE VOLTAGE LEVEL (SECTION 12)

1 spanner   3 adjusting screw
2 screwdriver   4 locknut

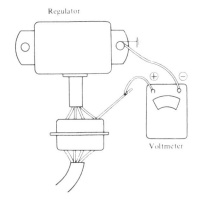

Fig. 10.21. Testing circuit for cut-out (Section 12)

Fig. 10.22. Voltage regulator connecting plug pins showing voltmeter connection for testing of unit (Section 12)

Fig. 10.24. Location of the fusible link (Section 13)

Fig. 10.23. Location of the fuse box (Section 13)

15 A	HEAD LAMP	BATTERY ALTERNATOR	PARK TAIL	10 A
15 A	WIPER WASHER HEATER	IGNITION SWITCH IG	RADIO CIGARETTE ROOM	15 A
10 A	METER REVERSE REGULATOR		HORN STOP HAZARD	15 A

Fig. 10.25. Fuse identification diagram (Section 13)

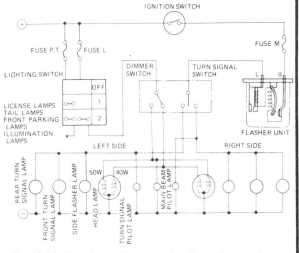

Fig. 10.26. Direction indicator and headlamp dipping circuit diagram (Section 14)

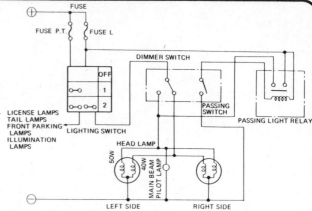

Fig. 10.27. Hazard warning lamp circuit diagram (Section 15)

Fig. 10.28. Headlamp flasher circuit diagram (Section 16)

FIG. 10.29. REMOVING A HEADLAMP SEALED BEAM UNIT (SECTION 17)

1   sealed beam unit   3   retaining ring
2   body   4   adjustment screws

Fig. 10.30. Renewing a front flasher bulb (Section 19)

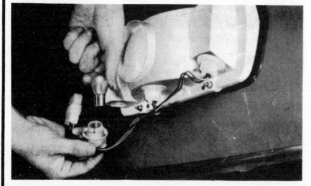

Fig. 10.31. Removing a bulb from a rear lamp cluster (Section 20)

Fig. 10.32. Renewing indicator repeater and license plate bulbs (Section 21)

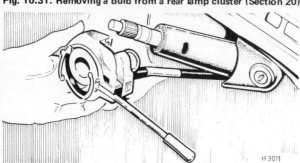

Fig. 10.33. Removing the combined direction indicator and headlamp flasher switch (Section 23)

119

21 Side flasher and license plate lamp - bulb renewal

1 The bulbs of these two units are accessible after removal of the lens securing screws and lens. (Fig.10,32).

22 Lighting switch - removal and refitting

1 Disconnect the cable from the battery negative terminal.
2 Working from behind the instrument panel, disconnect the connector from the lighting switch.
3 From the front of the instrument panel, depress the switch knob and turn the switch assembly anti-clockwise to remove it.
4 Installation of a new switch is a reversal of removal.

23 Direction indicator and headlamp flasher switch - removal and refitting

1 Disconnect the cable from the battery negative terminal.
2 Disconnect the switch by uncoupling the connector on the wiring harness and disconnecting the flasher relay.
3 Remove the horn ring or bar and push-buttons, according to type, by unscrewing the retaining screws from the reverse side.
4 Unscrew the steering wheel retaining nut and remove the steering wheel. If it is tight on its splines, use a suitable puller but protect the plastic surfaces of the steering wheel hub.
5 Unscrew the retaining screws and remove the steering column shroud.
6 Unscrew and remove the switch retaining screws and remove the switch from the steering column.
7 Refitting is a reversal of removal but note the switch locating hole in the steering column.

24 Horns - description and adjustment

1 Twin horns are fitted, adjacent to the radiator grille. Normal maintenance consists of checking the security of the connecting leads.
2 If the horns do not operate at all, check that the fuse has not blown. If the horn switch is working and all leads and connections are secure, then the relay has probably failed and must be tested by substitution of a new unit.
3 If the horns sound continuously then check the horn ring or push-button springs have not broken. If these are satisfactory, renew the relay.
4 Adjustment to the horn note can be made by loosening the locknut and turning the screw located on the back of the horn.

25 Combined ignition switch and steering column lock - removal and refitting

1 The unit is a combined lock and ignition switch, secured by a special clamp with shear-head bolts. A key-operated peg engages in a slot in the inner steering column. In the event of loss of keys without a record having been kept of the number or malfunction of the lock, then it should be removed as follows.
2 Disconnect the battery earth lead and steering column cowl.
3 Disconnect the ignition switch cables.
4 Centre punch each of the centre of the shear-head bolts. Do not remove the countersunk screws.
5 Drill out the centres of the shear-bolt heads.
6 Release the countersunk screws and remove the two halves of the unit.
7 Refitting is carried out by first setting the lock to the 'park' position so that the locking peg is disengaged.
8 Fit the new lock so that its locating tag engages correctly in the steering column hole and insert the shear-head bolts and countersunk screws finger tight at this stage.

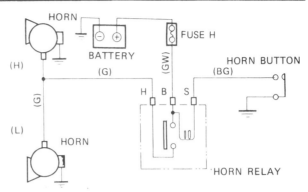
Fig. 10.34. Horn circuit diagram (Section 24)

Fig. 10.35. Adjusting the note of a horn (Section 24)

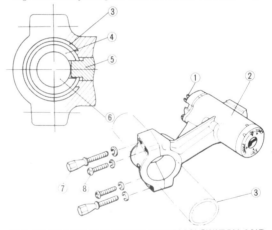
FIG. 10.36. THE COMBINED IGNITION SWITCH AND STEERING COLUMN LOCK (SECTION 25)

1 ignition switch leads
2 lock cylinder
3 steering column
4 collar
5 lock tongue
6 inner steering shaft
7 shear type securing screws
8 locating screws

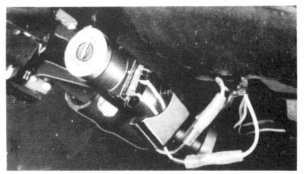
Fig. 10.37. Anti-theft switch and cable connections (Section 26)

9   Check the operation of the lock for smoothness and engagement by inserting the key and if necessary, give the lock unit a slight twist in either direction. When satisfied that the unit is correctly positioned, fully tighten the countersunk screws and tighten the shear-head bolts sufficiently to shear their heads.
10 Reconnect the ignition cable, the battery earth lead and refit the steering column cowl.

26 Anti-theft device - removal and refitting

1   This device may be fitted in conjunction with the combined ignition/steering column lock. The circuit of this warning system is closed when the door is opened and the steering is in the unlocked state. A warning buzzer sounds to indicate unauthorized entry to the vehicle.
2   In the event of failure of components of the system, disconnect the two cables by pulling their connectors apart, remove the cap at the side if the steering lock loosen the two switch securing screws and remove the switch.
3   The buzzer is located on the left hand side and at the rear of the facia panel. The door switch is a push fit in the hinge pillar.

27 Windscreen wiper and washer - description and maintenance

1   The wiper motor is of two speed type. It is mounted on the engine compartment rear bulkhead and drives the wiper arms through linkage located behind the facia panel.
2   The electrically operated windscreen washer unit (motor, tank and pump) is located to the left front of the engine compartment.
3   A combined wiper/washer switch is fitted. The switch operates the wipers by a two position push-pull action and the washer by twisting the switch knob clockwise. The washer knob is spring loaded and it should not be held in the 'ON' position for more than 30 seconds at a time.
4   At two yearly intervals or earlier if the screen is not being wiped effectively, renew the wiper blades.
5   Never operate the washer without liquid being in the tank.

28 Wiper mechanism - removal and refitting

1   Periodically check the wiper linkage for wear and renew as necessary.
2   To remove the linkage, unscrew and remove the nut which secures the wiper motor arm to the linkage crank, this is located behind the facia inside the vehicle.
3   From outside the vehicle, unscrew and remove the wiper arm securing bolts and lift the wiper arms off their driving shafts.
4   In the event of failure of the wiper motor, check for a blown fuse and security of electrical leads.
5   The wiper motor may be removed by first detaching the electrical connector from it and unscrewing and removing the three mounting bolts. It is recommended that the wiper motor is exchanged for a factory reconditioned unit rather than attempt to repair a faulty assembly.
6   Refitting is a reversal of removal but when fitting the wiper arms ensure that they are positioned as shown in Fig.10.39 when the motor is in the 'OFF' (parked position) before tightening the securing bolts.

29 Instrument panel - removal and refitting

1   This Section describes the removal of the instrument panel. Removal of the major facia panel assembly is described in Chapter 12.
2   Disconnect the cable from the battery negative terminal.
3   Push in and turn anti-clockwise each of the following switches to remove them and their escutcheon discs: the lighting

Fig. 10.38. Location of the wiper motor (Section 28)

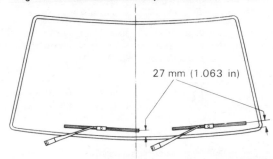

27 mm (1.063 in)

Fig. 10.39. Wiper arm fitting diagram (motor in parked position) (Section 28)

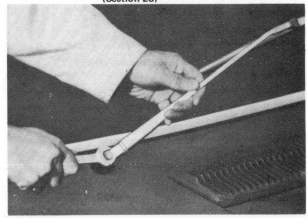

Fig. 10.40. Tightening a wiper arm to its driving spindle (Section 28)

Fig. 10.41. The instrument panel viewed from both sides (Section 29)

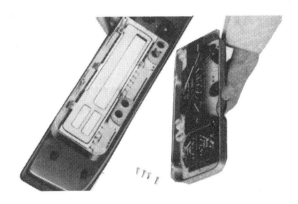

Fig. 10.42. Removing the instrument sub-assembly (Section 29)

Fig. 10.43. Removing the speedometer from the instrument sub-assembly (Section 29)

switch, the windscreen wiper switch, the cigarette lighter (if fitted) and the choke knob.

4 Insert the hand into the rear of the instrument panel and disconnect the cigarette lighter cable and remove the lighter switch completely.

5 Remove the radio and heater control knobs which are secured to their shafts and levers by grub screws.

6 Remove the shroud from the steering column.

7 Unscrew and remove the six screws which secure the instrument panel to the main facia.

8 Pull the instrument panel forward sufficiently to enable the speedometer cable to be disconnected from the speedometer head and the twelve pin electrical connecting plug and socket to be separated. Withdraw the instrument panel.

9 The instrumentation is secured to the rear of the panel by four screws and individual instruments may be removed from this sub assembly after unscrewing the small retaining screws.

10 Indicator/warning lamp holders are now accessible and may be withdrawn tor bulb renewal simply by pulling them from their sockets.

11 Refitting the instruments and panel is a reversal of removal.

30 Front seat belt switches

1 On vehicles operating in certain territories, a contact switch is incorporated in each front seat. Its purpose is to prevent the starting of the engine by means of an inhibitor switch and to illuminate a warning sign in the vehicle interior unless with the weight of a passenger sitting in a seat the safety belt is securely fastened.

2 The seat switches should be adjusted so that (using a test bulb) a weight of 24 lbs placed on a seat will close the switch contacts.

31 Heated rear window

1 Fitted as an option, the heater element is controlled by a switch and indicator lamp fitted under the left hand edge of the facia panel. The system is wired in conjunction with the ignition switch to prevent the heater being left on when the vehicle is parked.

2 The electric supply cable is routed on the floor inside the vehicle and on the nearside. A break in the heating element can be repaired by your Datsun dealer using conductive silver composition (Dupont 4817) without the expense of a new rear window being incurred.

Fault diagnosis appears on next page

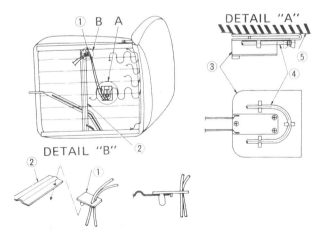

FIG. 10.44. DETAILS OF THE SEAT BELT SWITCH (SECTION 30)

1 clip
2 bar
3 switch
4 cushion spring
5 cushion pad

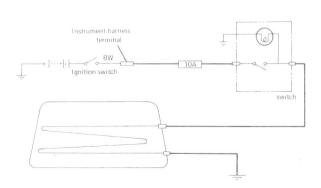

Fig. 10. 45. Circuit diagram for heated rear window (Section 31)

32   Fault diagnosis

Symptom	Reason/s	Remedy
STARTER MOTOR FAILS TO TURN ENGINE		
No electricity at starter motor	Battery discharged	Charge battery.
	Battery defective internally	Fit new battery.
	Battery terminal leads loose or earth lead not securely attached to body	Check and tighten leads.
	Loose or broken connections in starter motor circuit	Check all connections and tighten any that are loose.
	Starter motor switch or solenoid faulty	Test and replace faulty components with new.
Electricity at starter motor: faulty motor	Starter motor pinion jammed in mesh with flywheel gear ring	Remove motor, free drive and clean.
	Starter brushes badly worn, sticking, or brush wires loose	Examine brushes, replace as necessary, tighten down brush wires.
	Commutator dirty, worn or burnt	Clean commutator, recut if badly burnt.
	Starter motor armature faulty	Overhaul starter motor, fit new armature.
	Field coils earthed	Exchange starter motor.
STARTER MOTOR TURNS ENGINE VERY SLOWLY		
Electrical defects	Battery in discharged condition	Charge battery.
	Starter brushes badly worn, sticking, or brush wires loose	Examine brushes, replace as necessary, tighten down brush wires.
	Loose wires in starter motor circuit	Check wiring and tighten as necessary.
STARTER MOTOR OPERATES WITHOUT TURNING ENGINE		
Dirt or oil on drive gear	Starter motor pinion sticking on the screwed sleeve	Remove starter motor, clean starter motor drive.
Mechanical damage	Pinion or flywheel gear teeth broken or worn	Fit new gear ring to flywheel and, new pinion to starter motor drive.
STARTER MOTOR NOISY OR EXCESSIVELY ROUGH ENGAGEMENT		
Lack of attention or mechanical damage	Pinion or flywheel gear teeth broken or worn	Fit new gear teeth to flywheel, or new pinion to starter motor drive.
	Starter drive main spring broken	Dismantle and fit new main spring.
	Starter motor retaining bolts loose	Tighten starter motor securing bolts. Fit new spring washer if necessary.
BATTERY WILL NOT HOLD CHARGE FOR MORE THAN A FEW DAYS		
Wear or damage	Battery defective internally	Remove and fit new battery.
	Electrolyte level too low or electrolyte too weak due to leakage	Top up electrolyte level to just above plates.
	Plate separators no longer fully effective	Remove and fit new battery.
	Battery plates severely sulphated	Remove and fit new battery.
Insufficient current flow to keep battery charged	Battery plates severely sulphated	Remove and fit new battery.
	Fan belt slipping	Check belt for wear, replace if necessary, and tighten.
	Battery terminal connections loose or corroded	Check terminals for tightness and remove all corrosion.
	Alternator not charging	Remove and overhaul.
	Short in lighting circuit causing continual battery drain	Trace and rectify.
	Regulator unit nor working correctly	Check setting, clean and renew if defective.
IGNITION LIGHT FAILS TO GO OUT, BATTERY RUNS FLAT IN A FEW DAYS		
Alternator not charging	Fan belt loose and slipping or broken	Check, replace and tighten as necessary.
	Brushes worn, sticking, broken or dirty	Examine, clean or replace brushes as necessary.
	Brush springs weak or broken	Examine and test. Repla ce as necessary.
	Commutator dirty, greasy, worn or burnt	Clean commutator and undercut segment separators.
	Alternator field coils burnt, open, or shorted	Remove and fit rebuilt unit.
	Commutator worn	Remove and fit rebuilt unit.
	Pole pieces very loose	Remove and fit rebuilt unit.
Regulator or cut-out fails to work correctly	Regulator incorrectly set	Adjust regulator correctly.
	Cut-out incorrectly set	Adjust cut-out correctly.
	Open circuit in wiring of cut-out and regulator unit	Remove, examine, and renew as necessary.

Failure of individual electrical equipment to function correctly is dealt with alphabetically, item by item, under the headings listed below:

Symptom	Reason/s	Remedy
	HORN	
Horn operates all the time	Horn push either earthed or stuck down	Disconnect battery earth. Check and rectify source of trouble.
	Horn cable to horn push earthed	Disconnect battery earth. Check and rectify source of trouble.
Horn fails to operate	Blown fuse	Check and renew if broken. Ascertain cause.
	Cable or cable connection loose, broken or disconnected	Check all connections for tightness and cables for breaks.
	Horn has an internal fault	Remove and overhaul horn.
Horn emits intermittent or unsatisfactory noise	Cable connections loose	Check and tighten all connections.
	Horn incorrectly adjusted	Adjust horn until best note obtained.
	LIGHTS	
Lights do not come on	If engine not running, battery discharged	Push-start car, charge battery.
	Light bulb filament burnt out or bulbs broken	Test bulbs in live bulb holders.
	Wire connections loose, disconnected or broken	Check all connections for tightness and wire cable for breaks.
	Light switch shorting or otherwise faulty	By-pass light switch to ascertain if fault is in switch and fit new switch as appropriate.
Lights come on but fade out	If engine not running battery discharged	Push-start car, and charge battery.
	Light bulb filament burnt out or bulbs or sealed beam units broken	Test bulbs in live bulb holder, renew sealed beam units.
	Wire connections loose, disconnected or broken	Check all connections for tightness and wire cable for breaks.
	Light switch shorting or otherwise faulty	By-pass light switch to ascertain if fault is in switch and fit new switch as appropriate.
Lights give very poor illumination	Lamp glasses dirty	Clean glasses.
	Lamps badly out of adjustment	Adjust lamps correctly.
Lights work erratically - flashing on and off, especially over bumps	Battery terminals or earth connection loose	Tighten battery terminals and earth connection.
	Lights not earthing properly	Examine and rectify.
	Contacts in light switch faulty	By-pass light switch to ascertain if fault is in switch and fit new switch as appropriate.
	WIPERS	
Wiper motor fails to work	Blown fuse	Check and replace fuse if necessary.
	Wire connections loose, disconnected, or broken	Check wiper wiring. Tighten loose connections.
	Brushes badly worn	Renew wiper motor.
	Armature worn or faulty	Renew wiper motor.
	Field coils faulty	Renew wiper motor.
Wiper motor works very slowly and takes excessive current	Commutator dirty, greasy or burnt	Renew wiper motor.
	Armature bearings dirty or unaligned	Renew wiper motor.
	Armature badly worn or faulty	Renew wiper motor.
Wiper motor works slowly and takes little current	Brushes badly worn	Renew.
	Commutator dirty, greasy or burnt	Clean.
	Armature badly worn or faulty	Renew wiper motor.
Wiper motor works but wiper blades remain static	Wiper motor gearbox parts badly worn	Renew wiper motor.

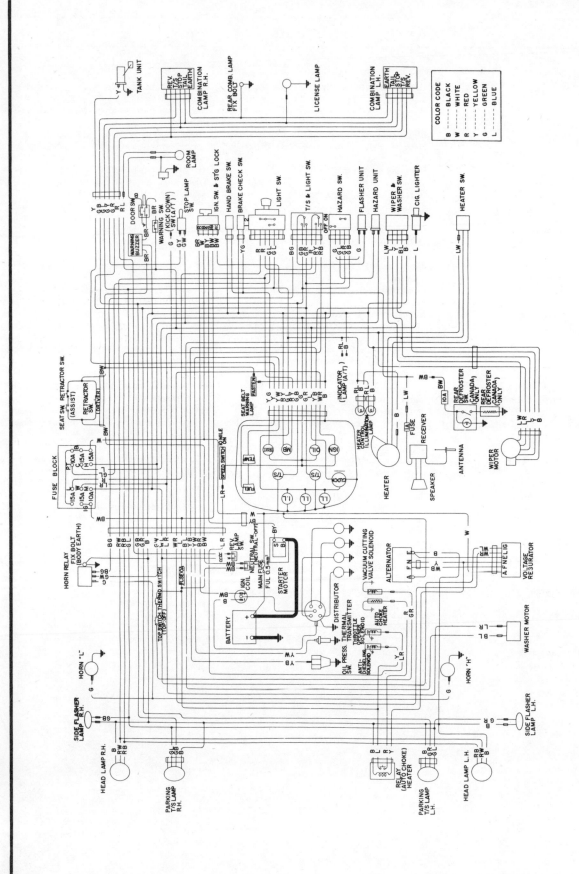

Wiring diagram - manual transmission

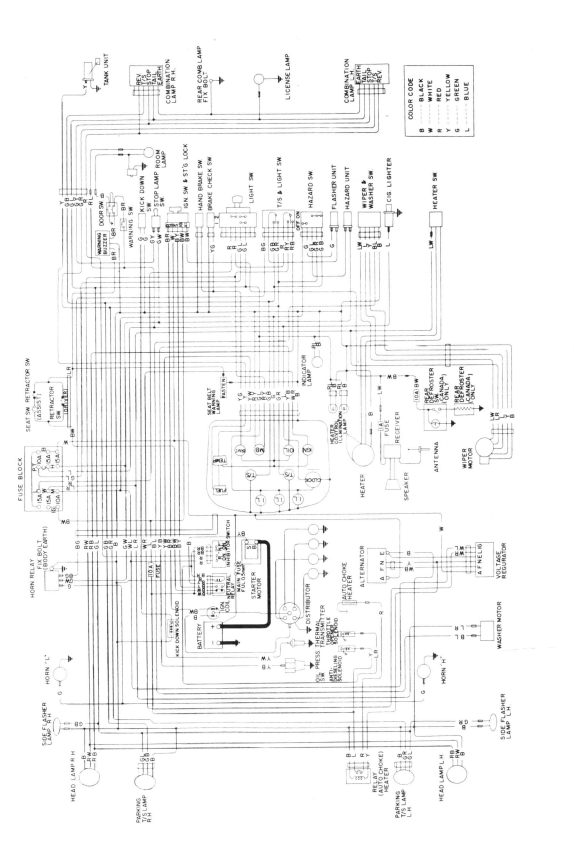

Wiring diagram - automatic transmission

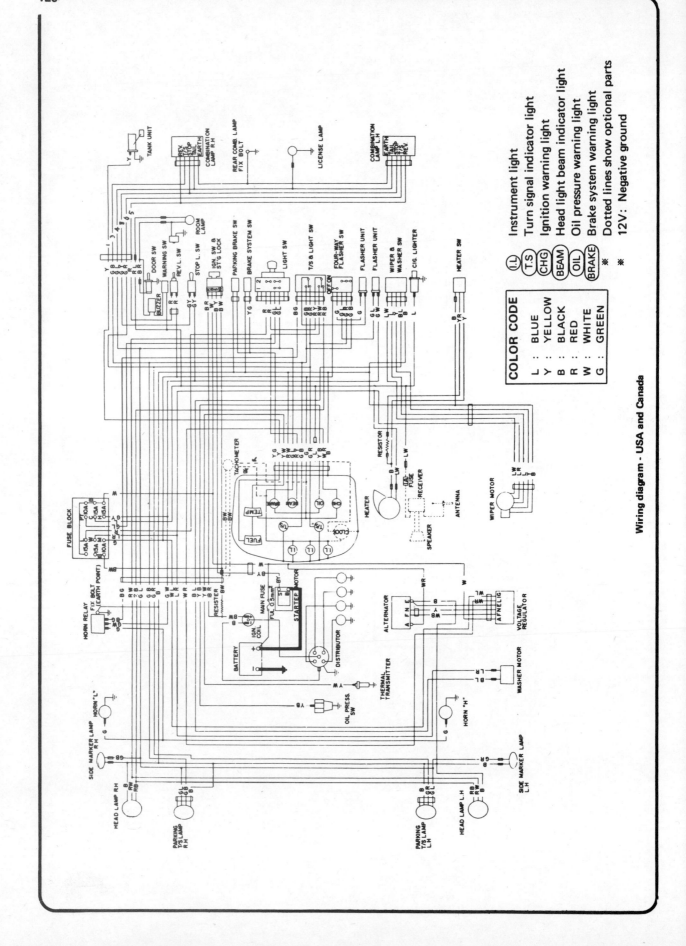

Wiring diagram - USA and Canada

Chapter 11 Suspension, and steering

Contents

General description 1
Maintenance and inspection 2
Suspension components - inspection for wear 3
Stabiliser bar - removal and refitting 4
Track control arm and ball joint - removal and refitting ... 5
Front suspension struts - removal and refitting ... 6
Front crossmember - removal and refitting 7
Complete front suspension assembly - removal and
installation 8
Front wheel bearings - adjustment 9
Front wheel hub and bearings - removal and refitting ... 10

Rear road springs and shock absorbers - removal,
servicing, refitting 11
Steering gear and linkage - inspection 12
Steering linkage and ball joints - removal and
refitting 13
Steering idler - servicing 14
Steering gear - removal and refitting 15
Steering gear - dismantling, servicing, reassembly ... 16
Steering lock stop bolts - adjustment 17
Front wheel alignment 18
Fault diagnosis 19

Specifications

Front suspension ... ... Independent by Macpherson strut, with stabiliser bar
   Shock absorbers ... ... hydraulic telescopic, integral with strut
   Springs:
      Number of turns 6.25
      Free length ... ... 13.3 ± 0.394 in.
   Stabiliser bar diameter ... ... 0.669 in.
   Front hub rotational starting torque (at wheel stud) ... ... new bearings 3.5 lb/ft   old bearings 1.5 lb/ft

Rear suspension ... ... Semi-elliptic leaf springs and double acting telescopic hydraulic
     shock absorbers
   Spring:
      Length ... ... 43.7 in.
      Width ... ... 1.97 in.
   Number and thickness of leaves:
      saloon and coupe ... ... 1 x 0.24 in.   2 x 0.28 in.
      estate and van ... ... 2 x 0.24 in. 1 x 0.28 in. 1 x 0.52 in.
   Spring eye diameter ... ... front 1.378 in.   rear 0.906 in.

Steering ... ... Worm and nut, recirculating ball
Ratio ... ... 15.1 : 1
Steering wheel diameter ... ... 15.7 in.
Oil capacity ... ... 3/8 Imp. pint

	Saloon and coupe	Van	Van (Heavy duty Springs)
Camber angle (positive)	5' to 2⁰ 05'	45' to 1⁰ 45'	45' to 1⁰ 45'
Caster angle (positive)	20' to 1⁰ 50'	1⁰ 05' to 2⁰ 05'	40' to 1⁰ 40'
Steering axis inclination	7⁰ 55'	7⁰ 45'	7⁰ 45'
Toe-in	0.16 to 0.24 in.	0.20 to 0.28 in.	0.20 to 0.28 in.

Torque wrench settings   **lb/ft**
   Suspension strut upper support nut ... ... 12 to 16
   Suspension strut piston rod nut ... ... 26 to 33
   Suspension lower swivel to strut bolts ... ... 33 to 44
   Suspension lower swivel ball joint nut ... ... 40 to 54
   Stabiliser bar securing bolts ... ... 7 to 9
   Ball joint to track control arm bolts ... ... 16 to 22
   Track rod ball joint nuts ... ... 28 to 36

					lb/ft
Track control arm pivot bolts (vehicle unloaded)			...	... ·	29 to 36
Front hub nut (initial setting)	...	...	...	...	16 to 17
Idler to body securing bolts	...	...	...	...	14 to 19
Steering box to body securing bolts	...	...	...	...	14 to 19
Steering wheel securing nut	...	...	...	...	22 to 25
Steering column to facia clamp bolts	...	...	...	6 to 7
Steering column to facia (collapsible type end bolts only)		...	11 to 13
Steering column to box flange bolts	...	...	...	11 to 18
Top cover to steering box bolts	...	...	...	...	12 to 20
Rocker shaft adjusting screw locknut	...	...	...	15 to 22
Steering drop arm to rocker shaft nut	...	...	...	100
Idler shaft nut	...	...	...	...	...	41 to 46
Track rod locknuts	...	...	...	...	...	58 to 72
Rear spring 'U' bolts	...	...	...	...	23 to 29
Rear road spring front bracket to body bolts	...	...	12 to 15
Rear road spring shackle pin nuts	...	...	...	12 to 15
Rear road spring shackle pin nuts (van)	...	...	23 to 29
Rear damper upper mounting nuts (van and saloon)	...	...	26 to 33
Rear damper upper mounting nuts (coupe)	...	...	7 to 9
Rear damper lower mounting nuts (van and saloon)	...	...	26 to 33
Rear damper lower mounting nuts (coupe)	...	...	7 to 9

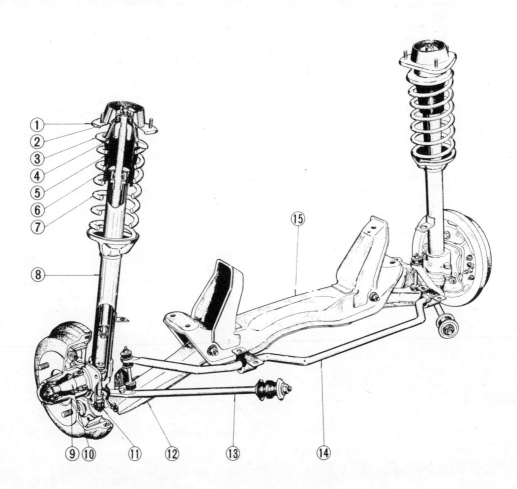

FIG. 11.1. LAYOUT OF THE FRONT SUSPENSION (SECTION 1)

1 mounting insulator	5 dust excluder	9 hub assembly	12 track control arm
2 upper bearing	6 piston rod	10 stub axle	13 radius rod
3 spring seat	7 coil spring	11 lower swivel ball	14 stabiliser bar
4 rubber bump stop	8 strut	joint	15 crossmember

1 General description

The front suspension is of the MacPherson strut type. Each strut is secured at its top end to rubber mounted thrust bearings while the lower end is secured to a swivel joint integral with the track control arm. The strut mounting points are non-adjustable, are set in production and determine the castor, camber and steering axis. Each strut contains an integral direct acting hydraulic shock absorber. Coil springs are mounted externally on the struts and rebound from them is controlled by an in-built stop.

At the lower end of each strut a stub axle carries the hub and brake assembly. The left and right hand struts are not interchangeable. Suspension movement is controlled during vehicle motion by drag links and a stabiliser bar. Fig.11.1 shows the front suspension layout.

Rear suspension is by conventional semi-elliptic leaf springs, the springs being mounted on rubber bushed shackle pins. Telescopic hydraulic shock absorbers are used.

The steering gear is a recirculating ball worm and nut unit which connects to the wheels via a drop arm, a centre track rod, a relay lever and two outer track rods connected to the steering arms on each wheel. 1973 and later models are fitted with a collapsible steering column and shaft.

2 Maintenance and inspection

1 Inspect the condition of all rubber gaiters, ball joint covers for splits or deterioration. Renew as necessary after reference to the appropriate section of this Chapter.
2 Check the security of the locknuts on the outer track rod ends, also the ball pin nuts.
3 Check the security of the front strut securing nuts and examine the condition of the radius rod and stabiliser bar rubber bushes and renew if necessary.
4 Every 30,000 miles, remove, clean, repack and adjust the front hub bearings and check the front wheel alignment (toe-in) as described in Sections 10 and 18 of this Chapter.
5 Every 30,000 miles, remove the threaded plugs from the ball joints, screw in a grease nipple and inject wheel bearing grade grease.
6 Every 10,000 miles, remove the filler plug from the steering box and top up if required with EP 90 grade oil.
7 No maintenance is required for the rear suspension other than periodically checking the security of 'U' bolt and shock absorber mounting bolts and nuts in accordance with the torque wrench settings given in the Specifications.

3 Suspension components - inspection for wear

1 The safety of a car depends more on the steering and suspension than anything else and this is the reason why the compulsory tests made for vehicles over three years old pay attention to the condition of all the steering and suspension components.
2 Have an assistant lift the rear of the vehicle body up and down and check any movement in the top and bottom rear shock absorber mountings. Renew the bushes as necessary.
3 Also check for movement in the road spring shackles and eyes and for a broken or cracked spring leaf and renew as described later in this Chapter.
4 Any sign of oil on the outside of the rear shock absorber bodies will indicate that the seals have started to leak and the units must be renewed as assemblies. Where the shock absorber has failed internally, this is more difficult to detect although rear axle patter or tramp, particularly on uneven road surfaces may provide a clue. When a shock absorber is suspected to have failed, remove it from the vehicle and holding it in a vertical position operate it for the full length of its stroke eight or ten times. Any lack of resistance in either direction will indicate the need for renewal.

5 The front suspension should be checked by first jacking the car up so that the wheel is clear of the ground. Then place another jack under the track control arm near the outer end. When the arm is raised by the jack any movement in the suspension strut ball stud will be apparent. So also will any wear in the inner track control arm bush. The ball joint end float should not exceed .060 in (1.5 mm). However, it is not possible to gauge this movement very accurately without removing the joint so if there is some doubt it is better to be on the safe side and dismantle it. There should be no play of any sort in the track control arm bush.
6 The top end of the suspension unit should have no discernible movement and to check it grip the strut at the lower spring seat and try pushing it from side to side. There should be no detectable movement either between the outer cylinder and the inner piston rod or at the top of the piston rod near the upper mounting.

4 Stabiliser bar - removal and refitting

1 Do not jack up the front of the vehicle but allow the weight of it to remain on the road wheels. Remove the splash shield.
2 Remove the nuts, washers and rubber bushes which retain the ends of the stabiliser bar to the drop links and track control arms.
3 Remove the rubber insulated brackets which secure the stabiliser bar to the bodyframe side members.
4 Withdraw the stabiliser bar and inspect all rubber bushes for deterioration, renewing them as necessary.
5 Refitting is a reversal of removal but note that the white identification mark must be located on the left hand side of the vehicle. Tighten all mounting bolts and nuts to between 7 and 9 lb/ft.

Fig. 11.2. Stabiliser bar attachment bracket (Section 4)

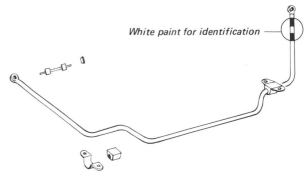

White paint for identification

Fig. 11.3. Stabiliser bar locating mark (Section 4)

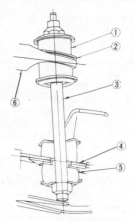

FIG. 11.4. STABILISER BAR AND DROP LINK MOUNTINGS (SECTION 4)

1 rubber bush	4 track control arm
2 washer	5 washer
3 drop link	6 stabiliser bar

Fig. 11.5. Jacking point on chassis crossmember (Section 5)

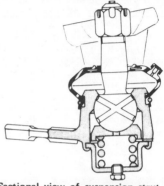

Fig. 11.7. Sectional view of suspension strut lower swivel ball joint (Section 5)

Fig. 11.6. Front and rear attachment points of radius rod (Section 5)

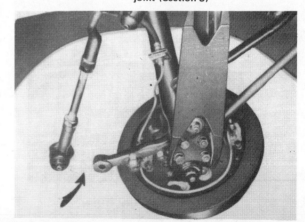

Fig. 11.8. Removing a track rod end ball joint from a steering arm (Section 5)

Fig. 11.9. Suspension strut lower swivel ball joint nuts viewed from both sides of the track control arm (Section 5)

5 Track control arm and ball joint - removal and refitting

1 Remove the stabiliser bar as described in the preceding Section.

2 Jack up the front of the vehicle, under the crossmember and remove the road wheel.

3 Unbolt both ends of the radius rod and remove it.

4 Unscrew and remove the nut from the outer ball joint on the outer track rod. Using a ball joint extractor or two wedges, separate the ball joint from the steering arm. Two club hammers of equal weight may be used to jar the ball joint taper pin from the steering arm eye. They should be used to strike the diametrically opposite edges of the eye simultaneously when the pin will be released.

5 Unscrew and remove the two track control ball joint housing nuts and bolts from the bottom of the suspension strut.

6 Remove the pivot bolt at the inner end of the track control arm and detach the track control arm assembly from the chassis crossmember.

7 Unscrew and remove the securing bolts which hold the ball joint assembly to the outer end of the track control arm.

8 Secure the steering arm portion of the ball joint assembly in a vice, remove the split pin and castellated nut from the ball joint taper pin and separate the ball joint from the steering arm.

9 Clean all the dismantled components in paraffin and examine for cracks. Check the ball joints for up and down movement of the ball pin and if the taper pin moves too easily from side to side, it is worn and must be renewed. Ensure that the rubber dust excluder is not perished or torn. If the rubber bush at the inner end of the track control arm is worn or has deteriorated it must be renewed. A suitable press will be required and the new bush when correctly fitted must protrude equally either side of the arm.

10 Reassembly and refitting is a reversal of removal and dismantling but the following must be observed.

11 Tighten the ball joint to track control arm bolts to a torque of between 16 and 22 lb/ft. Tighten the ball joint castellated nut to a torque of between 40 and 54 lb/ft. Use a new split pin and coat the nut all over with gasket cement to prevent corrosion.

12 Bolt the track control arm ball joint housing to the bottom of the suspension strut tightening the nuts to a torque of between 34 and 44 lb/ft. **Note that the shorter of the two bolts is located at the front of the strut.** Connect the track rod end to the steering arm and tighten the nut to a torque of between 28 and 36 lb/ft. Use a new split pin.

13 Locate the inner end of the track control arm to the crossmember and insert the pivot bolt but only tighten it finger tight at this stage. **Note that the pivot bolt nut is towards the front.**

14 Refit the road wheel, lower the jacks and refit the stabiliser bar as described in Section 4. With the vehicle unloaded, tighten the track control arm pivot bolts to a torque of between 29 and 36 lb/ft.

15 Check the front wheel alignment as described in Section 18.

6 Front suspension struts - removal and refitting

1 The strut assembly may be removed complete with hub, coil road spring and top thrust bearing unit. Removal for left and right hand assemblies is identical.

2 Apply the handbrake and jack up the front of the car, supporting adequately under the body side members.

3 Remove the road wheel from the side to be dismantled.

4 Disconnect the hydraulic pipe from the strut union and plug the fluid lines to prevent the entry of dirt and loss of fluid.

5 Remove the two nuts which secure the steering arm to the foot of the strut and withdraw the arm but allowing it still to be connected to the track rod and track control arm.

6 Remove the lower nut, rubber bushes and washers from the stabiliser bar drop link, through the track control arm.

7 Support the strut at its base and remove the three nuts and washers which secure the upper end of the strut assembly to the

Fig. 11.10. Track control arm to crossmember pivot bolt (Section 5)

Fig. 11.11. Removing the suspension strut lower swivel pin nut (Section 6)

Fig. 11.12. Suspension strut upper mounting nuts (Section 6)

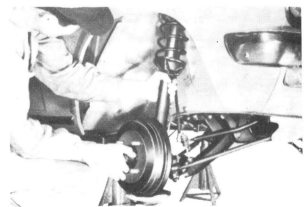
Fig. 11.13. Removing suspension strut assembly from the vehicle (Section 6)

inner wing valance. Do not remove the thrust bearing securing nut which is visible through the hole in the wing valance.

8 Lift the suspension strut assembly from the vehicle and remove the coil spring if required.

9 Using suitable coil spring compressing clamps, compress the coil springs. An alternative method of compressing the coil road springs is to make three clips from ½ inch diameter mild steel bar, of suitable length and with bent-over ends forming hooks, to span three coils of the spring. With the weight of a person on the wing before any dismantling takes place, the clips are slipped over the coils at equidistant points around the spring circumference. Whichever method is used for spring compression, a tough encircling safety strap should be used round the clips or compression after fixing them to the spring.

10 Remove the nut which secures the thrust bearing unit to the strut.

11 Remove the locating washer and bearing unit, push the damper rod into the strut and either gently release the spring compressors (evenly) or remove the coil spring complete with clips for subsequent detachment. The clips can easily be removed if a centrally placed screwed rod with nuts and end plates is used to further compress the coil spring.

12 When suspension struts become damaged, soft or faulty in action then it is recommended that they are renewed as units. The procedure described in this Chapter should be followed for dismantling the hub, brake and other components as the exchange or replacement unit will not include anything over and above the bare telescopic suspension leg.

13 Refitting of the suspension strut is a reversal of removal but the following points must be noted.

14 Check that the coil spring is located in its lower pan as shown in Fig.11.16.

15 Assemble the top bearing components in the sequence shown in Fig.11.17 greasing the area indicated.

16 Tighten the upper mounting nuts to a torque of between 12 and 16 lb/ft. Tighten the piston rod nut to a torque of between 26 and 33 lb/ft.

17 Where a new suspension strut is being installed it should be held vertically before fitting and the piston rod fully extended several times. Repeat the operation holding the strut upside down. This action will bleed the hydraulic fluid of any air which may have collected in the unit during storage.

18 When refitting is complete, bleed the brakes (Chapter 9) and check the front wheel alignment (Section 18).

7 Front crossmember - removal and refitting

1 Jack up the front of the vehicle and place stands under each side of the body side frame members making sure that they will not be in the way when the crossmember is withdrawn later.

2 Remove the road wheels.

3 Unscrew and remove the two track control arm pivot bolts from each side of the crossmember. Detach the track control arms from the crossmember and support them at their inner ends.

4 Using a suitable hoist take the strain of the weight of the engine and then unscrew and remove the upper nuts from the engine mountings.

5 Unscrew and remove the four crossmember securing bolts and lower the crossmember from the vehicle.

6 Check the condition of the engine mounting rubber insulators and renew them if necessary.

7 Refitting is a reversal of removal but tighten the engine mounting nuts to between 7 and 9 lb/ft torque and when the vehicle has been lowered (unloaded) tighten the track control rod pivot bolts to between 29 and 36 lb/ft.

8 Complete front suspension assembly - removal and installation

1 The suspension asssembly may be removed complete where major overhaul is to be carried out or accident damage repaired.

2 Jack up the front of the vehicle and support the body side frame members on stands or blocks.

3 Carry out the operations described in Sections 4,6 and 7 of this Chapter in that order. Note that radius rods are stamped left and right hand.

4 The suspension assembly may then be withdrawn from beneath the vehicle.

5 Installation is a reversal of removal but remember to bleed the brakes and check the front wheel alignment.

9 Front wheel bearings - adjustment

1 Jack up the front of the vehicle. Remove the road wheel. With drum type brakes, remove the drum to prevent shoe drag, with disc brakes, remove the friction pads (Chapter 9).

2 Knock off the cap from the end of the hub, remove the split pin from the castellated nut and wipe it free from grease.

3 Using a torque wrench, tighten the stub axle nut to between 16 and 17 lb/ft. Rotate the hub in both directions and re-check the torque wrench setting. Slacken the nut one flat so that the split pin lines up with the hole in the end of the stub axle. Insert a new split pin but do not bend it over at this stage.

4 If the adjustment is correct, there should be no hub end float and using a spring balance, the force required to rotate the hub should be (i) new bearings 3.5 lbs (ii) old bearings 1.5 lbs with the spring balance connected to a wheel stud. This bearing pre-load should be checked periodically at the intervals specified in the Routine Maintenance section of this manual.

5 When adjustment is correct, bend over the ends of the split pin, fit the cap to the end of the hub, refit the brake drum or disc pads, the roadwheel and lower the vehicle.

10 Front wheel hub and bearings - removal and refitting

a) Drum type front brakes.

1 Jack up the front of the vehicle, remove the road wheel and the brake drum.

b) Disc type front brakes.

1 Jack up the front of the vehicle, remove the road wheel and remove the friction pads. Disconnect the hydraulic brake pipe at the suspension strut bracket and plug the pipe to prevent loss of fluid. Remove the caliper unit as described in Chapter 9.

2 Knock off the cap from the end of the hub, remove the split pin and unscrew and remove the castellated nut and thrust washer.

3 Pull the hub assembly forward and extract the outer roller bearing then pull the unit from the stub axle.

4 Wash all internal grease from the hub using paraffin. If the bearings and seal are in good order, repack the interior of the hub and end cap with wheel bearing grease so that it occupies the area shown in Fig.11.25.

5 If the bearings are worn or damaged, prise out the oil seal from the inner end of the hub and extract the inner roller race. Drift out the inner and outer bearing tracks using a thin rod.

6 Fit the new bearing tracks using a piece of tubing as a drift. If both hubs are being dismantled at the same time, ensure that the bearings are kept as matched sets and do not mix up the races and tracks.

7 Press the new grease seal squarely into the inner end of the hub, with its lip towards the roller bearing.

8 Pack the hub with grease as described in paragraph 4.

9 Refitting is a reversal of removal, adjust the bearing pre-load as described in the preceding section and with disc type brakes, bleed the hydraulic system.

11 Rear road springs and shock absorber - removal, servicing, refitting

1 To renew the rear shock absorber jack up the car under the axle and remove the wheel for ease of access. Then remove the

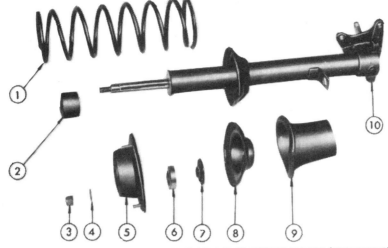

FIG. 11.14. EXTERNAL COMPONENTS OF A SUSPENSION STRUT (SECTION 6)

1 coil spring	3 piston rod nut	5 mounting insulator	8 spring upper seat
2 rubber bump stop	4 washer	6 bearing	9 dust excluder
		7 oil seal	10 strut assembly

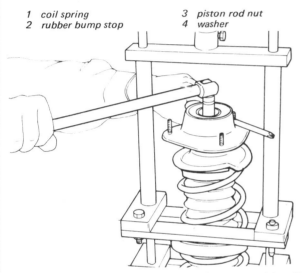

Fig. 11.15. Removing suspension strut piston nut with coil spring compressed (Section 6)

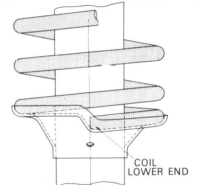

Fig. 11.16. Coil spring correctly located (Section 6)

COIL LOWER END

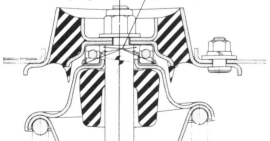

Fig. 11.17. Assembly sequence diagram for suspension strut top mounting (grease points arrowed) (Section 6)

Fig. 11.18. Location of engine mounting bolt (Section 7)

Fig. 11.19. Supporting the weight of the engine prior to cross-member removal (Section 7)

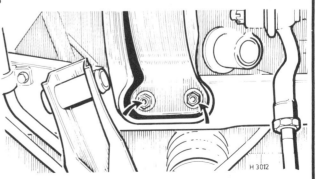

Fig. 11.20. Location of crossmember securing bolts (Section 7)

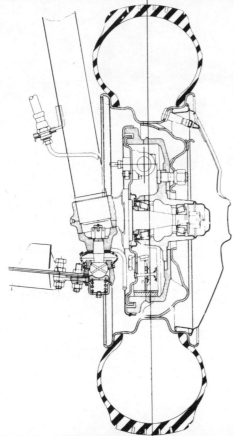

Fig. 11.21. Cross-sectional view of front hub and wheel assembly (Section 9)

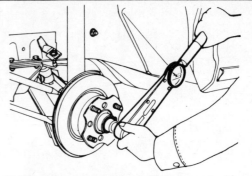

Fig. 11.22. Tightening a front wheel bearing nut with a torque wrench (Section 9)

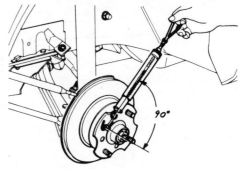

Fig. 11.23. Testing the front hub bearing pre-load (Section 9)

Fig. 11.24. Removing a front hub assembly (Section 10)

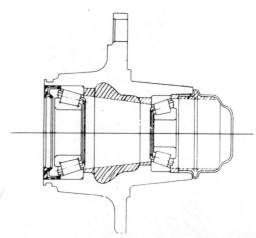

Fig. 11.25. Front hub and bearing grease packing diagram (pack shaded area) (Section 10)

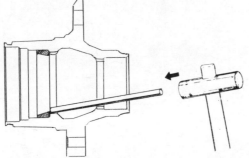

Fig. 11.26. Drifting out a front hub bearing track (Section 10)

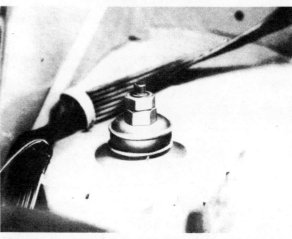

Fig. 11.27. Rear shock absorber upper mounting (Section 11)

lower anchor bolt, nut and lockwasher and pull the bottom of the shock absorber from its location.

2 From inside the boot remove the locknut from the top mounting spindle and then grip the flats on the spindle with a suitable spanner so that the second nut can be undone and removed.

3 The shock absorber may then be taken out from underneath. When refitting make sure first that all the rubber mountings and steel bushes are in good condition. Renew them if necessary. New bushes may come with the shock absorber.

4 To test a shock absorber, hold it vertically by gripping its lower mounting in a vice and push and pull its upper body to the full extent of its stroke ten or twelve times. If there is any lack of resistance in either direction then it must be renewed. it cannot be repaired.

5 The rear springs must be detached either to renew a broken leaf or to renew the mounting bushes at the front or rear. Jack up the car and support it on stands at the rear and then support the axle on a jack at a point away from the spring mountings. Remove the road wheel.

6 Detach the lower end of the shock absorber from the mounting.

7 Thoroughly clean off all the dirt from the 'U' bolts and shackle pins and soak the nuts and threads with a suitable easing fluid such as 'Plus-Gas'.

8 Remove the 'U' bolt nuts and jack up the axle a little way to separate it from the springs.

9 Unscrew and remove the nuts and washers from the front hanger assembly then remove those from the rear shackle. Lift the spring away.

10 A broken spring can be replaced as a complete unit or the individual leaf can be renewed. If the leaf only is being replaced new spring clips, rivets and inserts will be required to reassemble the leaves. A replacement unit can usually be found at a breaker's and this is the simplest and cheapest way to go about it.

11 Examine the condition of the shackle bushes and bolts and renew them if they are worn. Bush renewal is best left to a service sation, but they can be removed and refitted by using a threaded rod, nuts, washers and a tubular distance piece as an extractor.

12 When refitting a road spring, note that the centre bolt is offset toward the front.

13 When refitting the spring to the hangers it is usually easier to fit the front end first. Then replace the shackle pins and bushes. Replace the nuts but do not tighten them yet. Then lower the axle and position it so that it locates correctly onto the spring (and wedge if fitted) and put the 'U' bolts and clamp plate in position. Tighten up the 'U' bolt nuts only moderately.

14 The shock absorber should next be fitted to the lower mountings.

15 The car should then be lowered to the ground, bounced a few times to settle the bushes and then all the nuts tightened to the specified torque.

12 Steering gear and linkage - inspection

1 Wear in the steering gear and linkage is indicated when there is considerable movement in the steering wheel without corresponding movement at the road wheels. Wear is also indicated when the car tends to 'wander' off the line one is trying to steer. There are three main steering 'groups' to examine in such circumstances. These are the wheel bearings, the linkage joints and bushes and the steering box itself.

2 First jack up the front of the car and support it on stands under the side frame members so that both front wheels are clear of the ground.

3 Grip the top and bottom of the wheel and try to rock it. It will not take any great effort to be able to feel any play in the wheel bearing. If this play is very noticeable it would be as well to adjust it straight away as it could confuse further examinations. It is also possible that during this check play may be

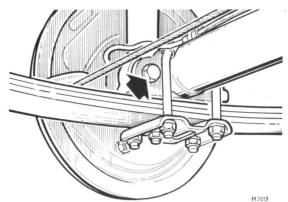
Fig. 11.28. Rear shock absorber lower mounting (Section 11)

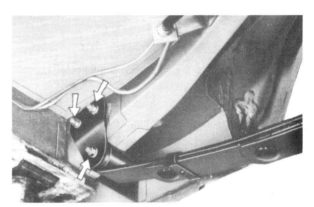
Fig. 11.29. Rear road spring front mounting bracket (Section 11)

Fig. 11.30. Rear road spring rear shackle mounting (Section 11)

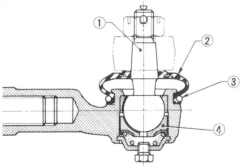
FIG. 11.31. SECTIONAL VIEW OF A TRACK ROD END BALL JOINT (SECTION 12)

1 taper pin
2 dust excluder
3 dust excluder retaining ring
4 sprung seat

discovered also in the lower suspension track control arm ball joint (at the foot of the suspension strut). If this happens the ball joint will need renewal as described in Section 5.

4   Next grip each side of the wheel and try rocking it laterally. Steady pressure will, of course, turn the steering but an alternated back and forth pressure will reveal any loose joint. If some play is felt it would be easier to get assistance from someone so that while one person rocks the wheel from side to side, the other can look at the joints and bushes on the track rods and connections. Excluding the steering box itself there are eight places where the play may occur. The two outer ball joints on the two outer track rods are the most likely, followed by the two inner joints on the same rods where they join the centre track rod. Any play in these means renewal of the ball joint. Next are the two swivel bushes, one at each end of the centre track rod. Finally check the steering box drop arm ball joint and the one on the relay or idler arm which supports the centre track rod on the side opposite the steering box. This unit is bolted to the side frame member and any play calls for renewal of the unit.

5   Finally, the steering box itself is checked. First make sure that the bolts holding the steering box to the side frame member are tight. Then get another person to help examine the mechanism. One should look at, or get hold of, the drop arm at the bottom of the steering box while the other turns the steering wheel a little way from side to side. The amount of lost motion between the steering wheel and the drop arm indicates the degree of wear somewhere in the steering box mechanism. This check should be carried out with the wheels first of all in the straight ahead position and then at nearly full lock on each side. If the play only occurs noticeably in the straight ahead position then the wear is most probably in the worm and/or nut. If it occurs at all positions of the steering then the wear is probably in the rocker shaft bush. An oil leak at this point is another indication of such wear. In either case the steering box will need removal for closer examination and repair.

13 Steering linkage and ball joints - removal and refitting

1   The ball joints on the two outer track rods and the swivel bushes on the centre track rod are all fitted into their respective locations by means of a taper pin into a tapered hole and secured by a self-locking or castellated nut. In the case of the four ball joints (two on each of the outer track rods) they are also screwed onto the rod and held by a locknut. The two other ball joints have left-hand threads.

2   To remove the taper pin first remove the self-locking nut. On occasion the taper pins have been known to simply pull out. More often they are well and truly wedged in position and a clamp or slotted steel wedges may be driven between the ball unit and the arm to which it is attached. Another method is to place the head of a hammer (or other solid metal article) on one side of the hole in the arm into which the pin is fitted. Then hit it smartly with a hammer on the opposite side. This has the effect of squeezing the taper out and usually works, provided one can get a good swing at it.

3   When the taper pin is free, grip the shank of the joint and back off the locknut. Move this locknut just sufficiently to unlock the shank as its position is a guide to fitting the new joint. Then screw the ball joint off the head.

4   It is most important when fitting new ball joints to first ensure that they are screwed on to the rod the same amount and then, before tightening the locknut, that they are correctly angled. So, after connecting everything up and before tightening the locknuts set the steering in the straight ahead position and see that the socket of the ball joint is square with the axis of the ball taper pin. If this is not done the whole joint could be under extreme strain when the steering is on only partial lock.

5   If the centre track rod bushes require that the track rod be renewed then it will be necessary first to detach the inner ball joints of the outer track rods from it. The two swivel joints can then be removed from the drop arm and idler arm respectively and the unit removed.

6   As has been mentioned already any play in the idler arm bush means that the centre track rod should be detached from it and the whole unit unbolted from the side frame and renewed.

7   When any part of the steering linkage is renewed it is advisable to have the alignment of the steering checked at a garage with the proper equipment.

8   Remove the plugs from the ball joints every 30,000 miles and fit a grease nipple to lubricate them. Check the condition of the rubber dust excluders at frequent intervals and renew if necessary.

14 Steering idler - servicing

1   The steering idler is of rubber bushed type and requires no maintenance.

2   In the event of wear developing, disconnect the ball joint at the end of the idler arm, remove the idler shaft nut and withdraw the idler shaft.

3   Remove the old rubber bush and insert the new one using soapy water or brake fluid as a lubricant. Push the idler shaft into the body, refit the thrust washer and tighten the shaft nut to a torque of between 41 and 46 lb/ft.

4   If the idler shaft assembly is removed from the vehicle to carry out the foregoing operations then the bolts which secure it to the bodyframe side members should be tightened to between 14 and 19 lb/ft.

15 Steering gear - removal and refitting

1   Disconnect the cable from the battery negative terminal.

2   Detach the horn ring or push-button assembly from the steering wheel. These are secured by two retaining screws inserted from the reverse side.

3   Unscrew the nut from the top of the steering column and pull off the steering wheel. Use a puller if necessary similar to the one shown in Fig.11.34.

4   Remove the shroud from the steering column.

5   Remove the combined direction indicator and headlamp flasher switch (Chapter 10).

6   If a steering column gearchange is fitted disconnect it at the hand control lever at the gearbox cross shaft.

7   Unscrew and remove the two bolts which secure the steering column to the lower edge of the facia panel.

8   Disconnect the steering box drop arm from the centre track rod by detaching the ball joint.

9   Remove the six bolts which secure the steering column blanking plate to the engine rear bulkhead.

10 Unscrew and remove the three bolts which secure the steering box to the bodyframe.

11 Withdraw the steering assembly through the vehicle interior, manoeuvring the blanking plate and steering box between the brake and clutch pedals. If preferred, the foot pedals may be renewed from their cross shaft to facilitate removal.

12 Refitting is a reversal of removal, tighten all bolts and nuts to their specified torque setting. Reconnect the battery and check the oil level in the steering box.

16 Steering gear - dismantling, servicing, reassembly

1   Secure the steering box securely in a vice. Unscrew and remove the nut which secures the drop arm to the rocker shaft. Mark the drop arm in relation to the rocker shaft splines.

2   Remove the drain plug and drain the oil from the housing. Using a suitable puller, remove the drop arm.

3   Loosen the locknut from the adjusting screw on the top cover and unscrew the adjuster two or three turns.

4   Remove the four top cover securing bolts and remove the cover and gasket.

5   Withdraw the rocker shaft. Remove the circlip from the upper end of the column shaft (collapsible type column only).

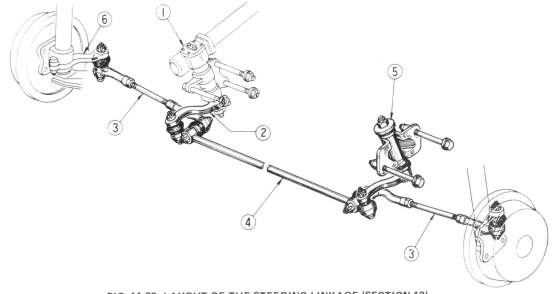

FIG. 11.32. LAYOUT OF THE STEERING LINKAGE (SECTION 12)

1 steering box	3 outer track rod	5 idler
2 drop arm	4 centre track rod	6 steering arm

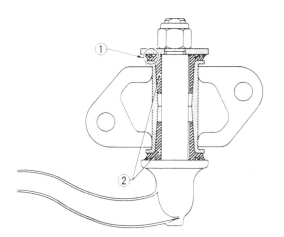

FIG. 11.33. SECTIONAL VIEW OF STEERING IDLER (SECTION 14)

1 seal   2 bush

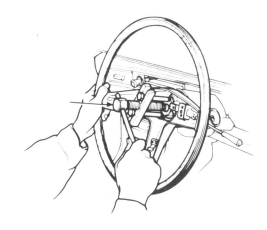

Fig. 11.34. Using a puller to remove a steering wheel (Section 15)

Fig. 11.35. Steering column (non-collapsible) bracket (Section 15)

Fig. 11.36. Steering column blanking plate and retaining screws (Section 15)

138

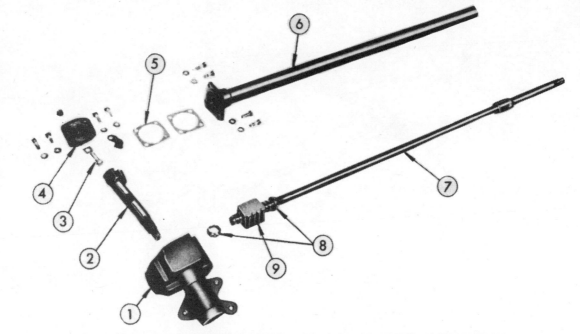

FIG. 11.37. EXPLODED VIEW OF STEERING UNIT (NON-COLLAPSIBLE) (SECTION 15)

1 steering box
2 rocker shaft

3 rocker shaft adjuster
4 top cover

5 shim
6 outer column

7 inner shaft
8 worm
9 nut

Fig. 11.38. Unscrewing a top cover securing bolt (Section 16)

Fig. 11.39. Withdrawing the steering column/shaft assembly (Section 16)

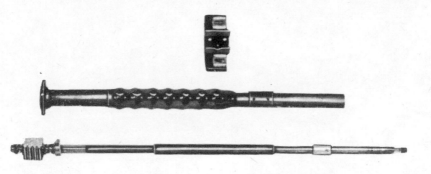

Fig. 11.40. Differing components of collapsible type column assembly (Section 16)

6 Unscrew and remove the four bolts which secure the steering column flange to the steering box. Withdraw the steering column/shaft assembly. During removal do not allow the steering nut to run to either end of the worm.

7 Slide the outer column from the shaft. If a collapsible type steering column is fitted, take great care not to bend or drop it, also ensure that the inner shaft is not compressed from end to end as its telescopic feature is based upon the shear strength of four plastic pins.

8 The steering gear is now completely dismantled into component parts. Inspect the rocker shaft for wear in the splines or to the nut mating surfaces and renew if necessary.

9 Check the worm and nut and bearings for wear. If there is slackness, renew the complete inner shaft, nut and bearings as an assembly.

10 Examine the bush which is located at the top of the steering column. If this is worn and allows side to side movement of the inner shaft, remove the bush and drift in a new one. Grease the bush liberally.

11 Drive the rocker shaft oil seal from the steering box using a suitable drift. Thoroughly clean the inside of the steering box and press a new seal into position.

12 Commence reassembly by securing the steering box in the vice and installing the inner and outer column assembly. Refit the original shims and tighten the column flange bolts to a torque of between 12 and 20 lb/ft.

13 Temporarily fit the steering wheel to the steering shaft and using a spring balance measure the force required to turn the wheel. With the spring balance attached to the steering wheel spoke at a point 8 inches from the centre, the turning effort should be between 4 and 9 ounces. If adjustment is required, remove the column assembly, and vary the shims. These are available in the following thicknesses: 0.0020 - 0.0028 - 0.0031 - 0.0039 - 0.0079 in. The worm, nut and bearings should be lubricated during the foregoing operation.

14 Insert the adjuster bolt in the recess in the top of the rocker shaft. Using a feeler gauge, measure the clearance at its lower frame. The correct clearance is 0.002 in. Use shims to adjust this clearance if necessary, they are available in the following sizes: 0.0596 to 0.0604 - 0.0608 to 0.0616 - 0.0620 to 0.0628 - 0.0632 to 0.0640 - 0.0644 to 0.0652 in.

15 Rotate the steering column shaft until the steering nut is mid way on the worm. Lubricate the steering box components with EP 90 oil and fit the rocker shaft so that its centre tooth engages with the centre groove in the steering nut. Fit the top cover and a new joint gasket and tighten the securing bolts to a torque of between 12 and 20 lb/ft. Fit the locknut to the top cover adjuster bolt but do not tighten it.

16 Refit the drop arm to the rocker shaft, aligning the marks made before removal. Ensure that the drop arm is correctly located with respect to its track rod connecting eye and that the alignment marks are mated with the steering gear control to provide a full lock in either direction for the drop arm. Do not drive the drop arm onto the rocker shaft splines but draw it into position with the rocker shaft nut, which should be tightened to 100 lb/ft.

17 Using the screwdriver slot in the end of the top cover adjuster screw, tighten the screw to between 14 and 22 lb/ft torque so that there is no up and down movement of the rocker shaft and any back lash in the drop arm is barely perceptible. Tighten the adjuster screw locknut and test for smooth movement of the steering gear from lock to lock. If there is stiffness or binding in any position, re-adjust.

18 With collapsible type steering columns, the column upper bush stands proud of the column tube. After fitting the washer and circlip, the end of the steering column must be staked at two points as shown in Fig.11.45. When refitting the collapsible type steering column to the vehicle, note the tightening torque of the upper brackets. This is essential to the in-built telescopic safety action of the design, Fig.11.46.

19 Fill the gear housing with EP 90 oil to the level of the filler plug.

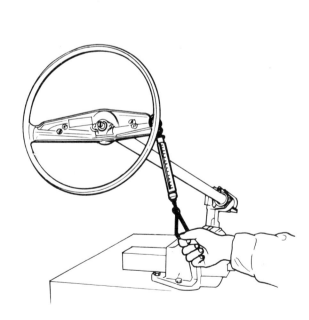

Fig. 11.41. Checking the rotational torque of the steering shaft (Section 16)

Fig. 11.42. Checking adjuster bolt end clearance in the rocker shaft (Section 16)

Fig. 11.43. Adjusting rocker shaft end-float (Section 16)

FIG. 11.44. SECTIONAL VIEW OF STEERING COLUMN TOP
BUSH ASSEMBLY ON COLLAPSIBLE TYPE STEERING
(SECTION 16)

1 outer column
2 washer
3 circlip
4 bush
5 inner shaft

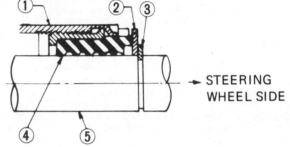

Fig. 11.45. Column top bush staking diagram (collapsible type
assembly)(Section 16)

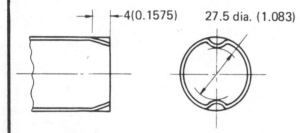

Fig. 11.46. Steering column clamp and bracket tightening
details (collapsible type assembly) (Section 16)

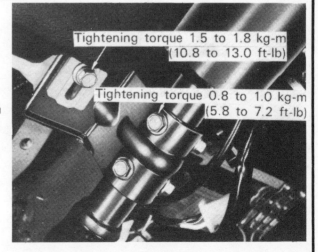

Tightening torque 1.5 to 1.8 kg-m
(10.8 to 13.0 ft-lb)

Tightening torque 0.8 to 1.0 kg-m
(5.8 to 7.2 ft-lb)

17 Steering lock stop bolts - adjustment

1 Turn the steering wheel to full lock with the vehicle on the ground.
2 Measure the clearance between the inside wall of the tyre and the suspension radius rod. If this is other than 1.2 in, adjust the stop bolt on the opposite wheel to provide the specified clearance.
3 Turn the wheels to full opposite lock and repeat the foregoing operations.

18 Front wheel alignment

1 Accurate front wheel alignment is essential for good steering and tyre wear. Before considering the steering angle, check that the tyres are correctly inflated, that the front wheels are not buckled, the hub bearings are not worn or incorrectly adjusted and that the steering linkage is in good order, without slackness or wear at the joints.
2 Wheel alignment consists of four factors:
Camber, which is the angle at which the front wheels are set from the vertical when viewed from the front of the car. Positive camber is the amount (in degrees) that the wheels are tilted outwards at the top from the vertical.
Castor is the right angle between the steering axis and a vertical line when viewed from each side of the car. Positive castor is when the steering axis is inclined rearward.
Steering axis inclination is the angle, when viewed from the front of the car, between the vertical and an imaginary line

drawn between the upper and lower suspension leg pivots.
Toe-in is the amount by which the distance between the front inside edges of the road wheels (measured at hub height) is less than the diametrically opposite distance measured between the rear inside edges of the front road wheels.
3 Due to the need for special gap gauges and correct weighting of the car suspension it is not within the scope of the home mechanic to check steering angles. Front wheel tracking (toe-in) checks are best carried out with modern setting equipment but a reasonably accurate alternative and adjustment procedure may be carried out as follows;
4 Place the car on level ground with the wheels in the straight ahead position.
5 Obtain or make a toe-in gauge. One may be easily made from tubing, cranked to clear the sump and bellhousing, having an adjustable nut and setscrew at one end.
6 With the gauge, measure the distance between the two inner wheel rims at hub height at the front of the wheel.
7 Rotate the road wheel through 180° (half a turn) and measure the distance between the inner wheel rims at hub height at the rear of the wheel. This measurement should be greater by between 0.16 and 0.24 in (saloon and coupe) or 0.020 and 0.28 in (van). This represents the correct toe-in of the front wheels.
8 Where the toe-in is found to be incorrect, slacken the locknuts on each outer track rod and rotate each track rod an equal amount until the correct toe-in is obtained. Tighten the locknuts ensuring that the ball joints are held in the centre of their arc of travel during tightening. If new track rods or ball joints have been fitted, a starting point for adjusting the front wheel alignment is to set each outer track rod so that the distance measured between the ball joint centres (located one at each end of the track rod) is 11.7 in.

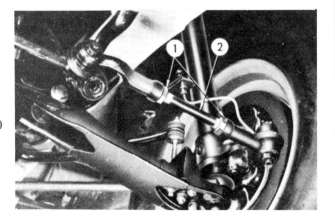

Fig. 11.47. A steering lock stop bolt (Section 17)

FIG. 11.48. AN OUTER TRACK ROD (SECTION 18)

1 locknuts   2 track rod

19   Fault diagnosis

Before diagnosing faults from the following chart, check that any irregularities are not caused by:
1   Binding brakes
2   Incorrect 'mix' of radial and cross-ply tyres
3   Incorrect tyre pressures
4   Misalignment of the body frame

Symptom	Reason/s	Remedy
Steering wheel can be moved considerably before any sign of movement of the wheels is apparent	Wear in the steering linkage gear	Check movement in all joints and steering gear and overhaul and renew as required.
Vehicle difficult to steer in a consistent straight line - wandering	As above Wheel alignment incorrect (indicated by excessive or uneven tyre wear) Front wheel hub bearings loose or worn Worn suspension unit swivel joints	As above Check wheel alignment. Adjust or renew as necessary. Renew as necessary.
Steering stiff and heavy	Incorrect wheel alignment (indicated by excessive or uneven tyre wear) Excessive wear or seizure in one or more of the joints in the steering linkage or suspension unit ball joints Excessive wear in the steering gear unit	Check wheel alignment. Renew as necessary. Adjust if possible or renew.
Wheel wobble and vibration	Road wheels out of balance Road wheels buckled Wheel alignment incorrect Wear in the steering linkage, suspension unit bearings or track control arm bushes Broken front spring	Balance wheels. Check for damage. Check wheel alignment. Check and renew as necessary. Check and renew as necessary.
Excessive pitching and rolling on corners and during braking	Defective shock absorbers and/or broken spring	Check and renew as necessary.

Chapter 12 Bodywork

Contents

General description 1	Rear door lock - removal, refitting, adjustment 11
Maintenance - bodywork and underframe 2	Winding windows - removal and refitting 12
Maintenance - upholstery and carpets 3	Doors - removal, refitting and adjustment 13
Minor body repairs 4	Bonnet and boot lid - hinge and lock adjustment 14
Major body repairs 5	Facia panel - removal and refitting 15
Maintenance - hinges and locks 6	The safety belts 16
Doors - tracing rattles and their rectification 7	Heater and ventilation system - general description 17
Front wing - removal and replacement 8	Heater - removal and refitting 18
Windscreen glass - removal and replacement 9	Heater - inspection and servicing 19
Front door lock - removal, refitting, adjustment 10	Body leaks and their rectification 20

1 General description

The body and underframe is of unitary, all-welded steel construction. The range comprises 2 and 4 door saloons, a 2 door coupe, an estate (and pick-up versions and a van in some territories). The coupe is fitted with tinted safety glass and other models with untinted.

The front wings are of bolt-on detachable type for economy of replacement in the event of accidental damage.

The bonnet is locked from the vehicle interior as are the passenger rear doors. The front doors are locked externally by key.

A front towing bracket is fitted and the rear towing point is at a rear road spring shackle. Two jacking points are located at both sides of the vehicle for which a jack is supplied as original equipment.

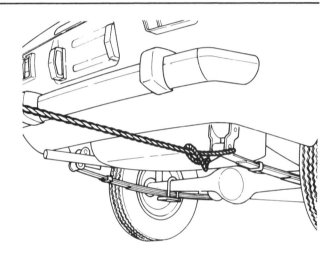

Fig. 12.2. Recommended rear towing point (Section 1)

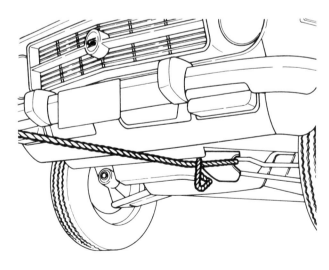

Fig. 12.1. The front towing bracket (Section 1)

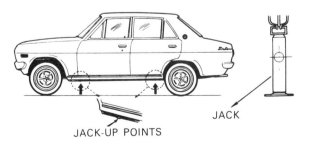

JACK-UP POINTS

JACK

Fig. 12.3. Jacking points (Section 1)

2 Maintenance - bodywork and underframe

1 The general condition of a car's bodywork is the one thing that significantly affects its value. Maintenance is easy but needs to be regular and particular. Neglect, particularly after minor damage, can lead quickly to further deterioration and costly repair bills. It is important also to keep watch on those parts of the car not immediately visible, for instance the underside, inside all the wheel arches and the lower part of the engine compartment.

2 The basic maintenance routine for the bodywork is washing - preferably with a lot of water, from a hose. This will remove all the loose solids which may have stuck to the car. It is important to flush these off in such a way as to prevent grit from scratching the finish.

The wheel arches and underbody need washing in the same way to remove any accumulated mud which will retain moisture and tend to encourage rust. Paradoxically enough, the best time to clean the underbody and wheel arches is in wet weather when the mud is thoroughly wet and soft. In very wet weather the underbody is usually cleaned of large accumulations automatically and this is a good time for inspection.

3 Periodically it is a good idea to have the whole of the underside of the car steam cleaned, engine compartment included, so that a thorough inspection can be carried out to see what minor repairs and renovations are necessary. Steam cleaning is available at many garages and is necessary for removal of accumulation of oily grime which sometimes is allowed to cake thick in certain areas near the engine, gearbox and back axle. If steam facilities are not available, there are one or two excellent grease solvents available which can be brush applied. The dirt can then be simply hosed off.

4 After washing paintwork, wipe off with a chamois leather to give an unspotted clear finish. A coat of clear protective wax polish will give added protection against chemical pollutants in the air. If the paintwork sheen has dulled or oxidised, use a cleaner/polisher combination to restore the brilliance of the shine. This requires a little effort, but is usually caused because regular washing has been neglected. Always check that the door and ventilator opening drain holes and pipes are completely clear so that water can drain out. Bright work should be treated the same way as paintwork. Windscreens and windows can be kept clear of the smeary film which often appears if a little ammonia is added to the water. If they are scratched, a good rub with a proprietary metal polish will often clear them. Never use any form of wax or other body or chromium polish on glass.

3 Maintenance - upholstery and carpets

1 Mats and carpets should be brushed or vacuum cleaned regularly to keep them free of grit. If they are badly stained remove them from the car for scrubbing or sponging and make quite sure they are dry before replacement. Seats and interior trim panels can be kept clean by a wipe over with a damp cloth. If they do become stained (which can be more apparent on light coloured upholstery) use a little liquid detergent and a soft nail brush to scour the grime out of the grain of the material. Do not forget to keep the head lining clean in the same way as the upholstery. When using liquid cleaners inside the car do not over-wet the surfaces being cleaned. Excessive damp could get into the seams and padded interior causing stains, offensive odours or even rot. If the inside of the car gets wet accidentally it is worthwhile taking some trouble to dry it out properly, particularly where carpets are involved. Do NOT leave oil or electric heaters inside the car for this purpose.

4 Minor body repairs

1 A car which does not suffer some minor damage to the bodywork from time to time is the exception rather than the rule. Even presuming the gate post is never scraped or the door opened against a wall or high kerb there is always the likelihood of gravel and grit being thrown up and chipping the surface, particularly at the lower edges of the doors and sills.

2 If the damage is merely a paint scrape which has not reached the metal base, delay is not critical but where bare metal is exposed action must be taken immediately before rust sets in.

3 The average owner will normally keep the following 'first aid' materials available which can give a professional finish for minor jobs:
a) A resin based filler paste
b) Matched paint either for spraying by gun or in an aerosol can
c) Fine cutting paste
d) Medium and fine grade wet and dry abrasive paper

4 Where the damage is superficial (ie not down to the bare metal and not dented) fill the scratch or chip with sufficient filler to smooth the area, rub down with paper and apply the matching paint.

5 Where the bodywork is scratched down to the metal, but not dented, clean the metal surface thoroughly and apply a suitable metal primer first - such as red lead or zinc chromate. Fill up the scratch as necessary with filler and rub down with wet and dry paper. Apply the matching colour paint.

6 If more than one coat of colour is required rub down each coat with cutting paste before applying the next.

7 If the bodywork is dented, first beat out the dent to conform as near as possible to the original contour. Avoid using steel faced hammers - use hard wood mallets or similar and always support the panel being beaten with a hardwood or metal 'dolly'. In areas where severe creasing and buckling has occurred it will be virtually impossible to reform the metal to the original shape. In such instances a decision should be made whether or not to cut out the damaged piece or attempt to recontour over it with filler paste. In large areas where the metal panel is seriously damaged or rusted the repair is to be considered major and it is often better to replace a panel or sill section with the appropriate piece supplied as a spare. When using filler paste in largish quantities make sure that the directions are carefully followed. It is false economy to rush the job as the correct hardening time must be allowed between stages and before finishing. With thick applications the filler usually has to be applied in layers - allowing time for each layer to harden. Sometimes the original paint colour will have faded and it will be difficult to obtain an exact colour match. In such instances it is a good scheme to select a complete panel - such as a door or boot lid - and spray the whole panel. Differences will be less apparent where there are obvious divisions between the original and resprayed areas.

5 Major body repairs

Where serious damage has occurred or large areas need renewal due to neglect, it means certainly that completely new sections or panels will need welding in and this is best left to professionals. If the damage is due to impact it will also be necessary to completely check the alignment of the body shell structure. Due to the principle of construction the strength and shape of the whole can be affected by damage to a part. In such instances the services of a Datsun agent with specialist checking jigs are essential. If a body is left misaligned it is first of all dangerous as the car will not handle properly and secondly uneven stresses will be imposed on the steering, engine and transmission, causing abnormal wear or complete failure. Tyre wear may also be excessive.

6 Maintenance - hinges and locks

1 Oil the hinges of the bonnet, boot and doors with a drop or two of light oil periodically. A good time is after the car has been washed.

2 Oil the bonnet release catch pivot pin and the safety catch pivot pin periodically.

3 Do not over lubricate door latches and strikers. Normally a little oil on the rotary cam spindle alone is sufficient.

7 Doors - tracing rattles and their rectification

1 Check first that the door is not loose at the hinges and that the latch is holding the door firmly in position. Check also that the door lines up with the aperture in the body.
2 If the hinges are loose or the door is out of alignment it will be necessary to reset the hinge positions, as described in Section 13.
3 If the latch is holding the door properly it should hold the door tightly when fully latched and the door should line up with the body. If it is out of alignment it needs adjustment as described in Section 13. If loose, some part of the lock mechanism must be worn out and requiring renewal.
4 Other rattles from the door would be caused by wear or looseness in the window winder, the glass channels and sill strips or the door buttons and interior latch release mechanism. All these are dealt with in Sections 12 and 13.

8 Front wing - removal and replacement

1 Jack up the front of the vehicle and secure with stands or blocks placed under the bodyframe side members. Remove the road wheel.
2 Disconnect the cable from the battery negative terminal.
3 Disconnect the headlamp electrical connections and remove the headlamp assembly (Chapter 10).
4 Remove the front bumper, the radiator grille and grille surround.
5 Prise off the side moulding from its body clip holes.
6 Unscrew and remove the wing lower securing bolt.
7 Unscrew and remove the remaining wing securing nuts from inside the engine compartment and from beneath the front and rear edges of the wing.
8 Break the sealant at the wing joints using a sharp knife if necessary.
9 Clean the wing mating joints on the body and apply a bead of fresh sealant. Refit in the reverse manner to removal.
10 Apply an underbody protective coating to the surface under the wing and have the outer surface re-sprayed to match the vehicle's original colour.

9 Windscreen glass - removal and replacement

1 Where a windscreen is to be replaced then if it is due to shattering, the facia air vents should be covered before attempting removal. Adhesive sheeting is useful to stick to the outside of the glass to enable large areas of crystallised glass to be removed.
2 Where the screen is to be removed intact then an assistant will be required. First release the rubber surround from the bodywork by running a blunt, small screwdriver around and under the rubber weatherstrip both inside and outside the car. This operation will break the adhesive of the sealer originally used. Take care not to damage the paintwork or cut the rubber surround with the screwdriver. Remove the windscreen wiper arms and interior mirror and place a protective cover on the bonnet.
3 Have your assistant push the inner lip of the rubber surround off the flange of the windscreen body aperture. Once the rubber surround starts to peel off the flange, the screen may be forced gently outwards by careful hand pressure. The second person should support and remove the screen complete with rubber surround and metal beading as it comes out.
4 Remove the beading from the rubber surround.
5 Before fitting a windscreen, ensure that the rubber surround is completely free from old sealant, glass fragments and has not hardened or cracked. Fit the rubber surround to the glass and apply a bead of suitable sealant between the glass outer edge and

Fig. 12.4. Location of radiator grille retaining screws (Section 8)

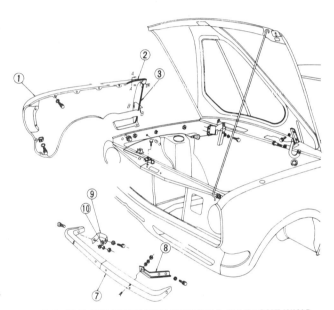
FIG. 12.5. DIAGRAM FOR REMOVAL OF FRONT WING (SECTION 8)

1 wing
2 sealing strip
3 rear sealer
7 bumper bar
8 bumper front bracket
9 bumper side bracket
10 distance piece

Fig. 12.6. Removal of wing lower bolt (Section 8)

Fig. 12.7. Sectional view of windscreen sealing rubber showing location of glass, body flange and decorative strip (Section 9)

FIG. 12.8. FRONT DOOR WITH TRIM REMOVED (SECTION 10)

1 door lock knob
2 interior handle
3 lock assembly

Fig. 12.9. Withdrawing a front door lock mechanism (Section 10)

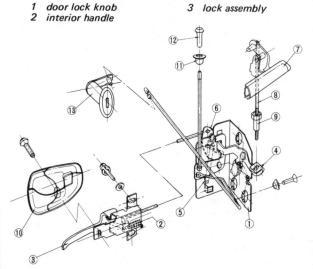

FIG. 12.10. EXPLODED VIEW OF THE FRONT DOOR LOCK MECHANISM (SECTION 10)

1 lock assembly
2 handle return spring
3 interior handle
4 plate
5 spring
6 stop
7 exterior handle
8 rod
9 adjuster nut
10 interior escutcheon
11 grommet
12 knob
13 lock cylinder

FIG. 12.11. REMOVING THE ASHTRAY FROM A REAR DOOR (SECTION 11)

1 ashtray
2 outer case

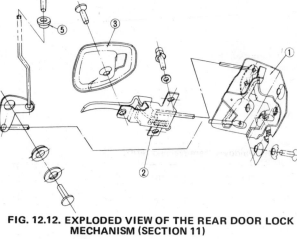

FIG. 12.12. EXPLODED VIEW OF THE REAR DOOR LOCK MECHANISM (SECTION 11)

1 lock assembly
2 interior handle
3 escutcheon plate
4 knob
5 grommet

Fig. 12.13. Removing a ventilator from the front door (Section 12)

the rubber.

6 Refit the bright moulding to the rubber surround.

7 Cut a piece of strong cord greater in length than the periphery of the glass and insert it into the body flange locating channel of the rubber surround.

8 Apply a thin bead of sealant to the face of the rubber channel which will eventually mate with the body.

9 Offer the windscreen to the body aperture and pass the ends of the cord, previously fitted and located at bottom centre into the vehicle interior.

10 Press the windscreen into place, at the same time have an assistant pulling the cords to engage the lip of the rubber channel over the body flange.

11 Remove any excess sealant with a paraffin soaked rag.

10 Front door lock - removal, refitting, adjustment

1 Wind the window to the fully closed position and remove the retaining screw from the window regulator. Remove the regulator handle.

2 Raise the door lock interior handle and remove the retaining screw now visible.

3 Unscrew and remove the door pull retaining screws and detach the door pull.

4 Insert a broad bladed screwdriver under one corner of the door trim panel and prise the trim retaining clip from the door frame. Now insert the fingers between the trim and the door frame and working round the panel pull all the retaining clips out of engagement. Remove the trim panel sideways so that the interior lock handle passes through the aperture in the escutcheon plate.

5 Unscrew and remove the lock knob from the upper sill of the door.

6 Remove the remaining screw from the interior lock handle and the two screws which secure the lock assembly to the door edge and withdraw the lock mechanism complete with remote control rod through the door aperture. The exterior door lock cylinder may be removed after releasing the retaining clip from within the door cavity and the exterior door release handle after removal of the securing screws and clips.

7 If the lock mechanism is worn, do not attempt to dismantle or repair it but renew the assembly complete.

8 Refitting is a reversal of removal but adjust the nylon nut on the exterior handle control rod so that the lock mechanism operates correctly and then secure the nut to the rod with a spot of adhesive.

11 Rear door lock - removal, refitting, adjustment

1 The procedure for the removal of the front door lock described in the preceding section will generally apply except that no exterior cylinder lock is fitted.

2 Rear doors are fitted with ash trays and these are withdrawn prior to removing the trim by first pulling out the tray to expose the securing screws.

3 Arm rests are secured by two self-tapping screws located at their base.

4 Refitting is similar to that described for front door locks.

12 Winding windows - removal and refitting

1 Remove the interior door trim and controls as described in Section 10.

2 Remove the glass stop and bracket from the bottom of the door cavity and by temporarily refitting the window regulator handle, wind the glass down to its fullest extent so that the roller on the end of the winder arm is detached from the window channel.

3 Remove the four ventilator (quarter light) securing screws. These are accessible through small holes in the rubber sealing

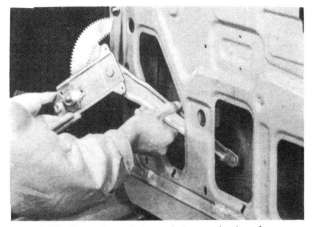

Fig. 12.14. Removing window winder mechanism from rear door (Section 12)

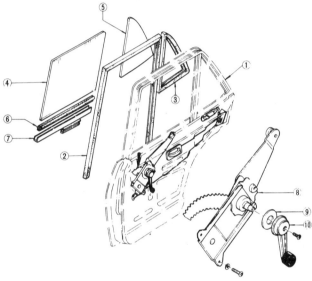

FIG. 12.15. EXPLODED VIEW OF REAR WINDOW AND REGULATOR MECHANISM (SECTION 12)

1 door frame	6 rubber channel
2 slide channel	7 metal channel
3 quarter light surround	8 window regulator
4 glass	mechanism
5 quarter light glass	9 thrust washer
	10 handle

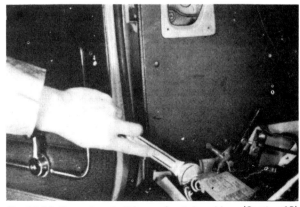

Fig. 12.16. Removing a bolt from a front door hinge (Section 13)

strip. Withdraw the ventilator from the door frame.

4 Pull the window glass up and out of the door cavity.

5 Unscrew and remove the three screws which secure the window regulator assembly to the door and remove it through the door aperture.

6 Refitting is a reversal of removal but adjust the lower ends of the window side channels so that the glass slides easily without any side ways movement.

13 Doors - removal, refitting and adjustment

1 Although the doors may be removed by unscrewing the hinge plates from their edges, it is recommended that the doors are removed complete with hinges by unbolting the hinges from the body pillars.

2 Whichever method is used, first mark round the hinges for ease of refitting.

3 Remove the blanking panels from the lower hinge bolt apertures. On right hand front doors, the upper hinge bolts are only accessible after removal of the parcels tray. On rear doors remove the trim from the centre pillar.

4 Support the bottom of the door on jacks or blocks and unscrew and remove the hinge bolts from the door pillars and lift the doors away.

5 If the original doors and hinges are refitted, locate them in previously marked positions. If new hinges or doors are used, then do not fully tighten the hinge bolts until the correct hanging of the door has been checked. Ensure that the gap all round the door is even and of consistent width, otherwise adjust the hinge plate position on either the door edge or pillar. Finally tighten the hinge bolts to a torque of 12 lb/ft.

6 Check the closure of the door and adjust the pillar striker plate if necessary, by loosening the three securing screws.

14 Bonnet and boot lid - hinge and lock adjustment

1 The bonnet lid is hinged at the rear and may be adjusted if necessary by loosening the retaining bolts and utilising the movement provided by the elongated hinge bolt holes. An assistant will be required to remove the bonnet lid for major engine overhaul.

2 The bonnet lock is controlled by a lever and cable located within the vehicle.

3 Adjustment of the lock is correct when the bonnet lid dovetail bolt engages centrally with the female section of the lock. Sideways adjustment of both units is made by slackening the lock securing bolts.

4 The bonnet lid should lock positively without excessive pressure being required and at the same time prevent rattle when closed. To adjust the effective length of the dovetail bolt, loosen the locknut and adjust the bolt by inserting a screwdriver in its end slot. Retighten the locknut. Always keep the slide of the bonnet lock and the nose of the dovetail bolt well greased.

5 The bolt lid or tailgate used on estate car versions are all counterbalanced with torsion rods. If the boot lid or tailgate is to be removed, first mark the position of the hinges and release the tension of the torsion rods using a lever or adjustable wrench as the hinge bolts are withdrawn.

6 The striker plate of the lock mechanism is adjustable after loosening the securing screws.

15 Facia panel - removal and refitting

1 The instrument panel may be removed from the facia panel as described in Chapter 10 or the facia panel removed complete with instrument panel as described in this Section.

2 Disconnect the lead from the battery negative terminal.

3 Disconnect all the multi-pin connectors at the rear of the facia panel, also the speedometer cable from the speedometer head and the heater control cable. Disconnect the choke cable,

remove the parcels tray and steering column shroud.

4 Unscrew and remove the three panel securing screws from the top edge. Due to their close proximity to the windscreen a cranked type screwdriver will be needed.

5 Remove the two bolts which secure the facia panel bottom brackets and the steering column clamp bolts.

6 Withdraw the facia panel forward and remove towards the passenger side to clear the steering wheel, ensuring that all electrical leads and control cables are disconnected.

7 Refitting is a reversal of removal.

16 The safety belts

1 Arrangement of the front seat safety belts and their locating points are shown in Fig.10.26. No alteration should be made to the fixing point positions as the original anchorages are especially strengthened.

2 The belts which are made from synthetic fibre should be cleaned in a warm detergent solution only.

3 Periodically inspect the belts for wear or chafing and renew if necessary. The belts should also be renewed when they have been subjected to accident impact shock of severe proportions.

4 When fitting new belts, ensure that the fixing point attachment bolt assembly is correctly made.

17 Heater and ventilation system - general description

1 The heater system delivers fresh air to the windscreen for demisting purposes and to the car interior. The flow to each may be varied in respect of volume and temperature by the two facia mounted controls. A flow-through fresh air ventilation system is fitted which delivers unheated air through the two facia mounted controllable ducts and exhausts the stale air through the flap valves at the rear of the rear side windows.

2 The heater assembly comprises a matrix heated by water from the engine cooling system and a booster fan controlled by a two-position switch. During normal forward motion of the car, air is forced through the air intake just forward of the windscreen and passes through the heater matrix absorbing heat and carrying it to the car interior. When the car is stationary or travelling at low speed then the booster fan may be actuated, Fig.12.27 shows the heater and ventilating airflow pattern.

18 Heater - removal and refitting

1 Drain the cooling system (Chapter 2) ensuring that the heater controls are set to the 'FULL HEAT' position.

2 Disconnect the two heater hoses at the engine rear bulkhead.

3 Remove the parcels shelf from below the facia panel.

4 Disconnect all electrical leads from the heater motor and control switch and the rods which connect the control levers to the heater assembly.

5 Pull off the two windscreen demister hoses and then remove the four heater securing screws and withdraw the heater unit taking care not to damage the matrix or to spill coolant in the vehicle interior.

6 If required, the demister nozzles, the heater control lever assembly and the scuttle grille may be removed after withdrawal of their retaining screws.

7 Refitting is a reversal of removal. Always refill the cooling system slowly with the heater controls full on.

19 Heater - inspection and servicing

1 The heater unit is simple and provided the electrical switches and wiring are securely connected, any fault must lie in the matrix or the booster motor.

2 If the heater fails to warm up, check the setting of the control levers and the control valve and ensure that the latter is

Fig. 12.17. Removing a bolt from a rear door hinge (Section 13)

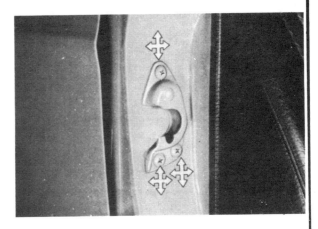

Fig. 12.18. Striker plate screws (Section 13)

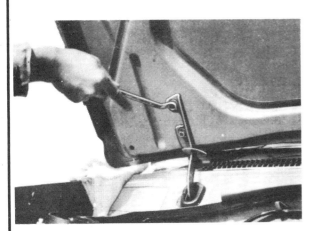

Fig. 12.19. Loosening a bonnet hinge bolt (Section 14)

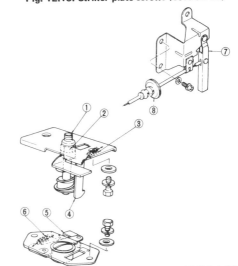

FIG. 12.20. EXPLODED VIEW OF THE BONNET LOCK
(SECTION 14)

1 dovetail bolt	5 lever
2 locknut	6 spring
3 spring	7 interior lock control lever
4 safety catch	8 grommet

Fig. 12.21. Adjusting the bonnet lock dovetail bolt (Section 14)

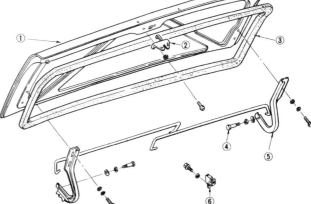

FIG. 12.22. COMPONENTS OF THE BOOT LID AND LOCK
(SECTION 14)

1 lid	4 hinge bolt
2 lock assembly	5 hinge
3 seal	6 striker plate

This sequence of photographs deals with the repair of the dent and scratch (above rear lamp) shown in this photo. The procedure will be similar for the repair of a hole. It should be noted that the procedures given here are simplified - more explicit instructions will be found in the text

In the case of a dent the first job - after removing surrounding trim - is to hammer out the dent where access is possible. This will minimise filling. Here, the large dent having been hammered out, the damaged area is being made slightly concave

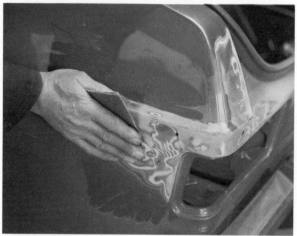

Now all paint must be removed from the damaged area, by rubbing with coarse abrasive paper. Alternatively, a wire brush or abrasive pad can be used in a power drill. Where the repair area meets good paintwork, the edge pf the paintwork should be 'feathered', using a finer grade of abrasive paper

In the case of a hole caused by rusting, all damaged sheet-metal should be cut away before proceeding to this stage. Here, the damaged area is being treated with rust remover and inhibitor before being filled

Mix the body filler according to its manufacturer's instructions. In the case of corrosion damage, it will be necessary to block off any large holes before filling - this can be done with zinc gauze or aluminium tape. Make sure the area is absolutely clean before ...

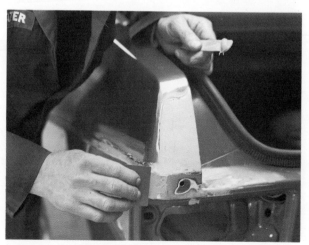

... applying the filler. Filler should be applied with a flexible applicator, as shown, for best results: the wooden spatula being used for confined areas. Apply thin layers of filler at 20-minute intervals, until the surface of the filler is slightly proud of the surrounding bodywork

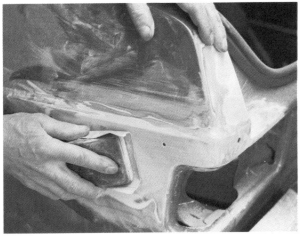

Initial shaping can be done with a Surform plane or Dreadnought file. Then, using progressively finer grades of wet-and-dry paper, wrapped around a sanding block, and copious amounts of clean water, rub-down the filler until really smooth and flat. Again, feather the edges of adjoining paintwork

The whole repair area can now be sprayed or brush-painted with primer. If spraying, ensure adjoining areas are protected from over-spray. Note that at least one-inch of the surrounding sound paintwork should be coated with primer. Primer has a 'thick' consistency, so will fill small imperfections

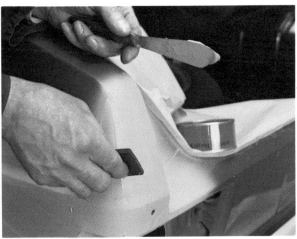

Again, using plenty of water, rub down the primer with a fine grade of wet-and-dry paper (400 grade is probably best) until it is really smooth and well blended into the surrounding paint-work. Any remaining imperfections can now be filled by carefully applied knifing stopper paste

When the stopper has hardened, rub-down the repair area again before applying the final coat of primer. Before rubbing-down this last coat of primer, ensure the repair area is blemish-free - use more stopper if necessary. To ensure that the surface of the primer is really smooth use some finishing compound

The top coat can now be applied. When working out of doors, pick a dry, warm and wind-free day. Ensure surrounding areas are protected from over-spray. Agitate the aerosol thoroughly, then spray the centre of the repair area, working outwards with a circular motion. Apply the paint as several thin coats.

After a period of about two-weeks, which the paint needs to harden fully, the surface of the repaired area can be 'cut' with a mild cutting compound prior to wax polishing. When carrying out bodywork repairs, remember that the quality of the finished job is proportional to the time and effort expended

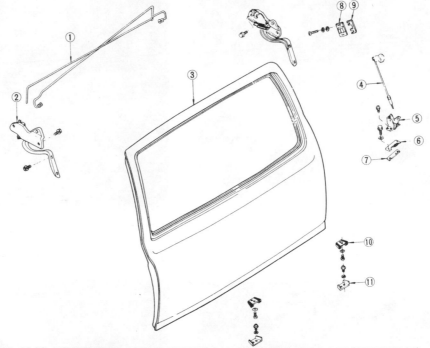

FIG. 12.23. COMPONENTS OF THE ESTATE CAR TAILGATE AND LOCK (SECTION 14)

1 torsion rods	4 rod	7 shim	10 buffer
2 hinge	5 lock assembly	8 dovetail	11 buffer
3 tailgate	6 striker plate	9 shim	

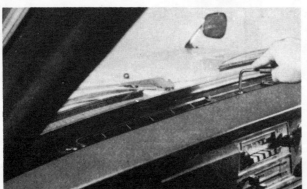

Fig. 12.24. Removing a facia panel top screw (Section 15)

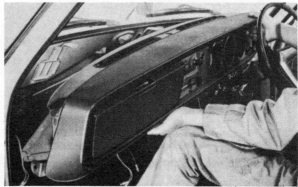

Fig. 12.25. Removing the facia panel complete with instruments (Section 15)

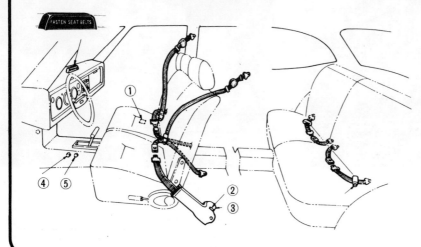

FIG. 12.26. SEAT BELTS AND INTERLOCKING ELECTRICAL CIRCUIT SWITCHES (SECTION 16)

1 seat switch
2 rotary switch
3 inertia reel
4 inhibitor switch for auto-matic transmission
5 cut-out switch for manual gearbox

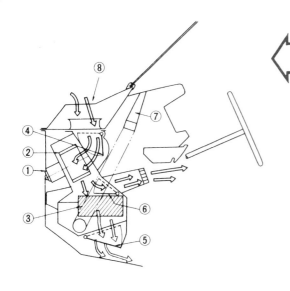

FIG. 12.27. HEATER AND VENTILATOR AIR FLOW DIAGRAM (SECTION 17)

1	heater motor	5	flap valve
2	fan	6	flap valve
3	matrix	7	demister nozzle
4	valve	8	scuttle

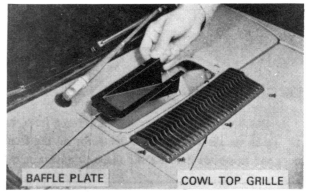

BAFFLE PLATE   COWL TOP GRILLE

Fig. 12.28. The scuttle mounted air intake grille (Section 17)

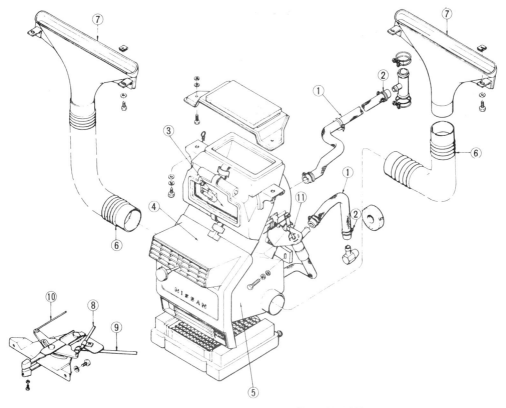

FIG. 12.29. THE HEATER UNIT (SECTION 19)

1	heater hose	4	air outlet	7	demister nozzle	10 control rod
2	hose clip	5	flap valve	8	control rods	11 water valve
3	flap valve	6	demister hose	9	control rod	

passing coolant by pulling off the heater connecting hose for a moment with the engine running.

3   Reverse flush the heater matrix with a cold water hose (the heater need not be removed from the vehicle) but if the unit is clogged do not use chemical cleaners but renew it.

4   If the heater matrix is leaking, do not attempt to repair it yourself but renew the unit.

5   Failure of the booster motor may be due to faulty brushes and these should be checked, otherwise remove the heater unit from the vehicle, dismantle the motor and refit a new one.

6   It should be remembered that the efficiency of the heater is largely dependent upon the engine cooling system and failure of the heater may be due to a defective thermostat or water pump or to air trapped in the heater pipes or matrix.

20 Body leaks and their rectification

1   The nuisance of water entering the interior of the car or the luggage boot can usually be overcome by proper attention to the windscreen seal and the rubber sealing of doors. A suitable sealant may be squeezed between the glass of the screen and the rubber surround and between the rubber and the body. The windscreen may be left in position during the operation and should the bright moulding become detached, it can be refitted with the use of a small screwdriver. Seelastik (black) is suitable for the sealing process and where a pressure gun is not available, then the small tubes available from most shops can have the nozzles pressed into a flattened spout to facilitate entry behind the rubber screen seal. Paraffin or white spirit, generously applied will clean off any surplus sealant and impart a smooth finish to the seal.

2   Inspection of rubber grommets used in floor holes and to seal cables and controls entering from the engine compartment, should be regularly carried out and renewal implemented where necessary.

Index

A

Accelerator linkage - 45
Air cleaner:
    automatic temperature control type - 40
    servicing - 40
Alternator:
    general description - 111
    maintenance - 111
    removal and refitting - 111
    servicing - 111
Anti-freeze mixture - 36
Automatic transmission:
    fault diagnosis - 88
    general description - 83
    kick-down switch and downshift solenoid - 85
    rear extension oil seal - 87
    removal and refitting - 85
    selector linkage - 85
    specifications - 83
    starter inhibitor and reverse lamp switch - 85

B

Battery:
    charging - 111
    electrolyte replenishment - 111
    maintenance - 110
    removal and refitting - 110
Big-end bearing:
    removal - 22
    renovation - 25
    replacement - 29
Bodywork:
    front wing - 145
    general description - 143
    hinges - 144
    leaks - 154
    locks - 144
    maintenance - 144
    repairs - 144
    winding windows - 147
Body repair sequence (colour) - 150/151
Bonnet - 148

Boot lid - 148
Braking system:
    bleeding hydraulic system - 99
    caliper unit - 103
    drum brakes adjustment - 99
    drum brake wheel cylinder seals - 101
    dual circuit pressure differential switch - 107
    fault diagnosis - 108
    flexible hoses - 101
    foot brake pedal - 107
    front brake disc - 105
    front brake shoes - 99
    front disc brake friction pads - 101
    front wheel cylinders - 101
    general description - 98
    handbrake - 107
    master cylinder - 105, 107
    rear brake shoes - 99
    rear brake cylinders - 101
    rigid brake lines - 101
    routine maintenance - 99
    specifications - 97
    stop lamp switch - 107

C

Camshaft:
    removal - 22
    renovation - 26
    replacement - 29
Capacities - 9
Carburettor:
    choke valve release adjustment - 46
    dash pot adjustment - 46
    dismantling and reassembling - 49, 51
    fast idle adjustment - 46
    float level adjustment - 46
    general description - 45
    housing cover setting - 46
    removal and refitting - 49
    slow running adjustment - 46
    throttle butterfly valves adjustment - 49
    vacuum break adjustment - 46

Clutch:
    adjustment - 64
    bleeding hydraulic system - 67
    fault diagnosis - 70
    general description - 63
    master cylinder - 67
    operating cable renewal - 67
    pedal - 64, 67
    refitting - 68
    release bearing - 68
    removal - 68
    renovation - 68
    slave cylinder - 67
    specifications - 63
Coil - 58
Condenser - 56
Connecting rod:
    removal - 22
    renovation - 25
    replacement - 29
Contact breaker points:
    adjustment - 56
    removal and refitting - 56
Cooling system:
    draining - 35
    fault finding - 38
    filling - 36
    flushing - 35
    general description - 35
    specifications - 35
Crankcase ventilator control system - 24
Crankshaft - renovation - 25
Cylinder bores - renovation - 26
Cylinder head:
    decarbonising - 28
    removal - 20
    replacement - 29

D

Decarbonising - 28
Dimensions - 9
Distributor:
    dismantling and reassembly - 58
    removal and refitting - 56
Doors:
    front lock - 147
    rattles - 145
    rear lock - 147
    removal, refitting and adjustment - 148

E

Electrical system:
    anti-theft device - 120
    cut-out - 115
    direction indicator and headlamp flasher switch - 119
    fault diagnosis - 122
    flasher circuit - 116
    front indicator and parking lamps - 116
    front seat belt switches - 121
    fuses - 116
    general description - 110
    hazard warning lamp circuits - 116
    headlamp flasher circuit - 116
    headlamps - 116
    heated rear window - 121
    horns - 119
    ignition switch and steering column lock - 119
    instrument panel - 120
    lighting switch - 119
    rear lamp cluster - 116
    side flasher and license plate bulb - 119
    specifications - 109
    voltage regulator - 115

windscreen washer - 120
windscreen wiper - 120
wiring diagram (automatic transmission) - 125
wiring diagram (manual transmission) - 124
wiring diagram (USA and Canada) - 126
Engine:
    adjustment after major overhaul - 33
    ancillary components removal - 20
    assembling - 29
    dismantling - 20
    fault finding - 34
    front mountings renewal - 25
    general description - 18
    major operations with engine in place - 18
    major operations with engine removed - 18
    method of removal - 18
    misfires - 62
    reassembly - 28
    refitting to the vehicle - 33
    removal - 18
    replacement - 33
    separation from automatic transmission - 20
    separation from manual gearbox - 18
    specifications - 15
Evaporative emission control - 43
Exhaust emission control - 53
Exhaust system - 53

F

Facia panel - removal and refitting - 148
Fan belt - 37
Fault finding:
    automatic transmission - 88
    braking system - 108
    clutch - 70
    cooling system - 38
    electrical system - 122
    engine - 34
    fuel system - 54
    gearbox - 82
    ignition system - 61
    propeller shaft - 90
    steering - 142
    suspension - 142
Flywheel:
    removal - 22
    replacement - 29
Flywheel starter ring gear - renovation - 28
Fuel filter - 40
Fuel lines - 43
Fuel pump - 41
Fuel system:
    fault finding - 54
    general description - 39
    specifications - 39
Fuel tank - 43
Fuel tank level transmitter - 45
Fuses - 116

G

Gearbox (manual):
    controlled vacuum advance - 80
    dismantling - 73
    fault diagnosis - 82
    general description - 71
    inspection - 74
    reassembly - 77
    removal and refitting - 73
    specifications - 71
    steering column gearchange - 80
Gudgeon pin:
    removal - 22
    replacement - 26

H

Headlamps - 116
Heater - 148
Horns - 119

I

Ignition system:
    fault finding - 61
    general description - 56
    specifications - 55
    timing - 57

L

Lubricants recommended - 13
Lubrication chart - 13
Lubrication system - description - 22

M

Main bearings:
    removal - 22
    renovation - 25
    replacement - 29

O

Oil pressure relief valve - 24
Oil pump - 24

P

Piston rings:
    removal - 22
    renovation - 26
    replacement - 29
Pistons:
    removal - 22
    renovation - 26
    replacement - 29
Propeller shaft:
    fault diagnosis - 90
    general description - 89
    removal and refitting - 89
    specifications - 89

R

Radiator - 36
Rear axle:
    differential carrier - 95
    general description - 91
    half shafts - 93
    pinion oil seal - 95
    removal and refitting - 91
    routine maintenance - 91
    shaft bearings - 93
    shaft oil seal - 93
    specifications - 91
Rocker assembly:
    dismantling - 22
    renovation - 28
Routine maintenance - 10

S

Seat belts - 148
Spare parts - ordering - 14
Spark plugs - 58
Spark plug chart (colour) - 59

Starter motor - 113
Steering:
    balljoints - 136
    fault diagnosis - 142
    front wheel alignment - 141
    gear - 135, 136
    general description - 129
    idler - 136
    linkage - 135, 136
    lock stop bolts adjustment - 141
    maintenance - 129
    specifications - 127
    track control arm - 131
Sump:
    removal - 22
    replacement - 29
Suspension:
    fault diagnosis - 142
    front assembly removal and installation - 132
    front crossmember - 132
    front struts - 131
    general description - 129
    inspection for wear - 129
    maintenance - 129
    rear road springs - 132
    shock absorber - 132
    specifications - 127
    stabiliser bar - 129

T

Tappets - renovation - 28
Thermostat - 37
Timing cover:
    removal - 22
    replacement - 29
Timing gears and chain:
    removal - 22
    renovation - 28
    replacement - 29

U

Universal joints - 89

V

Valve guides - renovation - 27
Valves:
    adjustment - 31
    removal - 20
    renovation - 26
    replacement - 31
Ventilation system - 148
Voltage regulator - 115

W

Water pump - 37
Water temperature gauge - 38
Wheel bearings - front - 132
Wheel hubs - front - 132
Windows - 147
Windscreen glass - removal and replacement - 145
Windscreen washer - 120
Windscreen wiper - 120
Wiring diagrams - 124, 125, 126

Printed by
Haynes Publishing Group
Sparkford Yeovil Somerset
England